Gender and the Writer's Imagination

GENDER
AND THE WRITER'S
IMAGINATION

From Cooper to Wharton

Mary Suzanne Schriber

THE UNIVERSITY PRESS OF KENTUCKY

Copyright © 1987 by the University Press of Kentucky

Scholarly publisher for the Commonwealth,
serving Bellarmine College, Berea College, Centre
College of Kentucky, Eastern Kentucky University,
The Filson Club, Georgetown College, Kentucky
Historical Society, Kentucky State University,
Morehead State University, Murray State University,
Northern Kentucky University, Transylvania University,
University of Kentucky, University of Louisville,
and Western Kentucky University.

Editorial and Sales Offices: Lexington, Kentucky 40506-0024

Library of Congress Cataloging-in-Publication Data

Schriber, Mary Suzanne, 1938-
    Gender and the writer's imagination.

    Bibliography: p.
    Includes index.
    1. American fiction—19th century—History and
criticism. 2. Women in literature. 3. Sex role in
literature. 4. Feminism and literature—United States.
5. Women and literature—United States. I. Title.
PS374.W6S37   1987   813'.009'352042   87-10919
ISBN 0-8131-1630-9

This book is for
A. MARIE JEANNOT SCHRIBER
my mother, my teacher, my friend

CONTENTS

ACKNOWLEDGMENTS

I owe particular thanks to Lynne M. Waldeland, my friend and colleague. She encouraged me in my work, boldly and courageously offering me the intellectual challenges from which this study has emerged. She persuaded me that this book could be written, and she then stood by me through revisions, disappointments, and stylistic trials and triumphs.

I am indebted, as well, to James M. Mellard, who has given me his time and his expert advice on editorial matters. Karen Blaser and her staff at the Word Processing Center, College of Liberal Arts and Sciences, Northern Illinois University, have been unfailingly pleasant, patient, and helpful. Northern Illinois University granted me a research sabbatical and a Graduate School Fund summer stipend to pursue this study.

PROLOGUE

Every text can be seen as in some sense a political
gesture and more specifically as a gesture determined
by a complex of assumptions about male-female
relations, assumptions we might call sexual poetics.
                                    —Sandra M. Gilbert

Hans Robert Jauss observes that literary works operate
through a modality of question and answer, problem and
solution. To understand their significance and therefore their
reception in the historical moment of their appearance, Jauss
says, we must recognize that literary texts are aesthetic solutions to problems that precede those texts and are rooted in
the "horizon of expectations" of a culture, in the presuppositions and values and attitudes of the writers who create them
and the readers who receive them. If we are able to reconstruct
the horizon of expectations on which a work in the past was
created and received, we can "find the questions to which the
text originally answered" and "discover how the reader of that
day viewed and understood the work."[1]

In the instance of nineteenth-century American culture,
historians and literary scholars have gathered from popular
publications, etiquette manuals, fiction, diaries, and the cur-
ricula of women's colleges a collection of ideas about woman
that informed nineteenth-century thinking and contributed to
an ideological framework that circumscribed the lives of actual women and prescribed norms of conduct for them. The
product of a dualistic habit of mind that assigned distinct
natures and roles to women and men, these ideas offer a
critical framework that brings to our attention, in novels
where heroines play important roles, a subtext of questions

about women to which cultural expectations gave rise and to which the novels seek aesthetic answers. This framework of ideas enables us to identify precisely those points in a text at which the culture's sociolect dictates the decisions and choices of the artist in the process of creating heroines and conceiving of situations for them that would seem plausible and meaningful to nineteenth-century readers.

Using the concept of woman's nature and woman's sphere (one-half of the culture's dualistic thinking about gender) as a frame of reference for nineteenth-century American novels points us toward answers to questions that inevitably arise for twentieth-century readers confronting nineteenth-century novels. When situations clearly intended to be serious strike us as preposterous, the perspective provided by this framework enables us to recover the meanings intended by the texts in their own century and to distinguish those meanings from the significance of the texts to us in our time. Since we view the world against a different horizon of expectations than did our ancestors,[2] this framework doubles our reading experience, giving us insight into both our own world and, insofar as it is accessible to us, the nineteenth-century world. It allows us to credit rather than dismiss what seem to us, from our later twentieth-century point of view, to be problematic scenes, while at the same time we identify in their sexual poetics the sexual politics that have constricted both genders. Conversely, when fictional scenes surpass in power and resonance the sum of their parts, this framework gives us, for our amplification as we attempt to explain the ways in which texts achieve their effects, the backdrop from which such scenes take their force. It enables us to account more fully for both artistic failings and achievements that otherwise remain only partially ex- plained in novels that include heroines in consequential roles. As the American Adam of R.W.B. Lewis and the frontier hypothesis of Frederick Jackson Turner enlarge our under- standing of the novelistic construction of male experience, so the nineteenth century's ideology of woman usefully informs our comprehension of the novelistic construction of female experience, delivering to us a new vision of old writers and an expanded sense of their enterprise and their art.

The novels of James Fenimore Cooper, Nathaniel Hawthorne, William Dean Howells, Henry James, and Edith Wharton register the impact of received ideas about woman on the literary imagination from the relatively tranquil 1830s, before feminism became a burning issue, through the stormy decades following the Civil War and beyond the turn of the century, when traditional understandings of woman were challenged mightily. In the novels of Cooper and Hawthorne, we see the pre-Civil War literary construction of the horizon against which heroines were projected. In the novels of Howells and James, the post-Civil War confirmation of the horizon takes place, as with varying degrees of success these writers wrestle with the problems and challenges that the culture's ideology of woman, now questioned, presents to the writer. The novels of Edith Wharton deconstruct the culture's horizon of expectations, asking previously unthinkable questions and exploring previously unimagined areas of "woman's nature" that were anathema or invisible to male novelists but were accessible to the imagination of a woman.

While resolving questions about literary texts, close analysis of the novels of these five writers, who collectively span the nineteenth century, against the culture's horizon of expectations discloses as well the tenacity, the pervasiveness, and the insidiousness of the culture's ideology of woman. Try as they sometimes did to escape the confines of the culture's commonplaces in the interests of their art and to imagine heroines in other terms, the imaginations of these writers were locked finally into the culture's frame of reference. Dualistic thinking, with its concept of woman's nature, exercised a tyrannical power over the literary imagination throughout the century, permitting these writers to experiment in their fiction with woman's sphere but shackling them to the notion of a generalized "woman's nature" in which all women were presumed to share. Between the birth of Cooper and the coming to artistic maturity of Edith Wharton, Americans fought three wars, freed slaves, became industrialized and urbanized and secularized, developed technologically, and were introduced to evolutionary theory and deterministic philosophies. In their literature they saw the waning of romance and the advent of realism and naturalism, but they held on to the notion of sexual differentiation and its ramifications. Cooper's characters would not recognize, for the most part, the physical world of Wharton's Lily Bart and Lawrence Selden, but they would feel quite at home there on the subject of men and women.

The fiction of Cooper, Hawthorne, Howells, James, and Wharton offers a particularly suitable laboratory in which to study the cooperation between cultural codes and imagination in the production of literary texts, as well as the power and seductiveness of the culture's horizon of expectations. While many scholars wisely insist that the American literary canon be made more inclusive, few would deny these writers canonical status. Further, reexamining "woman's fiction" and continuing to believe that "purely" literary criteria have "had a bias in favor of things male," Nina Baym confesses that although she found much to interest her in the novels of previously ignored writers like Catherine Sedgwick, Maria McIntosh, and Augusta Evans, she did not unearth "a forgotten Jane Austen or George Eliot, or hit upon even one novel that [she] would propose to set alongside *The Scarlet Letter*."[3] The gifts of imagination and artistry of writers like Hawthorne and James and Wharton, the one before and the other two after the Civil War, are undisputed. Despite their contested artistry, the historical importance of writers like Cooper and Howells, the one before and the other after the Civil War, is generally recognized. The fiction of these five writers collectively records the impact of ideology on the literary imagination in the accepted period pieces of the American novel tradition and in the presumably "best and brightest," as the traditional canon would have it, from the beginning of the nineteenth century until the modern era.

Moreover, it is generally agreed that these writers take critical positions in relation to the cultures that nurtured their imaginations. More than simply cataloging and transcribing the world in which they were raised, they turn an insightful, courageous eye on that world. Thus Cooper, for example, stood at a disapproving distance from his culture's press and jury system; Hawthorne perceived the devitalizing effects of puritanism on the human spirit; Howells stood critical of a declining morality and a rising business ethic; James rendered the vulnerability of innocence with a perceptiveness that almost appalls; and Wharton critiqued the incursions of uprooted and undisciplined people into a more civilized world. Each of these writers showed himself or herself ready to penetrate to the core of the dynamics of the culture and to consider not only the immediate effects but the long-term consequences of those dynamics. When these writers, therefore, enlist the culture's assumptions about woman not simply in the predictable way, to create a common ground of meaning with their audience, but sometimes unpredictably and unfortunately to reinforce the culture's predispositions at the expense of their art, we can be sure that we are in the presence of enormously powerful and persuasive notions.[4]

The writers examined in this study offer the opportunity to see the idea of woman working in its, perhaps, most subtle and insinuating way. Unlike the creators of "woman's fiction," and with the possible exception of William Dean Howells, they did not set out with the didactic intention to change the self-perceptions of their female audiences, to persuade them of their strengths and abilities, and to insist that women can ameliorate their lot.[5] Rather than programmatically seeking to subvert the horizon of expectations for woman, the subjects of this study most often have other artistic agendas in the forefront of their minds and imaginations. In the absence of either conscious defenses or programs pertaining to women, their work may provide the best examples of the power of the culture's horizon of expectations for woman to subvert the writer's imagination, to catch it unawares and exercise control over the artistic enterprise. Recognizing and, therefore, more accurately estimating at full value the insidious power of commonplaces about woman in the creative process, we can better comprehend the complexity of the artistic undertaking of these writers and credit those instances in which imagination bent the status quo to its own purposes or rose superior to it in the interests of art.

Reminding us in her introduction to *The New Feminist Criticism: Essays on Women, Literature, and Theory* that "feminist criticism has established gender as a fundamental category of literary analysis," Elaine Showalter divides feminist criticism into three stages. In the first, it exposed "the misogyny of literary practice," the stereotyped images of women in literature. Next, discovering that "women writers had a literature of their own," it recovered texts and journals and letters, and attempted to define a female aesthetic, "a uniquely female literary consciousness." In its third stage, feminist criticism demanded "a radical rethinking of the conceptual grounds of literary study" and of assumptions about reading and writing. This stage is marked by descriptions of *l'écriture féminine* as well as the reexamination of reader response and its relationship to gender.[6]

In the present time, hermeneutics, semiotics, deconstruction, and reader-response theory offer insights and methods of practical criticism with which to explore larger questions about the production of texts, about the writer's imagination and the gender-inflected problems and solutions that occur in the process of constructing fiction. Superimposing on the texts of Cooper, Hawthorne, Howells, James, and Wharton Roman Jakobson's grid of six elements—author, contexts, text, medium, codes, and reader—we are able to arrive at a more complete understanding of text production, an understanding that extends feminist criticism's recognition of, in Showalter's words, "gender as a fundamental category of literary analysis."

While the range of characteristics assigned to woman in the nineteenth century and the value invested in these characteristics varied with social class and with specific historical settings and moments, two generalizations can be made quite fairly about a habit of mind that characterized American thinking about woman. First, Americans in the nineteenth century, whether settling the frontier or conducting stock transactions on Wall Street, assumed a sharp dichotomy between the sexes. They conceived of woman as a creature substantially different from man, in ways that extended well beyond anatomy. Second, nineteenth-century Americans assumed that the home was woman's primary sphere. Whether the home was envisioned as a retreat from the outside world, a separate realm, or "a system of human relations" that, in a better world, would permeate the whole of society, Americans subscribed to an ideology of domesticity and assigned its implementation primarily to women. "Woman's nature" and "woman's sphere" were mental constructs laden with meanings to which Americans referred their actual experience and around which they organized their lives.

Sexual differentiation and its ally, the ideology of domesticity, gave order to basic human relationships, governing the interactions of men and women, husbands and wives, parents and children. Throughout the nineteenth century, these mental categories undergirded the dynamics of the family and the structure of society. Women's initiatives, whether with respect to property rights or professions or sexual conduct, took their force from these interlocking ideologies. Even the nineteenth-century conception of female behavior as a "problem" to be resolved depended upon a horizon of expectations marked by a priori ideas that envisioned woman almost as a distinct species. This was one of the culture's primary frames of reference, a source both of meaning and of outrage. Had it not been assumed that woman was a type of being quite distinct from man, matters such as professions for women and women's suffrage would not have provoked the controversy or enormous resistance such proposals received in some quarters.

While the twentieth century is particularly sensitive to gender distinctions and their potentially restrictive influence on the lives of men and women, historians remind us of the sometimes quite specific terms in which the nineteenth century couched the differences between the sexes and then took up rhetorical arms against those who challenged those terms. The specificity of those terms makes particularly clear the degree to which the phrase of Luce Irigaray about woman, *ce sexe qui n'est pas une*, is startling, the distance that thinking about woman has come. For example, one prominent set of nineteenth-century distinctions described woman's nature as uncompetitive, submissive, dependent, timid, intuitive, subjective, and unassertive, in contradistinction to the competitive, dominant, independent, adventurous, rational, objective, decisive, and assertive nature of man. Extending these perceived distinctions between the God-given natures of woman and man, this school of thought held that woman was ideally suited to a domestic role, defined as a sphere set apart from the hurly-burly of the masculine world. From within the protective confines of their arena, women were to nurture men and children and to promulgate those Christian virtues to which their intuitive and therefore spiritually attuned nature gave them special access. Thus Sarah Josepha Hale could write in all seriousness in 1868 that woman "was the last work of creation. Every step, from matter to man, had been in the ascending role. Woman was the crown of all...more finely organized in body, more sensitive in perception, more spiritual in nature, and closer [than man] to God."[7] Historians have labeled this school of thought the "cult of true womanhood" and have pointed out that the genteel, conservative segment of the American public devised "increasingly elaborate and poetic theories of the place and influence of women which by mid-century were marvelously complicated and flowery."[8]

After mid-century, the "woman question" came to be widely debated in America. Growing out of a philosophical climate that, similar to the climate described by Ian Watt in *The Rise of the Novel*, rejected universals and embraced individualism and the epistemology of John Locke, the "woman question" and the realistic novel converged. The escalating din of the debate over woman's nature and sphere that sounded through post-Civil War history and politics, and that found concrete expression in new-fangled manners and social modes, made its way into American fiction.[9] Yet the din was made not only by advocates of new values, attitudes, manners, and modes but by proponents of that older, conservative attitude toward woman, the "cult of true womanhood," still tenaciously embraced by numbers of people in the postwar world. As literary realists created heroines who pursued untraditional endeavors, questioned the culture's circumscription of their lives, articulated the conflict between old and new notions of female propriety and, in short, challenged the culture's ideology of woman, readers predisposed to dualistic thinking expressed their displeasure with such characters. The romantic novelist Amelia Barr, for example, berated girls in fiction who were not nice, "girls who were frank, highhanded, freethinking, and contemptuous of authority, girls who rode bicycles, played tennis, and rowed boats." Charles Dudley Warner, too, castigated the realists for creating "the silly and weak-minded woman, the fast and slangy girl, the *intrigante* and the 'shady.' " Mrs. Barr raised her voice in an appeal for girls who were "reverent…shrinkingly modest, and yet so brave in great emergencies…who yet had no higher ambition than to be the dearly loved wife of a noble-hearted man and the good house-mother of happy children."[10] The conventional woman was still the favored creature of many, despite the incursion of new notions of woman's potential and place. Judith Fetterley is all too accurate when she points out that in many fictions the female reader "is asked to identify with a selfhood that defines itself in opposition to her; she is required to identify against herself."[11] But there is reason to believe that many of our foremothers, far from recognizing this, found little to resist in fiction's images of women and, in fact, often subscribed to a sense of womanhood that many of us, in our time, find limiting and unacceptable.

The novels of Cooper, Hawthorne, Howells, James, and Wharton grew out of this gender-differentiating climate. The intersection between James Fenimore Cooper's imagination and the concept of woman's nature led to his main contribution to the literary American heroine, her potential within an American context. While he by no means ignored the time-honored focus on the sexual morality of heroines, his fiction demonstrates that he conceived of other, more original issues in the lives of American women. On some level he understood that the conditions of American life call out hitherto unexercised resources from women, as well as from men. While these resources are useful on the frontier, they may be problematic when they join the culture's ideals of woman. Cooper's fiction sets out to reconcile practical necessities and ideals and gives us heroines like Mabel Dunham who first wield a rifle in a block house and then proceed to tidy up the soldiers' living quarters. Pushing to their outer limits the characteristics desired in genteel women, Cooper imagines the original American heroine.

Cooper's fiction attempts to reconcile a second conflict that emerges in an American context, the conflict between admired, distinctively American qualities when they appear in women—spontaneity, freedom, simplicity, lack of artifice—and the manner and polish women need to execute their particular role. Cooper seemed, again, to understand on some level that the imposition of essentially aristocratic, European forms on the materials of American womanhood, desirable as they were for shaping first a woman's manners and then a man's, would put at risk a woman's identity as an American. His novels of manners send malleable young hero-

ines like Eve Effingham to Europe, where they learn to conduct the business of the drawing room and to inspire young
men to genteel behavior without taking on the hauteur and
artificiality, antithetical to the American spirit, that Cooper's
contemporaries associated with European womanhood. A
heroine such as Eve is Cooper's version of "the American
girl."

Although Cooper's art, regrettably, does not by any means
maximize his materials, the creakiness of his machinery allows
us to abstract from his novels a clear sense of the cultural
predispositions of which he made literary use. Cooper's didactic narrators and equally didactic characters generalize so
monstrously about "woman" that the norms of the texts are
seldom in doubt. More revealing of Cooper's assumptions
about his readers and their values are his method of characterization and the silences of his texts that presume such a
monolithic set of suppositions about woman as a class that his
implied authors can safely use kernel words like "woman"
and "her sex" to stimulate an undoubted and circumscribed
response. One need not, after all, spell out what everyone
already knows about females in order to communicate with
readers.

Like Cooper's fiction, the novels of Nathaniel Hawthorne
enlist the culture's ideas about woman to imbue heroines with
meaning and interest. Far more artistically adept than
Cooper, Hawthorne was able to join the culture's expectations and his heroines to accomplish a number of artistic
purposes. By projecting heroines against their cultural backdrop, he makes of them an arresting display, as when Hester
Prynne emerges from her prison and startles narrative and
authorial audiences alike, not simply because she holds an
illegitimate child in her arms but because she appears to be
profoundly, proudly beautiful at a moment when "woman" is
expected to appear disgraced and shamed. Hawthorne also
creates a version of "the American girl" in Phoebe of *The
House of the Seven Gables*, where he seeks to reconcile the

traits assigned to a lady in hereditary aristocracies with those of a woman in democratic America. In the depiction of Hepzibah Pyncheon, he creates a portrait whose comic dimension rests on unspoken ideas of the woman's sphere from which the spinster Hepzibah is displaced.

Perhaps most strategically of all, Hawthorne carefully manipulates received ideas in order to wrest from his authorial audience a complex moral view and a compassion for sinners that his audience might otherwise deny and withhold. He brings commonplaces about woman, such as kindness, self-sacrifice, and devotion, to bear in the fictional life of Hester Prynne when Hester engages in certain acts, such as meeting her illicit lover in the forest, that conventional moralists would condemn. The conjunction of a sinful rendezvous with a virtuous heart encourages the most harsh moralist to withhold or at least soften his judgment and complicate his vision of good and evil. Although Hawthorne himself may not have intended to valorize them, the very departures of his heroines from the cultural norms against which they are projected magnify their stature. Ironically, ideas about woman which would confine women to the ordinary contribute in Hawthorne's fiction to the creation of heroines of extraordinary interest.

The fiction of Howells is a remarkable instance of good intentions gone awry through the convergence of inferior artistry and unwitting allegiance to the idea of sexual differentiation. Howells identifies in his culture the problem of women who are freed by affluence to wear themselves out in idleness. He then asks questions about woman's sphere and quests for aesthetic answers, imagining en route all manner of heroines, from doctors and artists to civic volunteers and housewives. His fiction demonstrates through the depiction of narrative audiences that reductive notions of woman, such as assumptions about her incompetence, make extra-domestic careers for women into outsized if not insurmountable challenges.

Yet despite this seemingly avant-garde posture, Howells's

fiction fails to solve the very problem of woman's sphere that it raises as a source of dramatic conflict. This seems to stem from the fiction's failure to question the foundations of the ideology of domesticity, the idea of woman's nature. Unlike the heroines of "woman's fiction," who are called to independence and competence, the Howells heroine behaves like a bumbling idiot, incapable of elementary operations like arithmetic, and then not only is excused for it but is found charming because of it, as if the presumably inherent little foibles of "woman" are pleasing after all. Thus the culture's notions of woman's nature insidiously slip between Howells's imagination and his craft, causing his fiction to convey a sense of women as a protected class, to reduce them to vapid creatures, and to undo its own otherwise clear intent to expand the culture's understanding of women. Howells had apparently assumed and assimilated so completely the culture's sense of woman's nature as radically distinct from man's that he failed to notice its connection to woman's sphere. He failed to perceive, for example, that if women are irrational by nature, no amount of education will equip them for careers requiring logical thinking.

Henry James, like Cooper and Hawthorne before him, saw the culture's horizon of expectations for woman as a source of drama but also as a challenge to the artist. Society's reductive conception of woman's nature offers James an artistic problem whose resolution calls for the exercise of utmost creative ingenuity: the aggrandizement of female characters presumed in the culture to be unimportant, despite rhetoric to the contrary. James cares to make Isabel Archer matter not simply because Minny Temple, the model for Isabel, mattered to him but because the elevation of Isabel, and her counterparts throughout James's career, to the level of Subjects is a feat worthy of a great imagination, given the starting point of "female fry" in the world. To accomplish the feat, James enters the consciousness of his heroines to discover their complexity and surrounds them with other female figures who cast the heroines in relief. James enjoys making an ado of his heroines (and whether he believes in women's rights is immaterial) because he believes in the artist's power to create something from what the culture's horizon of expectations perceives to be precious little.

The culture's sense of woman became for James the artist's opportunity on a second front, that of the drama of consciousness. James turned fixed ideas of woman into a benchmark against which to measure the stasis of a mind like Rowland Mallett's in *Roderick Hudson*, hostage to the categories of fair and dark ladies (and the movement of a mind like Lambert Strether's, in *The Ambassadors*, as it breaks the boundaries imposed by preconceived ideas on one's vision of life). If the culture's attachment to traditional notions of woman and of her appropriate role is visceral (as it seems to be, given the longevity of these notions), then the ability of the human consciousness to modify or to abandon them is dramatic indeed. Perhaps this is why James deployed ideas about woman as often as he did to capture quality of mind and vision.

James elicited yet two more artistic coups from the culture's horizon of expectations. Perceiving in American culture gender differences magnified to the level of a sacred ideology, James wrested an entire novel, *The Bostonians*, out of the culture's assumption that human traits are apportioned along gender lines. In this novel, he used presumptions of sexual differentiation as his chief tool to capture what he saw as the most salient aspect of American life in the 1880s: the decline in the sentiment (as opposed to the idea) of sex. Secondly, he demonstrated the prowess of his imagination and his technical virtuosity by extending the culture's horizon of literary expectations, transforming the fair and dark ladies of popular fiction into his own prodigious heroines.

Cooper, Hawthorne, Howells, and James take a masculinist perspective, treating woman as a problem in their fiction. Edith Wharton takes a feminist perspective, treating the problems of women rather than woman as a problem. The culture's horizon of expectations joins her imagination to produce texts in which, unlike the fiction of Howells, woman's sphere, rather than the heroines assigned to occupy it, is shown to be trivial. Because of the insights that Wharton's female perspective provides, her imagination makes a more startling and outrageous use of the culture's frame of reference for woman. She deconstructs the components of that frame, exploring matters of intellect and of female sexuality and their consequences that were either invisible or unimaginable or frightening, or perhaps all of these, to the masculine imagination. In *The Touchstone, Twilight Sleep, Hudson River Bracketed,* and *The Gods Arrive,* Wharton dramatizes the ramifications of the assumption that man is the intellectual superior of woman. In Anna Leath of *The Reef,* Wharton imagines the consequences of a female character's fear of sexual frigidity. In Undine Spragg of *The Custom of the Country,* Wharton dares to create a heroine whose sexuality falls outside the culture's frame of reference, rendering it meaningless. The culture's horizon of gender expectations was the base from which Wharton's imagination, together with her craft, fashioned some of the most remarkable works of fiction that the American imagination has produced.

1. JAMES FENIMORE COOPER
The Point of Departure

What is civilization? I answer, the power of good
women.

—Ralph Waldo Emerson

It is a truism of literary criticism that James Fenimore Cooper
created the first distinctively American heroes. Natty Bumppo
has long been accepted as the prototype of the American
frontiersman grappling with American problems. Judith
Hutter and Mabel Dunham, on the other hand, have often
provoked amusement, followed by dismissal from the board-
rooms where serious literary discussions take place. Yet
Cooper should be credited with constructing from the
culture's ideology of woman the first distinctively American
fictional heroines, who deserve a place in American literary
history equal in importance to that of their male counterparts.
While critical schema like the Myth of the American Adam
have relegated Cooper's heroines to the sidelines, using the
framework of woman's nature reveals their meaning in Cooper's time, as well as their significance in ours, and thus begins
to restore these heroines to their rightful place alongside
Cooper's heroes. At his best, Cooper imagined and crafted the
first expression in our literature of "the American girl," a type
who demonstrates Cooper's imagination stretching the characteristics assigned to woman and adapting them to the conditions of American life.

Cooper's fictional world is governed by the conventions of
romance, part of the culture's horizon of literary expectations;
its plots include tests and trials, mysteries of birth and identity,

ritual marriages and characters lined up in contrasting pairs, and rewards and punishment meted out in keeping with poetic justice. The degree to which Cooper's implied authors draw on the literary expectations of their authorial audiences is suggested by their method of describing the physical qualities of heroines. Suggestive rather than prescriptive, the method relies on kernel words that, fitting mental models of the reality they represent, refer to such a well-constructed system of commonplaces that mentioning only one component of the system identifies the whole system. As Michael Riffaterre points out about literary practice in general, one such kernel word is "woman," and one component of the system it evokes is a list of an ideal woman's beauties.[1] A writer like Cooper can depend on his projected audience to create meaning out of its "amazing repertoire of conscious and unconscious knowledge,"[2] to finish his work for him, so to speak, to fill in the entire system behind "woman," if his implied authors simply sketch in one component. Elizabeth Temple of The Pioneers, for example, is identified by a list of her beauties: a noble forehead, a Grecian nose, arched brows, a mouth "only made for love," silken lashes, and a "soft, benevolent, and attractive" expression.[3] This description prophesies her role as the model woman of literary romance; her deeds and her rewards fulfill the prophesy.

The value ascribed to the appearance and conduct of an Elizabeth Temple transcends romance conventions, however, and connects as well to the culture's concept of woman's nature. The fair heroines of Cooper's fiction satisfy the culture's social and literary expectations, projecting a womanly model for the unformed American female;[4] the conduct of Cooper's models parallels the recommendations of etiquette manuals and women's magazines of the day for true womanliness. However, we need not look outside Cooper's fiction to substantiate its complicity in the values of Cooper's culture. The audiences inscribed in Cooper's texts establish that complicity.

There are at least two audiences inscribed in a literary text: the narrative audience, which includes the characters who witness and participate in a story and are addressed by the narrator; and the authorial audience, the readers whose knowledge, beliefs, and values the implied author assumes when making decisions about how to construct an understandable story. There is only one constant difference between these two audiences: a narrative audience believes a story is real and an authorial audience knows that a story is fictional. Apart from this constant, however, and in matters of attitude and values, these two audiences may be in absolute agreement or total disagreement; they may be identical or they may be radically dissimilar. How, then, can we distinguish these audiences and their values? Peter J. Rabinowitz points out that when the opinions of a narrative audience are not in some way corrected in a text, we can conclude that the authorial audience shares the opinions of the narrative audience. According to Rabinowitz, the coincidence of these two audiences suggests that, in the judgment of the implied author, the values of the text reflect those of the community the text addresses. Thus the relationship between narrative and authorial audiences provides the historian with insight into the extra-literary culture from which a text emerged.[5] In Cooper's fiction, narrative and authorial audiences are essentially one, signaling that in its treatment of heroines art is echoing the culture's ideological position on the subject of woman. Narrative audiences, right down to rakes and rogues, honor and approve, in one way or another, the virtues and conduct of fair heroines (and rue the vices of other females), and they do so with the full support of omniscient, editorializing narrators.

The most evident clues to this complicity are found in the statements of didactic narrators who generalize about woman to characterize their heroines. Cooper's fiction is rife with narrators who evocatively describe heroines by reference to gender in phrases like "the energy of her sex" and "the voice with which female affection is apt to greet a friend." This strategy, eschewing details and definitions, clearly assumes communal understandings about woman because the very possibility of meaning and communication depends on such understandings. What, after all, does the "energy of her sex" mean unless the audience draws on its social and literary understandings to supply meaning? Synonymns for the kernel word "woman" are economically enlisted to call up an entire network of commonplaces with which the implied author assumes his audience is acquainted.

Generalizations such as these are essentially methods of characterization and constitute one category of the practice of narrators in Cooper's fiction. A second category of generalizations, one that asserts while characterizing, is more complex. Theoretically, the rhetorical device of assertion, which is used to instruct an audience, implies that an audience does not know what a narrator knows; if it did, there would be no need to make an assertion.[6] For example, the narrator of *Homeward Bound* says that Eve Effingham recoils from a too familiar male with "the sensitiveness with which a well educated female distinguishes between one who appreciates her character and one who does not" (9:94). Superficially, the narrator is simply characterizing Eve's behavior; yet, infinitely more that that is going on in the narrator's statement. Words like "sensitiveness" and "well-educated" are of course value laden. The narrator not only tells what Eve's behavior is but asserts through these value words that her behavior is as it ought to be. Deconstructed, his statement says the following: well-educated women can distinguish gentlemen from rascals; well-educated women are sensitive; sensitive, well-educated women reject rascals; it is proper to reject rascals; women who do not reject rascals are insensitive, not well-educated, and guilty of impropriety; therefore, it is good to behave as Eve does. The narrator has indirectly instructed his audience in proper conduct for women. Reinforcing all of this is the character of Eve, previously established in the text as a model woman.

The narrator's assertion raises a question about the implied, authorial audience of the text. If the authorial audience is presumed to share the implied author's good opinion of Eve's behavior as asserted by the narrator, why is the narrator made to assert it at all? Why isn't Eve left simply to recoil? Does not the fact of assertion suggest that the implied author perceives a difference between his outlook and that of the authorial audience, which then prompts him to make assertions in the narrator's voice in order to instruct and convert that audience to his vision of conduct? The answer to this is both yes and no. Yes, the implied author apparently sees a need to teach proper conduct to his implied audience; his assertion does indicate a discrepancy between his perception and that of his audience. But no, his assertion does not suggest a difference in values. On the contrary, the grounds on which his narrator presumes to instruct the audience signal shared values and attitudes. Implicit in the narrator's assertion is the belief that his audience prefers "womanly" women and therefore will be susceptible to instruction in what conduct expresses womanliness. Precisely because the audience is presumed to value sensitivity in women, the audience will be receptive to the narrator's assertion, will be educable. When the audience values sensitivity and the deportment which is its expression, it manifests allegiance to the concept of woman's nature. It is this concept, then, that finally validates the narrator's instruction. Far from denying communal understandings, the assertions of narrators in Cooper's fiction ratify these understandings by teaching the behavior that will perpetuate them.

Narrators' generalizations about woman, carrying praise and blame and expressing the norms of the text, also contribute to plot. They serve to heighten the suspense surrounding the marriage questions endemic to romance. In *The Deerslayer*, for example, in keeping with the design of romance, Judith Hutter occupies the structural position of heroine: she stands opposite Deerslayer and thus is paired with him quite apart from her virtues or vices. According to the conventions

of the genre,[7] her structural position raises the expectation
that she may marry him, as a virtuous female character is most
often rewarded with marriage. Is Judith virtuous or not, and
therefore will she or will she not be worthy to marry Deerslayer? Within this generic romance context, the narrator attaches
to Judith generalizations about woman that heighten the
ambiguity of her character and thus increase the suspense of
the marriage plot. Using the norm of womanliness, the narrator alternately praises Judith and questions her "misguided" character; toying with audience expectations, the
narrator thus sustains the suspense that the structure and the
reward system of romance initiate. The implied author gets
double mileage out of the narrator's generalizations about
woman, using them simultaneously to supply norms and to
increase the tensions of the plot. Undergirding everything is
the culture's horizon of expectations with its belief in woman's nature. If the authorial audience, like the narrative
audience, subscribes to the idea that marriage is woman's
appropriate sphere and the arena of her happiness and fulfillment, as ideas about woman's nature propose, then the expectations of the audience are intensified and potentially raised to
their greatest pitch. Cooper's imagination coordinates literary
genre, characterization, and the ideology of woman in the
creation of suspense.

Cooper aligns his texts at every turn with the culture's
ordering of the sexes. Like his narrators, Cooper's heroines
enlist generalizations to explain their circumstances and their
actions, signaling in the process their acceptance of gender
distinctions. Lucy Hardinge of *Afloat and Ashore*, for instance, accepts the usual gender distinctions of her culture,
claiming that "men are not like us females, who love everything we love with our whole hearts. Men prefer wandering
about, and being shipwrecked, and left on desert islands, to
remaining quietly at home on their own farms" (1:382). By
reference to gender, Lucy accepts the wandering of men as a

simple fact; in keeping with the dictates of gender, she attributes it to a love of adventure rather than a failure to cherish the women left at home.

Indeed, heroines employ generalizations to assure other characters not only of their compliance in the system of gender distinctions but of their wish to conform to it. Alida of *The Water-Witch*, for example, performs a remarkable deed but fends off credit by saying, "Notwithstanding your generous interpretations of my character, Ludlow, I am but woman after all" (28:367). Depreciating her achievement by reference to her gender, Alida creates two effects: she poses as a properly humble woman and she reasserts the ordering of the sexes. She says, in effect, that her remarkable deed in no way threatens the social order because her deed is a fluke. She thus expresses her belief in the system and her desire to maintain her position within it. To us, such statements may seem forms of preposterous self-effacement; yet in such statements as these Cooper's novels embrace and perpetuate the ideological status quo. Generalizations are intended praise, marking qualities to which the system of sexual differentiation assigns value. It is only proper and womanly, in the vision of Cooper's implied authors and intended readers, that a woman be but a woman after all.

Every element of Cooper's work that touches the fictional lives of heroines so relies on gender that one is tempted to claim it as the sine qua non of his texts. In addition to providing the semes on which heroines are built and the content of narrators' and heroines' generalizations and norms, gender is consistently the benchmark against which all characters assess heroines. At times gender shows itself powerful enough to overturn long-standing, valued mental habits. *The Deerslayer* provides a most remarkable example of the subtle power of notions about gender. One of Natty Bumppo's most marked characteristics is his reliance on his own experience and perception in the wilderness to arrive at the truth in all matters—from the existence of God to the design of the universe. His contacts with Judith Hutter reveal Judith to be consistently honorable, compassionate, and dutiful. Were Natty to follow his usual procedure and rely on his own observation of Judith's behavior to arrive at the truth of her character, he would conclude that she is a virtuous woman. Natty, however, is told by Hurry Harry, a character he knows to be slippery, that Judith is guilty of coquetry: she has consorted with soldiers in the garrison. Despite the evidence of all his senses save his ears, Natty's judgment of Judith is poisoned and he rejects the possibility of marrying her.[8] On this one occasion, Natty relies on hearsay rather than observation as his source of knowledge.

What is intended by Natty's departing from his usual mental habits on the subject of Judith? For one thing, suspense is built into the plot through this gambit; questions surrounding Judith's character keep alive the uncertainty of whether Natty will marry. Still, the implied author must make Natty's rejection of Judith plausible to his intended audience because it does not make sense in terms of Natty's own observations of Judith or his usual method of analysis. It does make sense, however, in terms of the norms for woman's conduct that gossip says Judith has violated. Good women do not consort with strange men, men (like soldiers) to whom one has not been properly introduced, and women who do are blamable. Mere rumor destroys a woman's reputation. Yet, how do we know that this norm is not idiosyncratic and subscribed to by only the implied author? How do we know from the text that the hypothetical audience, for whom the implied author wrote, shares this norm and this vision of woman? We know because the implied author supplies nothing else to make plausible Natty's change of mental habit, reasons, and consequent decision. The implied author remains silent, apparently confident that his intended audience will feel this norm at work, accounting for Natty's procedure and decision. Reading *The Deerslayer* in our time, we may find Natty's reasoning to be priggish, if not inconsistent with his character. We are not, however, the audience inscribed in the text. That audience had to believe in the idea of woman's nature and the norms that accompany it in order to understand Natty Bumppo. Further, that audience had to attribute enormous power to the idea of woman's nature to accept as plausible that idea's ability to subvert a mental habit on which Natty prides himself.

Twentieth-century readers often find Cooper's heroines and their interaction with Cooper's heroes indisputably stupid. Cooper's artistry, his famous "literary offenses," may of course contribute to the present-day standing of his novels as period pieces. His flaws are accentuated by the impact of our own horizon of expectations on our responses to his heroines. Communication depends on shared systems of meaning, and the intended meanings of Cooper's romances tell us that some portion of Cooper's contemporaneous readers shared the beliefs, norms, and attitudes inscribed in the intended audiences of his texts. Their horizon of expectations, as perceived by Cooper, differed from ours. The meaning of his heroines within the literary and social context of their own time, as distinct from his heroines' significance to us in our own time, makes Cooper's contribution to our literary history in the persons of his heroines if not more palatable, at least more clear.

An example is Judith Hutter and her attitude toward Natty Bumppo. Judith not only yearns to marry Natty, but she continues her yearning in the face of Natty's remarkably patronizing—from our point of view—attitude toward her. Characterized as a homespun philosopher much given to the delivery of sermons, Natty has served scholars as a model of the American mentality and the experience of the frontier. He is particularly presumptuous, however, in the sermons he delivers to Judith, frequently instructing and correcting her. Judith could, for example, be presumed to know her feeble-minded sister, Hetty, as well as anyone, having lived with her for years. When Judith must decide whether Hetty's possessions should be used to ransom their father, she concludes that Hetty would certainly approve of such a use. Deerslayer, however, having met Hetty but a few days earlier, dares to question the correctness of Judith's sense of Hetty's wishes and even proceeds to deliver a lesson on the subject, saying: "It's a good rule, and a righteous one, never to take when those that give don't know the value of their gifts" (5:42). For all his apparent humility of origin and education, Deerslayer is surprisingly patronizing, especially to women. He goes so far as to tell Judith what women like in men. When Judith asserts that looks in a man are not terribly important to a woman, Deerslayer counters: "There I can't altogether agree with you" (5:435). It is astonishing to hear the bashful, inexperienced, and homely Deerslayer instruct the confident, experienced, and beautiful Judith on women's taste in men. Natty even advises Judith on marriage, telling her that he cannot understand her reluctance to marry Hurry Harry, although Judith emphatically has told Natty that "Hurry is a man I could never marry, though he were ten times more comely to the eye, and a hundred times more stout of heart than he really is" (5:435). Despite all this, Judith never murmurs against Natty, never contradicts him, never counters him. Surely, Judith is, to borrow James Russell Lowell's term, "sappy" in her silence before this patronizing rudeness.

Just as surely, the implied author does not intend to characterize Judith as "sappy" nor does he expect that his audience will read her this way. We know this because the text of *The Deerslayer* in no way registers surprise or criticism of Natty's presumption. On the contrary, Natty the hero articulates without qualification the values of the novel, and Judith tolerates submissively what is to us his presumptuousness. The implied author never undermines Natty or distinguishes the narrative from the authorial audience. He apparently assumes that Natty's attitudes and Judith's responses are plausible and acceptable to his audience. From our own perspective, we wonder how the interaction between Judith and Natty can possibly be taken seriously. The framework of woman's nature provides an answer, explaining the persuasiveness, to a pre–Civil War audience, of their exchange. According to the culture's idea of sexual differentiation, Natty behaves exactly as a man is allowed to behave, and Judith reacts exactly as she should, respectfully attending to Natty's wisdom. In terms of the ideology of gender, Natty is manly, Judith is womanly (sustaining the suspense of the marriage question, which the possibility of a virtuous Judith allows), and they both laudably conform their conduct, in these scenes, to their complementary genders. While this interpretation does not excuse Cooper's artistic flaws nor suggest that we should enjoy his novels more than we do, it does tell us why Cooper's contemporaries may have appreciated his novels more than we do. It also suggests that Cooper's creative powers and the uses to which he put his culture's ideology were greater than we may recognize, trapped in our own horizon of expectations.

Recognition of the intended meanings of texts, however, need not deter us from construing their significance to us. Indeed, as Hans Robert Jauss reminds us, the history of literary works and whatever continued life and influence they may have is inescapably made up of ongoing readings, inevitably projected against later and therefore new horizons of expectation.[9] The interaction of heroes and heroines in Cooper demonstrates the debilitating aspects, whether perceived by Cooper's contemporaries or not, of the culture's horizon of expectations for woman. First, the ideology of woman repeatedly distorts characters' perception of heroines. Natty sometimes cannot credit Judith for her virtues, indeed he cannot see them, because his a priori ideas about woman intercept his vision. Having asserted that all women are vain and love themselves better than anything else alive, Natty assumes that Judith will be incapable of sacrificing her feminine adornments to ransom her father from Indian captivity—despite the fact she has offered to do so. Second, presuppositions about woman, while they sometimes work in favor of heroines, at other times dilute praise when praise is warranted. When Judith generously thanks Natty for protecting her from an Indian attack, her gratitude is attributed not to her own sensitivity and appreciativeness but to "the quick instinct of a female's affection, and the sympathizing kindness of a woman's heart" (5:127). This strategy effectively denies Judith's individual initiative and in push-button fashion points instead to her gender as the real heroine, for which Judith can of course take little credit.

A third debilitating aspect of this ideology is that the characteristics assigned to "woman" limit the available range of virtues. When, for example, the Mingos instruct Natty to carry a call for compromise to his friend Chingachgook, and to return with an answer, Natty will not do so; he refuses to think that Chingachgook would so much as consider any dishonorable demands. Deerslayer says, "Lord; I could carry back his speech without hearing a word of it! I didn't think of putting the question to him at all" (5:410). When, however, the Mingos ask Deerslayer to ask Hist if she will do something equally dishonorable in the code of Indian women, namely, take a Huron husband, Deerslayer displays no equivalent confidence in her. He asks her the question, clearly not presuming honor in an Indian woman, although assuming it in an Indian man. Women may be honorable on some fronts, but there is a brand of honor that belongs to men alone. There are areas of achievement, whether spiritual or material, that arc not available to heroines.[10]

In general, Cooper's fiction betrays what is from our vantage point a masculinist view of the world, but it is a view that Cooper's contemporaries would identify as complete rather than partial. Although the sexes were theoretically complementary, separate and more or less equal, a presumption of male superiority and importance is unwittingly revealed in the economy of Cooper's fictional world. Elizabeth Temple of *The Pioneers*, for example, may be a remarkably competent heroine, but the world of Cooperstown rests easier when

Oliver Effingham at last shoulders her responsibilities.

The superior weight granted to male experience and problems is particularly evident in Cooper's handling of his doctrine of gifts, his valiant attempt to develop a cultural relativism in the interests of peace between Indians and whites.[11] The doctrine of gifts distinguishes nature from nurture, holding that human nature is shared but gifts are the products of circumstances and vary from culture to culture. As certain practices of the Indians, such as scalping, are the product of environment, so an Indian who scalps or engages in other practices shocking to whites is less blamable than a paleskin who perpetrates like deeds, for the paleskin's environment neither teaches nor condones such practices. If this doctrine is applied and circumstances are taken into account on behalf of the Indian, then American judgments of Indian practices will be tempered and the possibility of harmonious coexistence will be strengthened.

Introduced in *The Pathfinder* and more fully articulated in *The Deerslayer*, the doctrine of gifts is explained by Natty Bumppo in his tedious, sermonizing fashion:

A natur' is the creatur' itself; its wishes, wants, idees, and feelin's, as all are born in him. This natur' never can be changed in the main, though it may undergo some increase or lessening. Now, gifts come of sarcumstances. Thus, if you put a man in a town, he gets town gifts; in a settlement, settlement gifts; in a forest, gifts of the woods. A soldier has soldierly gifts, and a missionary preaching gifts. All these increase and strengthen until they get to fortify natur' as it might be, and excuse a thousand acts and idees. Still the creatur' is the same at bottom; just as a man who is clad in regimentals is the same as the man that is clad in skins. The garments make a change to the eye, and some change in the conduct, perhaps; but none in the man. Herein lies the apology for gifts; seein' that you expect different conduct from one in silks and satins from one in homespun; though the Lord, who didn't make the dresses, but who made the creatur's themselves, looks only at his own work. [5:455]

Natty's reference to "silks and satins" may suggest that gifts pertain to women as well as men, and clearly Cooper's im-

plied author would include women in the doctrine. When in
The Pathfinder Natty faces the difficulty of ferrying Mabel
Dunham over a waterfall, he says, "We know too well a
woman's gifts, to think of carrying the sergeant's daughter
over the falls" (17:41). On another occasion, Natty explains
Mabel's inability to marry an Indian with "That is her gift,
sergeant" (17:125). Raised in the settlements among whites
and being white, Mabel has the gift to marry into her own race
and to live in the manner to which she is accustomed.

Admittedly, the doctrine of gifts is never satisfactorily but
always erratically applied, whether to heroes or heroines.
Cooper's artistry was incommensurate with the demands of
the doctrine. Yet its application to heroines is particularly
confused, suggesting that Cooper more easily could imagine a
variety of manners and practices for men than for women.
Having included women under the umbrella of gifts, Cooper's
implied authors proceed to telescope nature and gifts in the
case of female characters. The different environments of Indian and white males may cause redskin and paleface men to
differ, but the same does not apply to Indian and white
women. Rather, as Natty tells Judith about her wish to rescue
Hurry Harry: "The same feelin's is to be found among the
young women of the Delawares. I've known 'em, often and
often, sacrifice their vanity to their hearts. 'Tis as it should
be...I suppose, in both colors. Woman was created for the
feelin's, and is pretty much ruled by feelin' " (5:151). A man is
Indian or white, but a woman is a woman is a woman, at least
when it comes to the codes of conduct for interacting with
men.[12] The behavior of men is attributable to nurture while
that of women is caused by nature. The concept of woman's
nature rather than the doctrine of gifts is finally the overarch-
ing system to which the actions of heroines are referred.

This returns us to the matter of Cooper's masculinist vision
of life. Cooper deployed the doctrine of gifts in the male
domain to account for the sins of men, mitigating those of
Indians and providing the grounds of condemnation for the
sins of white men. He did not perceive similar uses for the

doctrine in the female domain. Certain deeds of women are simply inexcusable, regardless of circumstances, a perception with which Theodore Dreiser would later wrestle in characterizing Carrie Meeber. A Cooper hero like Deerslayer is made to go well out of his way to explain the vicious deeds of men like Hurry Harry and the Indians and to develop a fairly elaborate philosophical scheme for that purpose. But when it comes to a heroine like Judith Hutter, that scheme is abandoned: the Cooper hero is not sufficiently motivated to make the effort to sort out nature from gifts to account for a heroine's behavior. An irregular upbringing and the frontier conditions in which she lives are not enlisted by Natty on Judith's behalf when it comes to her conduct with men. Although there is no textual evidence that the implied audience of *The Deerslayer* recovered this implication from the text, we can nonetheless take note of its significance. In a man's world, it is apparently important to reconcile men to one another. Problems with women are of a secondary order, and irresolvable in any case, because they are a product of the unchanging nature of the sexes. Change the environment of women as you will, a woman is a woman is a woman and can legitimately be held to certain standards whatever her circumstances.

Despite the fact that Cooper did not seize upon the doctrine of gifts to exonerate female characters for moral failings, nonetheless he must be credited with using the conditions of American life to expand the potential of his heroines in areas of practical abilities that did not violate the culture's notions of female virtue. The conception behind the doctrine of gifts, the impact of environment on human beings, enables one of Cooper's major contributions to American literary history— the creation of female characters who are distinctively American. Cooper's fiction suggests that just as the peculiar conditions of frontier life contributed to the formation of a distinctively American male, so these conditions inevitably impinged on the development of females as well. Cooper creates a model for the American woman, a particular manifestation of woman's nature as it is flavored by the New World.[13] His imagination pushes against the outer limits of the culture's horizon of expectations, as the conditions of American life require. As a result, his heroines sometimes transcend our usual conceptions of the Cooper heroine. Cooper perhaps best caught the distinctive range and vitality of the American woman in his frontier heroines. Unlike C.B. Brown's Clara Pleyel and Susanna Rowson's Charlotte Temple, whose placement in America is of no consequence, Cooper constructs female characters around both his sense of woman's nature and the practical demands of an American environment. As Kay S. House and Genevieve Belliglio put it, Cooper establishes "an androgynous paradigm which challenges the conventionally assigned roles of men and women."[14]

The characterization of Mabel Dunham in *The Pathfinder* demonstrates Cooper's use of presuppositions about "woman" as his starting point and his creative expansion of them, within the boundaries of the culture's norms, to provide an aesthetic solution to the problem of the American woman on the frontier. Mabel's story is occasioned by her journey into the territory of New York to visit her father, the commander of a military outpost. As in most of Cooper's fiction, the heroine provides the opportunity for men to have adventures and to prove their masculinity. But in the instance of *The Pathfinder*, the "tellability" of Mabel's character and adventures implicitly depends on the concept of woman's nature. Tellability requires a state of affairs "held to be unusual, contrary to expectations, or otherwise problematic,"[15] a state of affairs whose telling will produce a display. Mabel's adventures are interesting because woman's expected sphere is the home and the settlements, not a garrison or a frontier. Yet frontier conditions provide the occasion for Mabel to prove her mettle. Isolated in a blockhouse without male protection, Mabel, who understands systems of defense, coolly devises strategies to cope with her situation. More than simply courageous,

Mabel takes downright pleasure in adventurous though dangerous circumstances. Far from cowering helplessly in a corner, as a woman might be expected to do, Mabel undertakes a difficult exploit, feeling both "the novelty of her situation" and "a fair proportion of its wild delight" (17:278).

Unusually bold in her deeds, Mabel is also much more direct in her speech and less reticent in her mode than ideas about "woman" anticipate. Mabel is made to broach the subject of marriage with Pathfinder, a role reversal that Mabel's boldness and the conditions of the frontier allow. In a more civilized milieu, such a forward act could result in Mabel's banishment from the marriage market. Yet Mabel inoffensively manages to introduce this sensitive topic. She is allowed to possess the intelligence to assess given situations, discriminate among them, and adapt her behavior and responses accordingly, whether in a fort or in an intimate conversation with a man.

The implied author heightens Mabel's interest to the reader by playing her off against cultural assumptions that Mabel herself is made to articulate. She tells Pathfinder, for example, that he will not find her to be "a silly coward, as so many of my sex love to make themselves appear" (17:198). On some level Mabel understands that women often pretend to conform their deeds to the culture's norms even when their actual abilities outstrip them; women pretend to be ignorant or faint-hearted or weak even when they are not. She also knows that men will expect her to try to coddle them, to keep them home, to intervene between them and duty if that duty involves danger, for as she protests to Jasper Western, the man she loves: "I am not so feeble and weak-minded as you may think; for though only a girl from the towns, and, like most of that class, a little disposed to see danger where there is none, I promise you, Jasper, no foolish fears of mine shall stand in the way of your doing your duty" (17:91).

Mabel is both more wonderful and less silly than a woman is expected to be in Cooper's world. As Pathfinder magnanimously puts it, "Mabel is a woman, but she is reasonable and silent" (17:258). Frequently, the measure of her superiority is buried in the silences of the text, in those unstated assumptions that are the substrata of certain assertions. As a bullet rips through a corporal's body, for example, the narrator remarks: "Our heroine did not shriek—did not even tremble; the occurrence was too sudden, too awful, and too unexpected for that exhibition of weakness" (17:360). Were it not for the unarticulated assumption that females do tremble and shriek, not only would it be unnecessary to point out that Mabel did not do so, but Mabel would be a considerably less engaging character. Indeed, one purpose of display is to involve the audience in the state of affairs in the text; in this case Mabel is displayed by being allowed to rise above unstated assumptions. Further, Mabel rises above the usual expectations of woman because her circumstances on the frontier develop certain facets of her character. Her gifts become evident when there is occasion to exercise them. As the narrator tells us, "It was one of the peculiarities of the exposure to which those who dwelt on the frontiers of America were liable to bring out the moral qualities of the women to a degree that they must themselves, under other circumstances, have believed they were incapable of manifesting…presence of mind, fortitude, and spirit" (17:336). Heroines come to develop traits that mark them as women of the American frontier, characters with an American identity.

While Mabel is shown to be a remarkable woman, the implied author of *The Pathfinder* never transgresses, in her characterization, the limits of woman's nature and sphere, although he exploits those limits. Mabel takes possession of a hut, for example, and "with female readiness and skill she made all the simple little domestic arrangements of which the circumstances would admit, not only for her own comfort, but for that of her father" (17:312-13). Mabel's almost masculine relish of adventure supplements rather than replaces her attachment to woman's sphere. Caustic or witty with dishonorable men, a show of spirit that is a culturally approved female defense, Mabel is reserved and proper in the presence of honorable men. Her filial piety is shown to take proper precedence over her love for Jasper Western when she agrees to marry any man of her father's choosing. Mabel may wield a rifle in the blockhouse she defends, reminiscent of Catharine Maria Sedgwick's Hope Leslie, who was also granted unusual capacities, and she may encourage a squaw to do the same. But when that same squaw, Dew-of-June, is about to shoot her marauding husband, Mabel stays Dew-of-June's hand, not because bloodshed is wrong or even because killing is unwomanly but because a wife shouldn't kill her husband, even if he attacks her. Mabel honors her culture's disposition of the sexes in marriage.

Perhaps best of all from the culture and the implied author's point of view, Mabel is a marvelous example to others and an entirely salutary influence on her male companions, thanks not only to her deeds but to the way in which she executes them. For "Mabel had been religiously and reasonably educated; equally without exaggeration and without self-sufficiency. Her reliance on God was cheerful and full of hope, while it was of the humblest and most dependent nature" (17:471). A model of the ideal woman, at the deathbed of her father Mabel prays affectingly, "an instance of the influence and familiarity with propriety of thought, fitness of language, and decorum of manner, on the habits and expressions of even those who might be supposed not to be always so susceptible of receiving higher impressions of this nature" (17:472). In Mable woman's nature is in good working order as she executes her womanly role, the edification of others. Cooper's imagination uses the culture's ideology of woman to create a heroine who is an engaging aesthetic solution to the problem of the American woman. He does this by rearranging the semes of woman's nature and their prescriptions for conduct, expanding them to incorporate frontier influences, and allowing Mabel Dunham to live out to the edges of woman's nature without violating any of its norms.

Cooper's heroines are not always found on the frontier, however. His fiction goes further and grapples with the problem of the American woman in settlements and cities, enabling his second major contribution to the American literary history of heroines, the creation of the forerunner of "the American girl" later perfected by Henry James. Cooper's fiction looks beyond the frontier toward the time when the United States would be settled more completely. As Roy Harvey Pearce comments, Natty Bumppo must give way to civilization just as childhood must give way to maturity, a process that is right and natural.[16] Once the Nattys and other frontiersmen have passed into history, society—and woman's God-given role in its formation and conduct—will replace the frontier as the dominant force in American life. Discovering the uniquely American woman who, in keeping with the idea of woman's nature, will exercise a salutary influence over the men and children of America's civilized future becomes the challenge. Cooper accordingly develops his portrait of the American girl who, like her sisters on the frontier, must express woman's nature flavored by an American milieu. The American girl is of utmost importance because she is parent to the American woman, the guardian of society.[17]

Cooper saw that the formation of an American girl is problematic because it is threatened by two cultural poles of experience, American and European. The New World is both a blessing and a curse. It offers distinctively American, natural traits like simplicity, freshness, innocence, tenacity, and courage, but it does not offer the polish and manner that will form these traits into valuable tools in the execution of woman's role.[18] The rudeness of American life may create a female who is American but not a proper woman. An education in form, polish, and manner on the European model might resolve the dilemma. Yet the Old World, while it may be a blessing, may also be the sort of curse suggested in Margaret Bayard Smith's novel of 1824, *A Winter in Washington*, which heartily explores the danger to society of belles who adopt European manners. Education in European manners could strip a

young woman of her valued American traits. The artifice of
Europe may create a proper female who is not American.
How, then, can freshness and form, nature and art, innocence
and manner be combined to create "the American girl"?
Returning in 1833 from a sojourn in Europe, Cooper looks to
Europe to educate the American girl in those graces that will
enhance her essential, womanly contribution to a society in
the making. Shocked by the materialism and crassness of the
Jacksonian era, Cooper thought it an urgent matter to present
to the American public a model of the American girl who
could, in her maturity, refine and elevate American society. He
directs his attention to this matter in such novels as *Homeward Bound, Home as Found, Afloat and Ashore,* and *Miles
Wallingford,* major portions of which examine society and his
and his culture's notion of woman's proper sphere.

Cooper recognized that in the America of the 1830s and
1840s, when nationalistic pride was cresting and men like
Emerson were calling for Americans to be distinctively and
proudly American, it was no easy task to convince his compatriots that European manners were desirable. The entire
thrust of the national spirit of the time was in fact away from
things European, from those aristocratic ideas and manners
associated with class structures and artificiality, and inimical
to America's idea of itself. Cooper confronts American prejudice against Europe in his fiction, particularly in his heroines,
who are created to show the benefits of Europe as a finishing
school of sorts. Eve Effingham of *Homeward Bound,* for
example, is shown to have assimilated only the best that
Europe can offer a woman and to have melded it admirably
with American traits. Eve is described by another character as
"so *simple* and yet so *cultivated*; with a mind in which nature
and knowledge seem to struggle for the possession. One…so
little like the cold sophistication and heartlessness of Europe
on the one hand, and the *unformed* girlishness of America on
the other" (9:94, my italics). Eve is pure in keeping with
woman's nature, innocent and fresh in keeping with the New

World, yet formed and polished on the European model. Her American traits have not been dissipated or corrupted by her European acquisitions. Rather, her continental experience has merely rubbed the sharp edges from her American "unformed girlishness." *Homeward Bound* demonstrates in Eve that European manners and American womanhood are compatible.

Cooper takes up the same cause six years later in *Afloat and Ashore*. Emily Merton, an Englishwoman, becomes the mentor of Lucy Hardinge, the American heroine of the work. Lucy's future husband, Miles, wishes that "Lucy had a little more of Emily's *art*, and Emily a good deal more of Lucy's *nature*" (1:294, my italics). Lucy's nature is a woman's nature and Emily's art is the contribution of manner to it, manner that facilitates the execution of woman's role, the moral guidance of men and children. In this novel's ideal vision, the American girl is art and nature wed. Europe, the text suggests, is one of the better places in which to acquire art. Moreover, the experience of Europe will sharpen a woman's wit and intellect. In *Miles Wallingford*, Lucy Hardinge marries Miles and eventually travels abroad with him, where "the powers of the mind" were quickened in her through a "multiplicity of objects and events" without parallel in America. Lucy's mental attainments make her even more attractive to and admired by Miles.[19] Clearly, a European experience, if carefully handled, bodes well for American society and for American men and women.

Just as Cooper's fiction tethers the heroines of the Leatherstocking series to cultural presuppositions about woman while providing allowable latitude, it likewise tethers Eve Effingham, Emily Merton, and Lucy Hardinge. In the case of these heroines, however, the novels look to woman's education in manners, not the frontier, to render them the ideal American woman who acts appropriately out of her nature and exercises her role with maximum effectiveness. The bottom line in the characterization of all Cooper's heroines is consistently the culture's belief in woman's nature and sphere, but at this point in his career Cooper seems particularly interested in the way women will bring their nature to bear in the development of American society.

By 1850, when Cooper wrote his last novel, *The Ways of the Hour*, certain social and legal developments were constraining and complicating his imaginative freedom and inclining him to prose that approximates a tract. Although in 1798 C.B. Brown had published *Alcuin: A Dialogue* on the rights of women and Margaret Fuller's *Woman in the Nineteenth Century* had appeared in 1845, it was not until the 1848 woman's convention at Seneca Falls that agitation for woman's suffrage took form. The "woman question" was inescapable, though in a sense Cooper had been dealing with it in his own terms for years.

In 1848, New York state enacted into law the married woman's property bill, ending the reign of equity legislation and of Blackstone's *femme couverte* concepts, and giving women charge of their own property.[20] This legislation appeared to undercut traditional definitions of woman's nature and the ideology of domesticity cherished by Cooper and his culture. Woman's nature was thought to be violated by legislating away the economic necessity for dependency and submissiveness. Once women were freed from dependency, the stability of the family would be threatened and woman's role would consequently be weakened if not abolished, to the detriment of the society she was called to nurture. Women would no longer be so materially dependent upon their husbands as they had been in the past.

From Cooper's point of view, furthermore, public opinion had become dangerously powerful in America, and a confused notion of egalitarianism had infected the public mind, hopelessly muddling the concepts of the aristocrat and the gentleman and the gentlewoman. Cooper despaired of convincing his compatriots that the American girl could be a bracing combination of European manners and American innocence and morality. Out of this social context came *The Ways of the Hour*, Cooper's fictionalized battle with emerging feminism and rampant egalitarianism. The fierceness of Cooper's attack on feminism in *The Ways of the Hour* is evidence of the tenacity of a priori ideas about woman, the threat that any questioning of them constituted, and the degree to which they were cherished by Cooper and many of his contemporaries. It is evidence as well of the ability of the culture's horizon of gender expectations to overpower the creative process.

The heroine of *The Ways of the Hour*, Mary Monson, an American educated in Europe, is accused of murder and arson in the provincial town of Biberry, New York. In mystery story fashion, the plot revolves around her trial. In romance fashion, the tale involves secret family backgrounds, undisclosed identities, and love plots. In novel of manners fashion, the story critiques the manners of the time, largely through the speeches of characters. Cooper uses the plot of *The Ways of the Hour* to air a number of grievances that intersect somewhat unsatisfactorily in the person of the heroine. The trial of a woman educated in Europe gives Cooper his chance to take on the vulgarity of the American press, the gullibility of the American public, the fallibility of jurors, the stupidity of popular election of judges, and the culpability of proponents of women's property rights.

Like some of Cooper's previous fictions, *The Ways of the Hour* contains a triad of women. The fair-haired female is Sarah Updyke, a character who is so insubstantial that even the implied author loses track of her and drops her from the picture midway through the tale. Until her artistically indefensible disappearance, Sarah is a sweet young thing whose presence is necessitated by nothing more than the design of romance—each young man requires a potential mate. Sarah is joined by two other women who are important to the plot and its didactic intent. Anna McBain is the ideal "American girl" of the novel. Mary Monson, a Europeanized American, is the dark-haired lady who is discredited because she advocates women's property rights and divorce and usurps the male role during her trial by pleading her own case. While a twentieth-century reader senses that Mary Monson is the most substantial female character in the book, both the narrative and the authorial audiences of the work come to disapprove of Mary because of her liberal ideas.

Mary Monson (or Madame de Larocheforte, as we later discover) is a refined American gentlewoman. Foreshadowing Madame Merle of James's *The Portrait of a Lady*, she commands at least five languages, plays the harp, and reads widely. Her polished, reserved manner and her remarkable attainments are implicitly attributed to her immersion in Europe, where she met and married a vicomte. Her attunement to woman's nature is in question because of the crimes charged against her, and Mary is in fact tried by the vulgar press and the people of Biberry not for her crimes but for her accomplishments and manner. As the narrator points out, "a secret consciousness of inferiority" motivates the press and the public (29:30). Defensively proud and rampantly egalitarian, the narrative audience reacts against those aspects of European knowledge and finish that are capable of enhancing American life. Mary Monson is an instrument designed by Cooper to attack America's resistance at mid-century to things European. She is also an indication of Cooper's continued admiration for continental manners and the pleasing polish they provide. Cooper's Americans are, after all, misguided in their defensive reaction to Mary.

Despite her European refinements, which the implied author initially admires, Mary is finally as problematic for him as she is for the public he attacks. *The Ways of the Hour*, having established her attractiveness and accomplishments, then diminishes her at every turn. Mary's lawyer, Mr. Dunscomb, is convinced of her innocence until she uses a certain degree of "artifice" to counter false rumors and attempts to conceal her station and origins in order "to bring herself down, as nearly as possible, to the level of those around her" (29:42). Attorney Dunscomb reacts against this "slight proof of management" even though her strategy is both clever and eminently reasonable: public sentiment condemns her on the grounds of her genteel manners; her jury will be drawn from this same public; hence by all means she should attempt to win the public's favor. Dunscomb's suspicions about Mary escalate when she makes "several exceedingly shrewd and useful suggestions" marked by "singular acuteness" (29:228) about the conduct of her trial. Finally, Mary participates directly by cross-examining witnesses in court. She dares, that is, to act in a male domain—the law—and thus steps beyond woman's role in violation of woman's nature, which apparently calls for passivity even in the face of a death sentence. The reliable Dunscomb puts Mary's espousal of women's property rights together with her "ruling passion" for divorce and concludes that Mary is money-mad and driven by an unwomanly will to independence. Apparently forgetting that he has previously characterized Mary's husband as an old debauché from whom any woman might recoil, the implied author allows the narrator to join in Dunscomb's negative assessment of Mary, trivializing her marital discontent by reducing it to an objection to snuff. Thus the text becomes disunified, the narrator's remarks pulling in one direction and the characterization pulling in another.

Clearly, Cooper wrote himself into a box in his characterization of Mary Monson. He imagines her as a beautiful, refined, and accomplished woman. But he also imagines actions and ideas for her that are far too liberal for the confines of the culture's sense of woman's nature, to which both he and his implied audience subscribe. To write himself out of the box, Cooper, through the implied author, declares Mary Monson mad, a strategy that accomplishes three ends. It rescues from disgrace the value of Cooper's cherished European finish and manners for American women by depositing the blame for Mary's excesses on the doorstep of hereditary insanity rather than on the cultivation of intelligence and refinement. It thus allows to stand, as well, the indictment of a public that rejects the benefits of continental experience. Finally, it reaffirms ideal traits assigned to woman's nature by suggesting that only women who are insane would seek the freedom, independence, and activity that Mary Monson craves.

The closest approximation of "the American girl" in *The Ways of the Hour* is Anna McBain, a bundle of woman's nature, generous and loving in her exercise of woman's role; she attends to Mary's needs while Mary is in prison, and behaves generally in an appropriately submissive, charming, and deferential way. The source of her manner is apparently an American simplicity that guarantees a minimum level of good breeding, even without the experience of Europe. But of most interest is Cooper's use of this approximation of "the American girl" as a mouthpiece to counter new-fangled ideas about woman's role and the property rights perceived to violate that role. Anna recommends that all family property "should pass under the control of its [the family's] head" (29:179). She says she "should almost despise the man who could consent to live with me on any terms but those in which nature, the church, and reason unite in telling us he ought to be the superior" (29:181). The narrator, as if a forerunner of the husband in Louise Tuthill's *Reality* (1856), who insists that women are made to rule over hearts rather than heads, seconds Anna's sentiments and laments "that women should ever so mistake their natural means to influence and guide," in which case they sacrifice "womanly character and womanly grace" (29:363-64). Woman is intended by the Creator as "a 'help-meet' and not for the head of the family circles" (29:364). Anna and the narrator, both creatures of the work's implied author, stand firm on the rock of woman's nature.

From the perspective of literary history, it is unfortunate that Cooper, unequal to the challenge that the conception of Mary Monson offered, must declare insane this extraordinary mid-century female character who is interested in law, capable of cross-examining witnesses, and a proponent of women's independence and property rights. Had the implied author risen to the occasion of Mary Monson, Cooper would have begun to capture in his fiction an understanding of the multiple facets of women that female novelists all about him were dramatizing. But Cooper was not sufficient to the challenge. Rather, he allowed his implied author to turn away from a character whose possibilities seem contemporary. Mary Monson's final speech is a cry of the soul with which the modern reader sympathizes. Remembering her effective participation in her recent crisis, Mary exclaims: "Oh! the excitement of the last two months has been a gift of paradise to me, and, for the first time since my marriage, have I known what true happiness was!" (29:443). Clearly, the latitude of the social sphere thought appropriate for women is inadequate to Mary Monson's considerable talents. Yet the implied author does not applaud Mary's sense of paradise—excitement, self-direction, achievement in the world of action, even when not on the frontier. The circumscription of woman's nature that stands under the novel's norms and provokes discontinuities in its artistry requires that the likes of Mary Monson, while allowed to travel abroad, absorb Europe, and expand their horizons, should restrict their subsequent influence and action to a narrowly social and domestic sphere.

Threatened, Cooper took refuge in a priori ideas about woman and fell into the same graceless stridency on the subject of women's rights that also characterized his confrontations during this same period with the press, the law, and public opinion. The issue of women's property rights and its imagined ramifications became a pillory on which Cooper took out his discontent with numerous facets of American life and culture. Perhaps Cooper was particularly vociferous on the subject of woman because woman's nature, perceived to be designed and guaranteed by God, was thought to provide a point of order and stability in the human community. How much more would that nature be needed in the mid-century

American community where, Cooper thought, everything of value was under attack and chaos threatened society's reasonable, workable structure. Eradicate from American culture the concept of a distinctive female nature that provides woman's role as a stay against confusion, a domestic refuge into which the harried male can turn after his confrontation with the world, and the last hope for the restoration of order would be extinguished.

James Fenimore Cooper enjoyed the domestic life and "had one of those thoroughly happy old-fashioned marriages in which the husband's formal rights of mastery were rigidly respected and the wife, through her delicate sensibilities and the other arts of love, had her way. Susan's [his wife's] way was always in her husband's interest, and the gracefulness of her management left full room for the play of his independent vigor."[21] It is not surprising that Cooper clung tenaciously to the idea of sexual differentiation and the ideology of domesticity. They provided a structure in which his own life had achieved point and purpose. No doubt he could not understand why a scheme workable from his perspective and experience should be questioned. Cooper and all his characters, save Mary Monson, accept without question their culture's assumptions about woman's God-given nature and role. When these assumptions were challenged in the 1840s, Cooper reacted defensively. The idea of woman that stimulated Cooper's characterization of frontier heroines finally impeded his imagination and reduced him to writing tracts in which a heroine like Mary Monson appears, only to be discredited. Nevertheless, Cooper left in the process a record of the pervasiveness of concepts of woman and their artistic and cultural consequences. Out of the very value he attached to those ideas, he constructed a variety of heroines who demonstrate his creative use of the culture's received ideas and the sometimes subtle ways in which those ideas serve to discredit women and to constrict the writer's imagination.

2. NATHANIEL HAWTHORNE
A Pilgrimage to a Dovecote

> My point is that *certain* (not all) male texts merit
> a dual hermeneutic: a negative hermeneutic that
> discloses their complicity with patriarchal
> ideology, and a positive hermeneutic that
> recuperates the utopian moment—the authentic
> kernel—from which they draw a significant
> portion of their emotional power.
> —Patrocinio P. Schweickart

In "The New Adam and Eve," Adam and Eve walk through a deserted American village and visit the former haunts of a defunct people. Entering a drygoods store, Adam looks at a few items and throws them aside. Eve examines the same items, the "treasures of her sex," with "somewhat livelier interest."[1] She asks Adam what these treasures mean; he tells her not to bother her head with nonsense. In an abandoned home where "woman has left traces of her delicacy and refinement, and of her gentle labors," Eve "instinctively thrusts the rosy tip of her finger into a thimble" (10:257). As Eve passes a door with a broom tucked behind it, the narrator reports: "Eve, who comprises the whole nature of womanhood, has a dim idea that it is an instrument proper for her hand" (10:258). Adam barely notices the baby clothes in the nursery, but "Eve becomes involved in a fit of mute reflection, from which it is hardly possible to rouse her" (10:258). Eve's affinity for clothes, thimbles, brooms, and banquets apparently speaks for her humane vision of life, for when Adam and Eve go into the Hall of Legislature, Adam puts her in the speaker's chair and "unconscious of the moral he thus exemplifies," intones, "man's intellect, moderated by woman's tenderness and moral sense! Were such the legislation of the world, there would be no need of State Houses, Capitols, Halls of Parliament" (10:253). Already ameliorating the consequences of man's intellect, Eve drags Adam out of a library, preventing a second fall into knowledge. "Happy influence of woman!" (10:265) exclaims the narrator.

Nathaniel Hawthorne created this picture of woman's nature in 1843. Only seven years later, Hester Prynne walked through a prison doorway into the sunlight to become one of the most remarkable heroines in American fiction. Like the new Eve, Hester is associated with sewing, with "mute reflection," and with the halls of legislation. Hester, however, sews a badge of shame, reflects on the nature of her illegitimate child, and suffers the punishment of the law while throwing its efficacy into question. The implied author of the earlier story created a female type who ratifies his culture's concept of woman's nature; his counterpart in *The Scarlet Letter* challenged the culture's ideology in the radically imaginative characterization of Hester Prynne. Once the challenge of Hester's character is issued, however, he seemingly suffers a failure of nerve, investing his narrator with a series of speculations that serve to undermine the meaning of Hester's character and the unity of the romance.

Hawthorne's major work, with the character who is his Isabel Archer and Huckleberry Finn and Jay Gatsby, is both magnificent and flawed because of its relationship to a concept of woman's nature. *The Scarlet Letter* is perhaps the most dramatic example in our literature of the effects on the literary imagination of the culture's horizon of expectations, which enables achievements and impedes artistic fulfillment. In Hawthorne's other romances, the idea of woman's nature and sphere undergirds his female characters, drives comic portrayals, and contributes to his portrait of "the American girl." Yet the "new" Eve of his 1843 allegory continues to operate in

Hawthorne's romances as what E.H. Gombrich would call the ghost in the machinery.[2]

The opening scene of *The Scarlet Letter* depends heavily on implicit preconceptions of woman's nature to engage both the authorial audience assumed by the text and the narrative audience gathered at the scaffold. The situation is intrinsically interesting and would draw onlookers, no matter who mounted the scaffold. The implied author increases attention to the situation, however, by exploiting Hester's status as a woman as well as an accused sinner. He shows her to be a transgressor of woman's nature and of the law, a woman who apparently feels proper shame but also an improper defiance, manifested by her proud self-presentation. The town beadle first comes through the doorway, stretches forth his staff in his left hand, and lays "his right upon the shoulder of a young woman, whom he thus drew forward; until, on the threshold of the prison-door, she repelled him, by an action marked with natural dignity and force of character, and stepped into the open air, as if by her own free will" (1:52). This is clearly a woman who refuses to be restricted and guided; in repelling a representative of the law, she acts out her rejection of the law itself. This woman next resists the natural and motherly impulse to clutch the child she carries in her arms. Restraining herself, "wisely judging that one token of her shame would but poorly serve to hide another" (1:52), she makes a mental calculation and gives priority to herself rather than to her child. Looking first not to protecting the child but to coping with her own humiliation, "she took the baby on her arm, and, with a burning blush, and yet a haughty smile, and a glance that would not be abashed, looked around at her townspeople and neighbours" (1:52-53). Assertive, rather than submissive, Hester's ambivalent behavior, her defiant yet conventional nature, is paralleled in the scarlet letter itself, which uses the womanly craft of "elaborate embroidery and fantastic flourishes of gold thread" to draw attention to her shame. Although her handiwork may indicate a less than solemn attitude toward the community's instrument of torture, it may signify as well her acquiescence in the community's conviction that sin and retribution should be made public matters.

Just how perplexing Hester is intended to be, to narrative and authorial audiences alike, is registered in the narrator's description of the crowd around the scaffold and by his own reactions to Hester. He reports that some people were aware of a strange phenomenon in connection with her: "Those who had before known her, and had expected to behold her dimmed and obscured by a disastrous cloud, were astonished, and even startled, to perceive how her beauty shone out, and made a halo of the misfortune and ignominy in which she was enveloped" (1:53). It is almost as though adversity becomes Hester. She captivates the narrator with her "dark and abundant hair...a face which...had the impressiveness belonging to a marked brow and deep black eyes. She was lady-like, too, after the manner of the feminine gentility of those days; characterized by a certain state and dignity" (1:53). While drawn to her more conventional gentility, the narrator is also taken with her strength and her energy and her spirit.[3]

In short, Hawthorne imagined in Hester Prynne a complexity that defies the conventional understandings of woman in his time. The implied author gets the attention of his audiences by displaying Hester against the backdrop of societal norms; he holds their attention by evoking Hester's conventional, womanly dimension as proof that her adultery was not merely a venal act but was an expression of womanly love. Thus he attempts to soften and to intercept simple, hasty judgments of the adulterous woman who exceeds ordinary expectations, bringing the thematic implications of Hester's characterization into line with other revolutionary tendencies of his work. From start to finish, *The Scarlet Letter* seeks to puncture the complacency and self-righteousness of its narrative and authorial audiences alike, complicating their vision and forestalling absolute judgments by encouraging simultaneous perception of good and evil. Whether Hester's characterization successfully contributes to the work's overall intent depends on the ability of the implied author to sustain that complexity of character established in the opening scene. To "resolve" the problem that is Hester, it is essential to the unity and the intended meanings of the text that the implied author prevent Hester's character from being overwhelmed by either her defiant or her conventional dimension. A capitulation to either pole would simplify and deny the psychological complexity toward which the other elements of the text tend.

The conventional dimension of Hester's character, which eventually brings the community, one portion of the text's narrative audience, to side with her despite the blemish of her sin, is emphasized by the implied author in Hester's deeds and demeanor. Having isolated Hester, treated her child as a pariah, threatened to take her child from her, forced her to live without the comfort of friends, and even reviled her in her charitable acts, the community eventually comes around, attributing to Hester's *A* the meaning of "Angel" and "Able" rather than adultress. What accounts for this change of heart on the part of the community is Hester's faithfully playing the part of the repentant woman restored to virtue. She has cared for her little Pearl, tended the sick and dying, and comported herself in a humble manner. She "submitted uncomplainingly" to the "worst usage" of the public and "made no claim upon it" until finally "the blameless purity of her life ...was reckoned largely in her favor" (1:160). Meeting people in the street, she "never raised her head to receive their greeting...she laid her finger on the scarlet letter, and passed on" (1:162). Adopting the demeanor of repentance, Hester finally wins the respect of her jurors, but this is the public Hester.

To sustain the unconventional dimension of her character, the plot is complicated by a secret meeting between Hester and her cuckolded husband, Chillingworth, and by a rendezvous in the forest between Hester and her lover, Dimmesdale. The community, ignorant of these acts, would have been shocked by them (and perhaps provoked to revise its softened judgment of Hester in the light of them). The authorial audience, witnesses to these events, knows that Hester, separated from her legal spouse, proposes to Dimmesdale that they run off together; it knows that Hester remains more defiant and less conventional than the community within the novel suspects. The authorial audience overhears Hester's radical speech to Dimmesdale in the forest when she declares that "what we did had a consecration of its own. We felt it so! We said so to each other!" (1:195). Hester never does admit that in her deed she sinned *with* Dimmesdale, as the community would have her admit. Instead, she holds that she sinned *against* Dimmesdale by concealing Chillingworth's identity. She is not a repentant sinner but, rather, a repentant lover.

Further, the authorial audience is instructed in the ambiguity of Hester's behavior, in her complexity, by an editorializing narrator who offers at least two interpretations of Hester's deeds: one substantiates her conformity to the standards of the community and another details her rebellion against them. While reporting that Hester eventually appears to the community as an exemplary figure, humble and acquiescent in her fate, the narrator explains that her behavior "might be pride, but was so like humility, that it produced all the softening influence of the latter quality on the public mind ... society was inclined to show its former victim a more benign countenance than she cared to be favored with, or, perchance, than she deserved" (1:162). This apparently humble woman, the narrator insightfully notes, may not be humble or repentant at all. Rather, she may be remarkably proud and unworthy of the gentle treatment she eventually evokes so self-deprecatingly from the community. The narrator also observes that Hester dresses with a "*studied* austerity" (my italics) and shows a careful "lack of demonstration in her manners" (1:163). This is a woman, the narrator implies, who very possibly is posing and playing at repentance, the same woman who will later meet her lover in the forest and insist on the consecration of an adulterous act.

Successfully sustaining Hester's complexity before his authorial audience, the implied author faces another challenge: eliciting audience sympathy for Hester despite her defiance of conventional norms, particularly as they apply to the woman taken in adultery. The implied author must manipulate Hester's characterization in a way that will prevent his audience from dismissing her out of hand and reverting, in the process, to the same simplistic judgments that her complex character is designed to forestall. He achieves this by referring Hester's motives to her "womanly" nature.

In depicting Hester with Chillingworth, for example, the narrator draws a "womanly" Hester. The narrator reports that Hester was absolutely frank with Chillingworth when she married him. Chillingworth knew it was not a love match and, in fact, asserts that he committed the first wrong when he married a younger woman. Nonetheless and quite admirably, if notions of woman's nature are normative, Hester insists to Chillingworth, "I have greatly wronged thee" (1:74). Although unfaithful to Chillingworth, Hester is shown to believe in the ideal of fidelity and in woman's responsibility to honor it. Hester's act of adultery transgressed against the system, but Hester does not challenge the values on which the system stands. She does not reject the system itself. In her meeting with Chillingworth, Hester agrees to Chillingworth's request that she conceal his identity as restitution for her failure to keep her vows. Her promise unwittingly facilitates his torture of Dimmesdale. Having discovered the evil that her promise unleashed, Hester reacts in ways that elicit sympathy for her. Rather than simply accusing Chillingworth of heinous deeds, she again takes responsibility and blame upon herself. When Chillingworth asks who made him a fiend, Hester cries out, shuddering, "It was myself!...It was I, not less than he. Why hast thou not avenged thyself on me?" (1:173). By conceding Chillingworth's right to some sort of revenge, Hester's statement expresses her willingness to protect Dimmesdale and shoulder his burden, and casts Hester in the role of a woman who loves as the culture's horizon of expectations would have it—absolutely and self-sacrificially. Surely the authorial audience will be unable to condemn peremptorily a woman who acts consistently out of love rather than revenge.

In the forest meeting with Dimmesdale, those aspects of Hester's character are reinforced that make it unlikely that the authorial audience will simply dismiss her. In this scene, Hester finally reveals Chillingworth's identity to her lover, the minister. Aware of the "deep injury for which she was responsible to this unhappy man," Hester cries out, "O Arthur,... forgive me! In all things else, I have striven to be true!" (1:192-93). Ironically, all these years Hester has held herself to a standard to which she has not held Dimmesdale, the man who has, after all, hidden his truth, his sin, for seven years, leaving Hester to suffer alone. She now invokes this standard against herself, and she does not invoke it against Dimmesdale. Her love conquers any conceivably base motives, even in the face of Dimmesdale's rather despicable (from a twentieth-century perspective) response to her plea for forgiveness: "Woman, woman, thou art accountable for this! I cannot forgive thee!" (1:194). Despite his office of minister, and despite his failure to be true to Hester and to share her lot publicly, Dimmesdale presumes that he can withhold forgiveness. Worse, he refuses to forgive the human being who has born the brunt of the community's scorn while he has cowered in his study and his pulpit. Nonetheless, compassionate and guilt-ridden and in love, Hester collapses before Dimmesdale and passionately reveals her commitment to him despite his abandonment of her. " 'Thou shalt forgive me!'" cried Hester, flinging herself on the fallen leaves beside him. 'Let God punish! Thou shalt forgive!' " (1:194). Finally Dimmesdale condescends to say, "I do forgive you, Hester,...I freely forgive

you now" (1:195). Having appeared on the scene a weak and
defeated man, Dimmesdale is temporarily restored by
Hester's courage, love, and persistence. While the authorial
audience can see, of course, that the very fact of this rendezvous transgresses the moral law as understood in Hester's
community, the scene shows that Hester's motives uphold the
spirit of the law of woman's nature. Hester supports the man
she loves, as a woman should. A sinner, she nonetheless
behaves as a woman can be expected to behave, accepting
guilt, humbling herself, and sacrificing her pride for her beloved. The implied author would encourage his audience to
believe that because Hester has loved much, much is to be
forgiven her. Thus the private, unconventional acts of Hester,
serving to develop the defiant and potentially alienating side
of Hester's character, are justified by the narrator's implicit
appeal to acceptable, "womanly" motives for Hester's behavior. The implied author forces the authorial audience to
see and to sustain a complex view of Hester.

Yet, having done all this, the implied author seems to lose
his courage. He allows the same construct of woman's nature
to which he has appealed in Hester's behalf to intervene in the
text against her. Much to our astonishment, the narrator who
could see that Hester's humility was perhaps pride and that
her manner was perhaps calculated is suddenly made to turn
away from his own perceptions and to deny his own in-
sightfulness. He imposes on Hester an idea of woman's nature
that deprives her character of that manipulative dimension
that has appeared since the first chapter of the romance. He
converts her "studied" austerity of dress into a change in her
attractiveness, as if unaware of the implications of his own
word "studied." He claims that "all the light and graceful
foliage of her character had been withered up" by the scarlet
letter and that the fact that Hester cut her hair or hid it "by a
cap" signifies that Hester's womanhood is being snuffed out:
"There seemed to be no longer any thing in Hester's face for
Love to dwell upon....Some attribute had departed from her,

the permanence of which had been essential to keep her a woman" (1:163).

Ignoring the gains in the public's estimate of her that he himself claims Hester has achieved, the narrator goes on to attribute the change in Hester to matters that pertain to the culture's assumptions about woman's nature and role: "Such is frequently the fate, and such the stern development, of the feminine character and person, when the woman has encountered, and lived through, an experience of peculiar severity. If she be all tenderness, she will die. If she survive, the tenderness will either be crushed out of her, or—and the outward semblance is the same—crushed so deeply into her heart that it can never show itself more....She who has once been woman, and ceased to be so, might at any moment become a woman again, if there were only the magic touch to effect the transfiguration" (1:163-64). Apparently being a "woman" has nothing to do with anatomy but is, rather, a state of mind and emotion. In any case, the narrator here is most baffling. He has, after all, just reported Hester's many errands of mercy that, although perhaps calculated to ease her lot, nevertheless also indicate a certain kindness on her part. Moreover, Hester's attachment to Pearl is far from hard and unaffectionate. Because Hester's deeds, as recorded by the narrator, do not correspond with the narrator's analysis of Hester's state of heart and soul, he must base his analysis on something other than the evidence Hester's deeds provide.

The narrator goes on to lay Hester's condition at the doorstep of intellect: "Much of the marble coldness of Hester's impression was to be attributed to the circumstance that her life had turned, in great measure, from passion and feeling, to thought....She assumed a freedom of speculation, then common enough on the other side of the Atlantic, but which our forefathers, had they known of it, would have held to be a deadlier crime than that stigmatized by the scarlet letter. In her lonesome cottage, by the sea-shore, thoughts visited her, such as dared to enter no other dwelling in New England"

(1:164). The narrator would have his audience believe that not only has Hester ceased to be "a woman" but that this has happened because she turned from passion and feeling to thought and freedom of speculation. This is a most perplexing position for the narrator to assume and a most odd direction for the meanings of the text to take. After all, Hester has withstood the onslaught of her accusers. She has manipulated their expectations in a way that allows her to wrest as much freedom as she can from severely constricting circumstances. Surely, it must be that her intelligence, her ability to think and to speculate that the narrator finds "unwomanly," has permitted Hester to direct and control the minimally satisfactory life she has. Her intelligence has enabled her to abstract from her own experience certain countercultural convictions about the nature of sin and guilt. Because Hester has arrived at her own norms of conduct and definitions of sin and guilt, she can respond to Dimmesdale in the forest in the "womanly" way she does. Hester's ability to think prevents her from absorbing the strictures of her community and this, in turn, enables her to remain admirably, self-effacingly, and self-sacrificially faithful to Dimmesdale. Were Hester Prynne all passion and feeling as the narrator wishes, she would have been crushed long since.

Moreover, the narrator is incorrect when he claims that Hester is no longer capable of feeling, a distorted vision that comes from the culture's horizon of expectations with its multifarious assumptions about woman. Contrary to the narrator's statement, Hester is moved to considerable compassion for Arthur Dimmesdale when she encounters him at midnight on the scaffold, as he attempts in a convoluted way to purge himself of his sin. She goes to him in this night vigil and joins her hand with his. Further, Hester is brought to ask herself if she has failed Dimmesdale and if she should correct that failure despite society's disapproval. Her feeling here is prompted by her assessment of fact, an intellectual process. The narrator creates a dichotomy between thought and feeling that the text does not substantiate but that the gender distinctions of the culture, with their assignment of different traits to men and women, encourage. Having described Hester as "unwomaned" because especially thoughtful, the narrator himself says that she was "strengthened by years of hard and solemn trial....She had climbed her way...to a higher point" (1:167). Surely the "unwomanly" speculation that her isolation and her rebellious nature encouraged contributed to Hester's ascent.

Textual evidence forces the conclusion, then, that the implied author here brings to the narrator's analysis of Hester an idea of woman and her relationship to thought that exists outside *The Scarlet Letter* and is wheeled in to be imposed on Hester's fictional life, although unsupported by her actions and circumstances. That this is in fact the case becomes abundantly clear in the chapter entitled "Another View of Hester," in a passage which is particularly problematic because it is difficult to determine to whose mind the content is to be attributed—the narrator's or Hester's.

The frame sentences of the paragraph suggest that the narrator is reporting Hester's thoughts through indirect discourse. Unfortunately, the matter is not this simple because the narrator seems to render his own mind as well as Hester's. For example, the narrator says, "A tendency to speculation, though it may keep woman quiet, as it does man, yet makes her sad." To whom does this generalization belong? Eschewing the more usual practice of putting a "she thought that" or a "in her case" before "a tendency to speculation," a strategy that would tie the tendency unambiguously to a specific mind, the narrator launches directly into the thought without identifying the subject who performs the speculation, allowing the reader to ascribe it to Hester or to the narrator or to both. Then he says, "She discerns, it may be, such a hopeless task before her." Who is "she"? Woman? Hester? Both? And what are we to make of "it may be?" Does Hester speculate that women who think about woman's lot *may* discern a hopeless task before *them*? Or does *Hester* see the task as hopeless? And why does the narrator equivocate in any case? Or is it the narrator who imagines what a woman in Hester's situation would imagine? This last is the most likely possibility. The narrator straightforwardly tells us what "it may be" that Hester thought. He tells us *his* imagination of her thoughts rather than telling us *her* thoughts.

Whether the reader concludes that the narrator's imagination and Hester's thoughts are the same depends on whether the reader finds that the thoughts here ascribed to Hester (or is it to the narrator?) square with her character and with the dramatic action of the novel. I find that sometimes they do and that, at other times, they clearly do not. When they do not, they coincide most handily with cultural presuppositions about women. The problematic paragraph is this:

Indeed, the same dark question often rose into her mind, with reference to the whole race of womanhood [frame sentence]. Was existence worth accepting, even to the happiest among them? As concerned her own individual existence, she had long ago decided in the negative, and dismissed the point as settled. A tendency to speculation, though it may keep woman quiet, as it does man, yet makes her sad. She discerns, it may be, such a hopeless task before her. As a first step, the whole system of society is to be torn down, and built up anew. Then, the very nature of the opposite sex, or its long hereditary habit, which has become like nature, is to be essentially modified, before woman can be allowed to assume what seems a fair and suitable position. Finally, all other difficulties being obviated, woman cannot take advantage of these preliminary reforms, until she herself shall have undergone a still mightier change; in which, perhaps, the ethereal essence, wherein she has her truest life, will be found to have evaporated. A woman never overcomes these problems by any exercise of thought. They are not to be solved, or only in one way. If her heart chance to come uppermost, they vanish. Thus, Hester Prynne, whose heart had lost its regular and healthy throb, wandered without a clew in the dark labyrinth of mind. [Frame sentence] [1:165-66]

In the opening frame sentence, the narrator begins to talk about Hester. But then, as if so overwhelmed by her gender that he forgets her individuality, he slips from Hester's mind into that perceived universal, "woman's" mind. From that point forward, the narrator assumes, apparently, that Hester is "woman" and that he can therefore generalize from his male point of view about woman as a class and simultaneously explain Hester's thoughts. When he does so, he gives us his own mind, the frame sentences notwithstanding. Speculation, for which woman is, strictly speaking, unsuited in the first place will lead to sadness (as if Hester didn't have sufficient cause for sadness, never mind speculation about larger issues). The sadness is caused by the immensity of reforms that, even if possible to achieve, may destroy woman's "ethereal essence." Apparently the narrator and the authorial audience know so well what "ethereal essence" means that it need never be defined. Whatever it is, it can evaporate. In any case, "a woman," and therefore Hester, presumably, cannot resolve these problems because they are pseudoproblems; when a woman's heart is touched, they vanish, we are told. This must be the thought of the narrator rather than of Hester Prynne; in the chapter preceding this, "The Minister's Vigil," the degree to which Hester's heart was and is touched by Dimmesdale has been abundantly demonstrated during the midnight meeting on the scaffold. This thought, belonging to the narrator alone, is of course among the most patronizing possible. It dismisses what women perceive to be problematic as non-problems that dissolve when woman assumes her proper place—when she gets her priorities in order—according to the Divine design of woman's nature.[4] In the concluding frame sentence, the narrator says that Hester is confused because her heart has lost its "healthy throb." Yet as we have seen, Hester's heart throbs quite soundly, even as her head devises strategies to cope with her situation.

Conflating Hester Prynne with "woman," the implied author of *The Scarlet Letter* allows the words of his narrator to contradict the deeds of Hester Prynne. He creates a work in which the editorializing of the narrator and the norms he articulates are at odds with the implications of dramatic action, as if he finally must pull Hester back into line with the ideology of woman or make her seem less "womanly" for transgressing its boundaries. Thus norms are obscured and the intended meanings of the work lead to irreconcilable oppositions, calling on the authorial audience to take up, on the one hand, a sympathetic attitude toward Hester because her deeds stem from her conformity to woman's nature and yet, on the other hand, to understand that Hester is "unwomaned" by the very speculation that makes her able to sustain her "womanly" fidelity and love.

The sexual poetics that emerge from the text when it is referred to the culture's horizon of expectations explain this disjunction. The narrator exercises the privileges of omniscience, taking up a position that demands both interpretation and value judgment. The narrator is an instance of that neutral omniscience that expresses universal wisdom, establishes norms, and forecloses the possibility of an intellectual and moral distance between the implied author and the narrator.[5] The narrator is, then, a spokesperson for the implied author, and Hawthorne stands behind both. Hawthorne's ambiguity has become celebrated,[6] and we know that Hawthorne chose to write romances rather than novels in order, as he declares in his prefaces, to claim the latitude the romance tradition offers. We know as well that Hawthorne, like Cooper, deploys all the devices of the romance tradition in order to suggest an ambiguous world that by its very nature escapes our rational explanations and categories. Hawthorne uses shadowy family backgrounds, coincidences, suspense, and all the other tools of the romancer to set a mood and to create a sense of the mystery of life. Ambiguities introduced in the interests of a complex world view, however, must not be confused with an artist's ambivalence with respect to norms. Reliable authorial intrusions into fiction have a particular purpose and must follow certain laws in order to fulfill their purpose. As Wayne Booth points out, narrative intrusions define for us "the pre-

cise ordering of values on which our judgment should depend
...in fiction the concept of writing well must include the
successful ordering of your reader's view of a fiction...an
author has an obligation to be as clear about his moral
position as he possibly can be."[7] Hawthorne fails us in this
regard in *The Scarlet Letter*. His implied author admirably
complicates the romance heroine type, but he falls into a
confusing ambivalence in his evaluation of her conduct because of his very success in rounding her character. He suggests that we apply to Hester norms of judgment that are at
variance with the facts of Hester's fictional life.

Hawthorne hangs *The Scarlet Letter* on the same romance
frame that Cooper used, but he imagines more powerfully
than Cooper when he creates Hester Prynne. Her character
pushes against the boundaries of romance and of the culture's
ideology as well. But the implied author could not break away
from the horizon of expectations to which Hawthorne's assumptions finally held him. Hawthorne's artistic achievement
in *The Scarlet Letter* is foiled by the restrictions that a priori
ideas of woman lead him to place on Hester. Given the splendor of Hester Prynne that emerges even amidst the narrator's
ambivalences, imagine what she might have been had Hawthorne been more bold.

Like *The Scarlet Letter*, *The Marble Faun*, Hawthorne's
last completed romance, becomes entangled in the problem of
norms and value judgments with which the implied author
evaluates his characters. Hawthorne uses the romance frame
that literary tradition offers him, and his implied author
complicates that frame by making complex the simple categories of good and evil, virtue and vice, as these are conventionally ascribed to fair and dark heroines. The implied
author establishes unconventional heroines but forces them
into conventional postures that conform to the expectations
of romance types. In so doing, he violates the integrity of the
characters that he has established. Finally, he forces these

same characters, now subverted, to fit a romance plot that completes a cycle, rewards good, punishes evil, and restores order. The questions raised about the fair Hilda's virtue exemplify the problem. They are ultimately abandoned in favor of easily resolving the romance pattern, which also allows the implied author to escape the problem of woman raised by the characterization of his heroine.

At issue is the fair heroine, Hilda, a copyist working in Rome. She is a "slender, brown-haired, New England girl" (4:7), everyone's friend but reserved to a degree that "kept those at a distance who were not suited to her sphere" (4:63). The narrator adores Hilda, praising her humble, almost religious approach to the Old Masters, whom Hilda serves as "handmaid" (4:61). The implied author complicates Hilda's simple romance beginnings by having her witness a crime. Exposed to the knowledge of good and evil, which, according to the narrator, gives her character a "sturdier quality," Hilda ceases her copying work, exercising a coldness of heart that her actions reveal and the other characters articulate. The dark lady of the romance, Miriam, had earlier observed to Hilda that "[your innocence is] like a sharp steel sword...your judgments are often terribly severe, though you seem all made up of gentleness and mercy" (4:66). Nonetheless, following her crime, Miriam turns to Hilda for comfort, and Hilda rejects her. Despite their friendship, Hilda tells Miriam that she will henceforth avoid her because God has bid her [Hilda] to return to Him with her white robe unstained.

Hilda proves to be a woman without compassion, and her coldness of heart is not transformed in the course of the romance. After much sorrow and after confessing her sin (her "tattling," as Nina Baym calls it) in church, events that give us cause to anticipate some change in Hilda, she remains the same except for her inability to copy Old Masters. Her view of life remains as simple and as rigid as ever, we realize, when she chastises Kenyon for being unduly sympathetic with the sinners Miriam and Donatello: "There is, I believe, only one right and one wrong....This is my faith; and I should be led astray, if you could persuade me to give it up." Kenyon responds, "Alas, for poor human nature, then!" (4:384). But he continues to seek Hilda's cold hand in marriage. As the romance concludes, Kenyon again raises the question of the complexity of sin and advances the proposition that good may come from evil. Hilda is shocked: " 'Oh, hush!', cried Hilda, shrinking from him with an expression of horrour....'Do not you perceive what a mockery your creed makes, not only of all religious sentiment, but of moral law, and how it annuls and obliterates whatever precepts of Heaven are written deepest within us?' " (4:460).[8] Whatever the theological validity of Hilda's position, her judgments of others are chilling.

It seems odd that the implied author does not allow the experience of evil to affect Hilda in some substantial way. Yet as if ignoring the implications of Hilda's conduct and attitudes, he imposes a romance frame on her fate and gives her the conventional reward of marriage, a problematic conclusion despite generic conventions. Fair heroines of romance may be admired for their rectitude, but they are not expected to be perceived as cold and heartless by the narrative audience of the text (even though they may seem so to us, in our time). The marriage proposal of Kenyon, Hilda's future husband, remains unpersuasive despite the design of romance; it seems implausible that a man who has identified Hilda's severity wishes nonetheless to marry her.[9] Thus the plot of *The Marble Faun* and the characterization of Hilda work against one another. This raises three questions. Why does the implied author sustain Hilda's innocence rather than allow her to mature as a result of her experience? If he wishes to leave her untouched, why does he not cause the narrator to condemn her coldness rather than remain silent and thus implicitly extend his admiration? Finally, presuming that the implied author thought his audience would find the marriage persuasive, what attributes does he assume in his audience that make him confident that they will accept this resolution of his plot? The narrator allows to stand, without comment, the other characters' accusatory reactions to Hilda. The implied author must be depending on an attitude in the authorial audience to answer these problems. The ideological ground that the implied author believes he shares with the authorial audience is revealed by the terms in which Kenyon's marriage proposal is cast. The ground that will persuade the audience of the plausibility of the marriage proposal is a shared concept of woman's nature. Kenyon asks Hilda to undertake woman's typical role, to serve as his guide and his conscience, his "counsellor" and his "inmost friend, with that white wisdom which clothes you as with a celestial garment....Oh, Hilda, guide me home!" (4:460-61). Hilda agrees to be the angel in Kenyon's house. Woman's duty is to counsel men, to guide them and to serve as their conscience, the transcendent importance of which the authorial audience must accept in order to find Hilda's marriage persuasive.[10] The culture's horizon of expectations makes possible the conclusion of The Marble Faun and accounts for the implied author's commitment to Hilda's innocence, her imperviousness to experience. Having taken Hilda to the brink of a complex humanity that might enlarge her soul, the implied author turns back, preferring to retain Hilda's innocence rather than to risk her purity, a woman's pearl beyond price. That pearl impedes the characterization of Hilda and allows the implied author to close his romance with a marriage he trusts his audience to accept. Their shared horizon of social expectations is presumed to override those literary expectations frustrated by Hilda's heartless character.

When Hawthorne's imagination remained safely within the boundaries of his culture's ideology, his romances remained unified. The culture's ideology of woman, however, sometimes intervened between Hawthorne's imagination and his craft in artistically useful ways. The House of the Seven Gables best exemplifies how Hawthorne's imagination benefited by a concept of woman's nature that allowed the creation of a satisfying aesthetic whole. The major concerns of the romance are property rights in America and hereditary guilt. The heroines serve primarily to demonstrate the democratizing of American culture as it moves away from aristocracy and hereditary rights toward democracy and egalitarianism. The deceased Alice Pyncheon, subject of a family legend, was a "lady"; Hepzibah Pyncheon, a withered spinster, is a "lady" forced to assume a plebian role; and Phoebe Pyncheon, the final step on the long road to democracy, is a young, middle-class woman.

Hawthorne uses his female characters here as Paul Eakin and Leslie Fiedler claim females are most often used in American narrative: as symbols of the culture's values. In this case it is the value democracy places on achievement rather than heredity. The "lady" is a cultural throwback to be replaced in Hawthorne's novel by American women of common blood, prepared for common toil. As in the fiction of Cooper, the problem of woman occurs. Tied to hereditary rank and aristocratic societies, the "lady" must be recast into "the American girl," nurtured in a classless society but behaving like a lady nonetheless. Notions of woman's nature provide an opportunity for comic effect in the character of Hepzibah Pyncheon, and they provide, as well, the foundation on which the character of Phoebe, Hawthorne's American girl, is built.

The implied author introduces Hepzibah "at the instant of time when the patrician lady is to be transformed into the plebian woman" (2:38) by opening a cent-shop. She is "overpoweringly ridiculous," according to the narrator, because she is incompetent: too nearsighted to sew and too "torpid" to be a schoolteacher. The narrator attributes her bumbling efforts to a lady's lack of training and work experience: Hepzibah has been idle for sixty years. Her idleness and incompetence anticipate William Dean Howells's heroines, who often suffer from the same disease. By force of circumstance, Hepzibah is about to begin to make a contribution to the world. The rank and privilege of a "lady," it seems, not only offend egalitarian principles but are highly impractical as well.

Hepzibah is incompetent in another realm. She is a spinster and is thus a woman displaced from woman's sphere. The narrator's comments implicitly appeal to understandings of woman's sphere in order to render Hepzibah a comic figure. The narrator is made to look in on Hepzibah at her toilette. This personal ritual, in itself of no particular interest, is made so in relation to her spinsterhood, to a horizon of expectations that woman will marry. The narrator says: "We suspect Miss Hepzibah, moreover, of taking a step upward into a chair, in order to give heedful regard to her appearance, on all sides, and at full length, in the oval, dingy-framed toilet-glass, that hangs above her table. Truly! Well, indeed! Who would have thought it!" (2:31). Far from behaving decorously in the presence of a woman as she performs her personal routine, the narrator gently mocks this woman and draws out her comic dimension. He first seduces the authorial audience into complicity with him and away from Hepzibah by using the editorial "we." Then, not content with simply reporting that Hepzibah looks in a mirror, he piles up details that serve to exaggerate her procedure as she checks herself "on all sides, and at full length." Further, three concluding exclamatory sentences are added to also establish comic exaggeration. What does the narrator mean when he exclaims, "who would have thought it?" Why wouldn't his intended audience have thought "it," and to what does "it" refer?

Although the narrator declares that Hepzibah's age and reclusiveness render her preening peculiar, another tacit assumption underlies the comedy of Hepzibah's toilette: given a woman's role and sphere, she dresses to appeal to the opposite sex, which in turn provides her with the arena in which to exercise her womanly nature. A marriage partner is out of the question for the old Hepzibah. Thus it is comic that she should preen at length before a mirror. Significantly, the implied author is so confident about shared assumptions that he does not bring in the narrator to articulate the norm that is violated to render Hepzibah amusing.

The implied author uses Hepzibah's unmarried state for further comic purposes. He uses it, condescendingly, to wed the audience to the narrator in a marriage based on shared superiority to a comic figure whose very debilities prove the need for an American Phoebe. As Hepzibah completes her toilette and then looks fondly at a miniature she carefully takes from a drawer, the narrator asks: "Can it have been an early lover of Miss Hepzibah? No; she never had a lover— poor thing, how could she?—nor ever knew, by her own experience, what love technically means" (2:32). Just as the comic effect of Hepzibah's toilette depends on a tacit understanding of woman's designated sphere, so the rhetorical question about Hepzibah's miniature relies on shared suppositions so common that they need not be spelled out in the text. The narrator's rhetorical question, joined by the interjection of "poor thing" and the "how could she," is implicitly connected with Hepzibah's state in life. It joins Hepzibah's unattractiveness with her failure to win a husband, and it asks the implied audience to pity her, not simply for her personal eccentricity but for her displacement from woman's sphere. Hepzibah is a "poor thing" on the presupposition that an unmarried woman is pitiable. Furthermore, the narrator's comic treatment of Hepzibah is a narrative interlude that neither forwards the plot nor adds to Hepzibah's characterization; she already has been seen as bumbling and comic. The implied author assumes that the narrator's dawdling over Hepzibah's private affairs will please his readers rather than annoy them, so assured is he of the comic interest of a spinster.

Except that she is not situated on the frontier, the characterization of Phoebe replicates "the American girl" of Cooper. Like her less skillfully drawn predecessors, Phoebe must be American and plebian, but with the manner of the lady trained.[11] The narrator claims that it is difficult to decide whether Phoebe is a lady because she has so many "ladylike attributes" (2:80) but not hereditary rank, and he proceeds to produce a catalogue that might have been compiled from the documents of the cult of true womanhood: "She shocked no canon of taste; she was admirably in keeping with herself, and never jarred against surrounding circumstances" (2:80); her figure is so small as to be childlike, her face pink and freckled and surrounded by ringlets. She is pretty and "graceful as a bird...pleasant...the example of feminine grace and availability combined, in a state of society, if there were any such, where ladies did not exist" (2:80). Given this catalogue, one might anticipate that Phoebe's assigned sphere will also be conventional: "There [in a society where ladies do not exist], it should be woman's office to move in the midst of practical affairs, and to gild them all—the very homeliest, were it even the scouring of pots and kettles—with an atmosphere of loveliness and joy" (2:80). Clearly, any future utopia over which Phoebe presides in feminine splendor will not include a new definition of woman's sphere. Yet Phoebe embodies hope in *The House of the Seven Gables*, a possibility for a future that would have been radically different under Hester Prynne's direction but for which Hawthorne's early "The New Adam and Eve" should have prepared us.

As Hawthorne's answer to the problem of woman in an egalitarian society, Phoebe bears out Henry James's contention that "in women his [Hawthorne's] taste was conservative."[12] The characterization of Phoebe gives body to a concept of woman's nature and sphere. Hawthorne's implied author simply replaces the rank of "lady" with a genteel young woman. Even Cooper's American girl is allowed more wit and assertiveness than Hawthorne's. Locked in the status quo in *The House of the Seven Gables*, the implied author allows Phoebe to leap to her destiny, as her future mate Holgrave outlines her role and sphere. " 'Ah, Phoebe!' exclaimed Holgrave.....'The world owes all its onward impulse to men ill at ease. The happy man inevitably confines himself within ancient limits. I have a presentiment that, hereafter, it will be my lot to set out trees, to make fences—perhaps, even, in due time, to build a house for another generation—in a word, to conform myself to laws, and the peaceful practice of society. Your poise will be more powerful than any oscillating tendency of mine' " (2:306-07). Holgrave would make of Phoebe exactly what Cooper's Deerslayer most fears in woman: a domesticator, a tamer of man. Holgrave wants Phoebe to make a home for him, first to create and then to inhabit woman's sphere. With her love of flowers and her feminine graces, Phoebe agrees to do so. Her union with Holgrave marks the restoration of balance and justice in the romance of *The House of the Seven Gables*, where every man and every woman is delivered into his or her culturally assigned place— including Hepzibah, who is given a surrogate husband in her brother, Clifford, once he is restored to health and can therefore assume the role of Hepzibah's protector.

A year after creating the conventional Phoebe, Hawthorne resumed, in Zenobia of *The Blithedale Romance*, the work begun in the heroine of *The Scarlet Letter*. Zenobia's feminist speeches testify to Hawthorne's acquaintance with the woman question of his time, a fact that may make the casting of Phoebe as the ideal American girl a statement of Hawthorne's preference in women rather than a simple use of a romance schema. *The Blithedale Romance* is distinguished not only by the titanic Zenobia but by its narrative point of view; it is Hawthorne's only long first-person narrative. The story of Blithedale is thus filtered through the eyes of Miles Coverdale, who characterizes himself as he tells the story. The meanings of the text must be derived from the character of Coverdale as well as from the events and characters he records and his assessment of them.[13]

The presence of Coverdale as teller makes *The Blithedale Romance* a challenging problem in interpretation, a problem that discloses the time-bound nature of social expectations and attitudes. If one accepts the Victorian perspective of

Coverdale as a translucent rather than a "crazy" window on reality, as the contemporary audience of this romance may have thought, *The Blithedale Romance* is another of Hawthorne's works that ratifies the attitudes of his time. If, however, Coverdale's "perspective" is construed as a system of prejudices that distorts vision, as we may see it in our time, *The Blithedale Romance* is a revolutionary work about the relationship between creativity and received ideas. Because *The Blithedale Romance* is a first-person narrative, this problem in interpretation exceeds a simple distinction between intended meaning and significance. If Coverdale's perspective is not to be read as a debilitating bias, then his readings of Zenobia are accurate, and Zenobia stands condemned of transgressing her God-given nature. Yet if Coverdale's perspective is intended as a limitation, his readings of Zenobia are a distortion of her character; in that case the romance condemns Coverdale's conservatism and isolates it as the facet of his character that promises to make him a mediocre poet.

As reported by Coverdale, a group of reformers, including a dark lady, Zenobia, and a facsimile of a fair lady, Priscilla, come to Blithedale to build a socialist community. Zenobia is a woman who is startling not only because of her beauty and her sexual allure, but because she is a militant feminist who speaks for women's rights and creates poems, essays, and feminist tracts. While at Blithedale, she falls in love with Hollingsworth, the man who has spearheaded this utopian experiment. Hollingsworth, however, selects the fair Priscilla to be his wife. Zenobia is later found drowned.

In his role as narrator and romancer, Coverdale creates a plot from these events. He links Zenobia's death to her disappointed love of Hollingsworth. Despite her previous protestations that woman's life should not be ruled by a single event, marriage, Zenobia's acts are perceived by Coverdale as if, indeed, that one event were all that made her life worthwhile. According to Coverdale, she commits suicide because of a broken heart, her act disproving her own theories. Thus the

dark lady and her ideas are discredited and punished, and the
fair lady Priscilla, who comports herself properly, is rewarded
with marriage. The romance design completes itself; the
events and their plotting are consistent with the conventional
meanings of the design of romance, meanings that would be
accessible to Hawthorne's audience because of their literary
expectations.

The straightforwardness of genre is complicated in *The
Blithedale Romance*, however, by Coverdale's character. In
the telling of Zenobia's story, Coverdale characterizes himself
as well as his dark lady. He describes himself as a "frosty
bachelor" (3:9) who, before coming to Blithedale, led a life of
"sweet, bewitching, enervating indolence" (3:19) in bachelor
parlors, following the routine of a genteel Victorian gentleman: eating at his club, visiting galleries, writing a few
stanzas, and spending his evenings at billiards or at the theater. He has come to Blithedale, he claims, "in quest of a
better life" (3:10), wishing to be an artist rather than a mere
poetaster.[14] Upon arriving at Blithedale, he suffers a fever,
after which he feels he has "crept out of a life of old coven-
tionalisms" and become "quite another man" (3:61).

Coverdale is by no means cleansed of his former, genteel
habits of mind, however. He remains a proper gentleman,
assessing Zenobia's movements as pure but not quite "decorous" (3:17). He takes comfort in conventional family structures, abandoning the irregular life of Blithedale and rejoicing
in a cute scene in which "prettily dressed" children are kissed
and teased by "papa," stealing "as softly behind papa, as he
had stolen behind the children" (3:150). In addition, Coverdale registers a number of generalizations about women that
reveal his mental set. He claims that women are more cautious
in their hospitality than men (3:28); that female reformers
instinctively attack society in its most vital spot (3:441); that
the female sex is prone to lavish worship on saints and heroes
(3:71); and that women are always ready with pitiless rebukes
when offended (3:159). Coverdale will no doubt see the wo-

men of Blithedale against the horizon of expectations that
provides such ideas.

The character of Zenobia, disclosed in her speech acts, is
certain to offend a gentleman like Coverdale. Her appearance
alone would set a genteel man on edge. She is said to be
dressed simply "but with a silken kerchief, between which
and her gown there was one glimpse of a white shoulder....
Her hair—which was dark, glossy, and of singular abun-
dance—was put up rather soberly and primly, without curls,
or other ornament, except a single flower. It was an exotic"
(3:15). She is critical of the status quo, unlikely to "steal
behind" papa or anyone else. She says that "when our individual adaptations begin to develop themselves, it may be that
some of us, who wear the petticoat, will go afield" (3:16). In
conversation with Coverdale she reveals her discontent with
the narrowness of woman's sphere: "Did you ever see a happy
woman in your life?...How can she be happy, after discovering
that fate has assigned her but one single event, which she must
contrive to make the substance of her whole life? A man has
his choice of innumerable events" (3:60). Zenobia is a female
reformer and a woman who pushes against the restrictiveness
of woman's role. Enacting her revolt, she writes poems and
essays, accepts speaking engagements, and writes feminist
tracts.

Coverdale's reaction to such a woman is hardly surprising,
in light of his unwitting self-portrait. He claims that the
freedom of Zenobia's deportment, her "mellow tones," and
her "unconstrained and inevitable manifestation" mean that
Zenobia is "a woman to whom wedlock had thrown wide the
gates of mystery...Zenobia is a wife! Zenobia has lived, and
loved! There is no folded petal, no latent dew-drop, in this
perfectly developed rose!" (3:47). Coverdale's reaction to
Zenobia's needs, compared with those of the slight Priscilla, is
also predictable; he will protect the fair one, but as for
Zenobia: "I saw no occasion to give myself any trouble. With
her native strength, and her experience of the world, she could

not be supposed to need any help of mine" (3:79). Zenobia's independence and seeming self-sufficiency give the unimaginative Coverdale no role to play in her presence. He seems not to know how to proceed with such an unconventional woman. Operating from an unstated assumption about male protectiveness of the female, he says that undertaking the "guardianship" of Zenobia "would be quite a super-erogatory piece of quixotism in me" (3:94). He fears that if Zenobia ever had knowledge of any attempt on his part to protect her, she would make him "the butt of endless ridicule" (3:94). Zenobia makes Coverdale feel insecure because she violates the expectations that ordinarily guide a man's conduct.

When Coverdale listens to Zenobia's speeches, he listens without anticipating any playfulness or irony, both of which he himself lacks, and he hears what he expects to hear. When Zenobia tells him that his poetry has stolen into her memory, Coverdale assumes she is praising him. When Zenobia recommends that Coverdale use Priscilla as a subject for his poetry because he sees her "in so poetical a light" (3:33), Coverdale assumes Zenobia is sincere. When Zenobia has been shunted aside by Hollingsworth, and Coverdale overhears the conversation in which she tells Hollingsworth that she is "a woman—with every fault, it may be, that a woman ever had, weak, vain, unprincipled (like most of my sex; for our virtues, when we have any, are merely impulsive and intuitive") (3:217), Coverdale thinks her assessment of woman is sincere rather than satirical because it corresponds with his own. Thus when Zenobia is found dead, it is consistent with his character and predispositions, and therefore entirely predictable, that Coverdale would name suicide as the cause of death and unrequited love as the cause of suicide.

Coverdale interprets Zenobia's deeds as the intended audience of the implied author would interpret them: in keeping with received notions of woman's nature and sphere. Because Zenobia flirts with violating all of these, she is finally rendered miserable. Foiled in love, she has no further reason to live. In keeping with poetic justice, she dies, and the fair heroine marries, with one caveat that looks forward to the conclusion of *The Bostonians*: Priscilla goes off with Hollingsworth who is as monomaniacal in his desire to reform society as James's Basil Ransom is in his desire to shape Verena Tarrant. *The Blithedale Romance* thus resolves the problem of the dark, feminist lady within a romance frame. The intended meanings of the text, in the context of the culture's understandings, are both clear and entirely conventional.

The Blithedale Romance, however, is a striking instance of the difference between meaning and significance, which in this case testifies to the enormous role of social expectations and the literary schema of romance in the creation and likely reception of art. In order to read *The Blithedale Romance* as a work that reinforces the status quo, it is necessary to assume that the Victorianism and gentility that are Miles Coverdale's framework of meaning provide accurate perceptions rather than biased or prejudiced distortions. If, that is, woman's nature and its ramifications are accepted as true to nature and experience, than all Coverdale's assessments of Zenobia are adequate, and he is to be taken as a fairly reliable narrator who reports to the implied readers of the text what they already know in one way or another: love is a woman's whole existence, and feminism is a violation of nature that nature will punish. But if Coverdale is understood to be an unreliable narrator in his assessments of Zenobia because his conservatism and tepidity distort his view of reality, then *The Blithedale Romance* may be seen as a revolutionary work. Its significance, to those of us whose horizon of expectations does not include a concept of woman's nature as an article of faith, is iconoclastic. *The Blithedale Romance* then becomes an example of the contention of Hans Robert Jauss that "the resistance that [a] work poses to the expectations of its first audience can be so great that it requires a long process of reception to gather in that which was unexpected and unusable within the first horizon."[15] In the absence of nineteenth-century predispositions and the filter those provide, Zenobia's speeches reveal a clever, witty, and insightful woman whose stature indicts the meanness of her world and particularly its representative, Coverdale, whose assumptions about woman's nature impede his vision and his imagination, guaranteeing that he shall always be a poetaster and never a poet. *The Blithedale Romance* is thus a drama of the relationships among preconceptions, vision, and the creative imagination in which the figure of Zenobia tests Coverdale's imaginative reach and flexibility.[16]

The key to Coverdale's inadequate vision is the character of Zenobia as it is revealed in her speeches. Zenobia's rhetoric, closely attended to and unmediated by nineteenth-century preconceptions of exotic-seeming women, reveals a person of wit who sees life in perspective and is able to declaim humorously as well as seriously on the subject of woman's sphere. Speaking with Coverdale about the assignment of duties at Blithedale, Zenobia piles up infinitives and compound constructions that signal a whimsical stance: "Oh, we of the softer sex…we women (there are four of us here, already) will take the domestic and indoor part of the business, as a matter of course. To bake, to boil, to roast, to fry, to stew—to wash, and iron, and scrub, and sweep, and, at our idler intervals, to repose ourselves on knitting and sewing—these, I suppose, must be feminine occupations for the present" (3:16). Zenobia's use of the clichéd "softer sex" is accompanied by a laugh, and a series like "to bake, to boil, to roast, to fry, to stew" is surely intended as a mock-epic catalogue. Her further, exhaustive list of cleaning methods plays a humorous change on the old theme that a woman's work is never done. Zenobia's comic approach to what is to her a serious issue, women's rights, reveals another of Zenobia's traits: a capacity to control her responses, reminiscent of Hester Prynne's capacity to manipulate her manner. Zenobia can be playful, as we have seen, on subjects she takes seriously, but she can also show anger on the same subjects. Her response depends upon her intelligently assessing the situation. She reacts angrily to Coverdale's condescending smile at her mention of "woman's wider liberty" (3:120), for example, refusing to allow a topic important to her to be devalued by others. Far from being a plaything of circumstance, Zenobia chooses her mode and her moment.

Given that Hawthorne assigned to Zenobia the role of poet and essayist, it should come as no surprise that her language is acute and colorful. Her rhetoric proves her acquaintance with the literature of her time and her sensitivity to matters of style. An example is Zenobia's legend. Often read seriously as a significant allegory of high philosophical import, it is at least in part a parody of melodramatic literature. Zenobia delivers her legend in the stilted diction of eighteenth-century gothic romance, complete with "thee" and "thy" and "-est" verb endings, which are not typical of her speech. She allows herself literary clichés that are finally humorous, such as " 'my lips are forbidden to betray the secret!' said the Veiled Lady" (3:112). Of some 114 sentences that comprise the legend, thirty-one (or 28 percent) are exclamatory, and a notable number of the rest are interrogatory, heightened sentence structures that emphasize the melodramatic nature of the narrative. Moreover, the list of young Theodore's fears of kissing the Veiled Lady of the legend is climaxed by this: "Even should she prove a comely maiden enough, in other respects, the odds were ten to one that her teeth were defective; a terrible drawback on the delectableness of a kiss!" (3:113). This legend is not serious fare but a clever parody of the popular literature of the time, a parody that demonstrates Zenobia's literary acumen as she playfully weaves this melodramatic tale for the susceptible Blithedalers.

A witty command of language marks all Zenobia's utterances. Joined with the serious, conservative character of Coverdale as *her* narrative audience, her language becomes playfully ironic and a judgment on this Victorian gentleman who presumes to the rank of artist. When the subject is literature, Zenobia's exchanges with Miles Coverdale are the dialogues of one writer with another, as well as one human temperament with another. They suggest that Zenobia scorns genteel literature and the work of Miles Coverdale. Coverdale's poetry is the first subject of conversation between Coverdale and Zenobia. She tells him that his poetry has "stolen into my memory, without my exercising any choice or volition about the matter" (3:14), which Coverdale takes to be a compliment. Knowing Zenobia's way with words, however, we must wonder if she is not damning Coverdale's verse rather than praising it. His poetry may haunt her for the same reasons that advertising jingles and genteel versifying lodge in the mind: their deadly regularity of rhythm and rhyme makes them eminently memorizable.

The suspicion that Zenobia may be deftly mocking Coverdale is confirmed somewhat later, when Zenobia decks out Priscilla-the-fair with flowers and then offers her to Coverdale for his "artistic" use. In no way admiring Priscilla, Zenobia in fact finds this evanescent shadow of a person irritating and worthy of disdain. Having covered Priscilla with blossoms that include, as the satiric Zenobia would have it, "a weed of evil odor and ugly aspect," Zenobia says to Coverdale, "Is not she worth a verse or two?" (3:59). Earlier, Zenobia had recommended to Coverdale that because he saw Priscilla "in so poetical a light" he should turn her and her advent at Blithedale into "a ballad. It is a grand subject, and worthy of supernatural machinery" (3:33). Zenobia speaks archly here, with her considerable irony rendered unmistakable by the fact that she finds Priscilla to have "probably no more transcendental purpose than to do my miscellaneous sewing" (3:33). Zenobia clearly does not believe that a creature like Priscilla can inspire grand and passionate poetry. Offering Priscilla to Coverdale as a subject minimizes Coverdale's literary pretensions. As Zenobia puts it: "As she has hardly any physique, a poet, like Mr. Miles Coverdale, may be allowed to think her spiritual!" (3:34). Zenobia's respect for Coverdale's talent is not much greater than her love for Priscilla.[17]

This is the character who, rejected by the archreformer Hollingsworth, still defends him, seemingly like a schoolgirl who has been hurt but is still in love—or at least this is how Coverdale and critics of *The Blithedale Romance* have interpreted her words. Disappointed in love, Zenobia says to Coverdale, "Presume not to estimate a man like Hollingsworth!" (3:225). If a Victorian frame of reference like Coverdale's is imposed on these words, then Zenobia is protecting the man she loves from the criticism of others. Is she not, then, a woman in love like any other woman? Not wholly. Zenobia is not blinded by her feelings for Hollingsworth. On the contrary, she sees him as a victim of "the fiend" and herself as finally "awake, disenchanted, disenthralled" from his clutches (3:218). She nonetheless feels compelled to defend him before Coverdale because, a passionate soul herself, she will not tolerate an attack on greatness, even greatness gone astray, by the mediocre. As she says, Coverdale probably does not know that a great man "attains his normal condition only through the inspiration of one great idea.…There can be no truer test of the noble and heroic, in any individual, than the degree in which he possesses the faculty of distinguishing heroism from absurdity" (3:166). Coverdale does not possess this faculty nor any aspect of character that speaks of grandeur of soul. Because Hollingsworth does, Zenobia is attracted to him. She seeks her own level, her own height.[18]

Still, in her final scene in the romance Zenobia delivers speeches that, read in the context of genteel ideas and out of the context of the character established earlier in the work, are taken by Coverdale and by critics to mean that Zenobia does embrace woman's nature and place as defined by her culture. Her previous rhetoric about woman, then, would seem to have been bogus, but her words prove to be consistent with her feminist ideals.[19] Zenobia addresses Coverdale in the midst of a bitter quarrel between Hollingsworth and herself. She claims that she has been "on trial" for her life, but her statement is accompanied by a laughter that must be sardonic. Hollingsworth has just claimed that he does not judge

Zenobia, though he does not love her, upon which she turns to Coverdale and says: "Ah, this is very good!...What strange beings you men are, Mr. Coverdale!—is it not so? It is the simplest thing in the world, with you, to bring a woman before your secret tribunals, and judge and condemn her, unheard, and then tell her to go free without a sentence. The misfortune is, that this same secret tribunal chances to be the only judgment-seat that a true woman stands in awe of, and that any verdict short of acquittal is equivalent to a death-sentence!" (3:215). Zenobia's tone must be considered here. Because she speaks in anger, it is entirely likely that she means to describe woman's life as it is and not as, according to Zenobia, it should be. Zenobia has in fact been "tried" by Hollingsworth, as all women are tried by men in a patriarchal society such as she inhabits. Moreover, woman was expected to pass "unheard" in Zenobia's world.

The angry Zenobia is also capable of cynicism on the subject of "true" womanhood. A "true woman" does stand in awe of the male tribunal, whether "true woman" is the culturally-defined woman who submits to male authority, or the woman who sees the power vested in the male before whom she must of necessity, then, stand in awe. Finally, a woman judged guilty of ambitions beyond her proper domestic sphere was metaphorically sentenced to death in Zenobia's society—witness the declared preference of both Coverdale and Hollingsworth, representatives of the conventional and the exceptional dimensions of male society, for the insubstantial Priscilla.

Shortly after this speech, Zenobia says to Hollingsworth: "At least, I am a woman—with every fault, it may be, that a woman ever had, weak, vain, unprincipled, (like most of my sex; for our virtues, when we have any, are merely impulsive and intuitive,) passionate, too, and pursuing my foolish and unattainable ends, by indirect and cunning, though absurdly chosen means, as an hereditary bond-slave must—" (3:217). This is Zenobia the consummate parodist, whom we have

seen at work earlier, recounting her legend. This seemingly
self-deprecating Zenobia, in her anger, now parodies to these
men in hyperbolic fashion what she knows they think women
to be, driving home at the last moment an intensely feminist
charge against male society—namely, that male images of
woman finally make women slaves. This is of course a red flag
to social reformers, such as Hollingsworth, and to any Victorian male, such as Coverdale, who fancies himself the protector of women.

Zenobia's final conversation with Coverdale before her
untimely death must be read with the understanding provided
by her literary awareness, rhetorical gift, and insight into
Coverdale as a poetaster. Zenobia is aware of the conventional
readings of woman's heart and motives that genteel Victorian
Americans make. Aware of Coverdale's pretensions to literature, she is able, in her legend, to parody the kind of literature
that a conventional soul like Coverdale will undoubtedly
produce, if he writes at all, and therefore creates a script for
him. She patronizingly recommends that he write "this ballad," a popular form, and even provides, lest his own insights
fail him, two possible morals: "that, in the battlefield of life,
the downright stroke, that would fall only on a man's steel
head-piece, is sure to light on a woman's heart, over which she
wears no breastplate, and whose wisdom it is, therefore, to
keep out of the conflict. Or this:—that the whole universe, her
own sex and yours, and Providence, or Destiny, to boot, make
common cause against the woman who swerves one hair's
breadth out of the beaten track...with that one hair's breadth,
she goes all astray, and never sees the world in its true aspect,
afterwards!" (3:224). Zenobia here proposes alternative endings for some conventional literary endeavor of Coverdale's.
The clue to the irony of her proposal lies in the ridiculously
exaggerated imagery in which she presents these scenarios,
the first epic and the second sentimental. Even after the angry
confrontation with Hollingsworth and after his rejection of
her, Zenobia is here once again at play, hilariously proposing

forms to help the insipid Coverdale navigate the tempestuous waters of human interaction.

When in a more serious vein Zenobia complains that Hollingsworth "flung away what would have served him better than the poor, pale flower he kept" (3:224), she is merely stating a self-evident fact. She is self-assured enough to recognize that she would be a heartier, more challenging companion for a man of Hollingsworth's dimensions. Finally, Zenobia imagines that many a woman in her position would blush under the eyes of those who knew she had loved and lost and would, she says, "mortify herself, I suppose, with foolish notions of having sacrificed the honor of her sex, at the foot of proud, contumacious man" (3:225). Again, Zenobia expands on the script that a genteel poetaster like Coverdale is likely to write. She knows that his understanding of woman is so conventional that he is likely to depict women in the stock postures, images, and responses of genteel literature, and she responds that this business of sacrificing "the honor of her sex" is a "foolish notion."

Zenobia then continues: "Poor womanhood, with its rights and wrongs! Here will be new matter for my course of lectures, at the idea of which you smiled, Mr. Coverdale, a month or two ago" (3:225-26). This hardly sounds like a person about to take her own life. Nevertheless, Zenobia goes on to dramatize herself and her situation in a highly stylized message that she asks Coverdale to deliver for her to Hollingsworth: "Tell him something pretty and pathetic, that will come nicely and sweetly into your ballad—anything you please, so it be tender and submissive enough" (3:226). Zenobia is, of course, not herself converted to submissiveness as woman's proper posture before man and the world. Rather, she plays against Coverdale's expectations. She knows what the culture likes women to be and therefore what it would prefer in a popular ballad. This proves to be incontrovertibly so when later in the same conversation Zenobia tells Coverdale: "Lip of man will never touch my hand again. I intend to

become a Catholic, for the sake of going into a nunnery"
(3:227). (Whether this is to be before or after her projected
lecture tour, she does not say.) This is obviously a self-drama-
tizing, literarily acute Zenobia; the same woman who wore a
luxuriant flower in her hair; a woman who is casting herself,
granted all we have seen of her nature, in the unlikely role open
to a romance heroine. Certainly no further indication is
needed of her wit, her distance from heartbreak, her literary
acumen, and her estimate of Coverdale.

Zenobia's parting talk with Coverdale, together with her
complexity of character and her talent and inclination for
parody, hardly lead us to anticipate a suicide.[20] On the contrary, she tells Coverdale that she plans to continue her lectures. Suicide over unrequited love is out of character for
Zenobia, but reading a woman's death along the lines of
sentimental romance is not out of character for Coverdale.
The bare facts of Zenobia's death are few and straightforward:
she is found drowned, her body inflexible, her arms "grown
rigid in the act of struggling" and "bent before her" (3:235).
That is all. The conventional poetaster who came to Blithedale with a priori ideas of woman proceeds to impose his
genteel, literary, sentimental ideal on Zenobia's death and to
construct a story from it. Coverdale describes her knees not as
simply "bent" but "in the attitude of prayer." He imagines her
soul comes "bubbling," no less, "out through her lips" to give
itself "up to the Father, reconciled and penitent." He describes her arms, too, not simply as "bent" but "as if she
struggled against Providence in never-ending hostility" while
her hands are said to be "clenched in immitigable defiance"
(3:235). Would Coverdale have us believe she had defied the
divine design for woman? Casting about for tried and true
images in which to capture Zenobia's death, Coverdale does
not seem to notice that he has contradicted himself, giving a
praying Zenobia in one image and a defiant one in the next.
His words obviously embroider the facts of Zenobia's death,
facts that do not in themselves clearly point toward suicide.

Removed from the culture's horizon of expectations but aware of the horizon's significance to the narrator, the implied author of *The Blithedale Romance* delivers a final, devastating indictment of Coverdale in the thoughts he grants Coverdale on Zenobia's death. Zenobia's dead body before him, Coverdale is shown to lack the imaginative reach to speculate on the particular emotions that the real Zenobia may have experienced at the moment of her death. Rather, the limited Coverdale falls back on literary convention and stock ideas of woman and heroines and wonders if Zenobia would have done the deed had she "foreseen all these ugly circumstances of death, how ill it would become her, the altogether unseemly aspect which she must put on," exhibiting herself "to a public assembly in a badly-fitting garment!" (3:236). Coverdale's implication is: Woman, thy name is vanity, even if you despair to the point of death. Coverdale here descends to inhuman depths of insensitivity and callousness. Unfortunately, he doesn't stop there. He imagines, despite the implications of a death by suicide, which he believes her death to be, that Zenobia was merely playing a part: "She had seen pictures, I suppose, of drowned persons, in lithe and graceful attitudes. And she deemed it well and decorous to die as so many village-maidens have, wronged in their first-love, and seeking peace" (3:236). If we ever doubted Coverdale's shallowness of soul, we no longer can. Coverdale is conventional and mediocre. Even in the face of a woman's death, he sees only a literary and cultural abstraction, and a melodramatic one at that, rather than flesh and blood. The implied author could not more severely judge the quality of soul of the representative Victorian gentleman and the would-be artist who is unable to shed his culture's preconceptions of woman. With a great story before him in the person of Zenobia, Coverdale fails as an artist—and as a human being.

Like many first-person narratives, *The Blithedale Romance* is ultimately about its narrator, Coverdale, whose whole purpose in going to Blithedale is to test his literary talent. "The woman question" becomes the vehicle to explore a larger issue: the nature of art and its relationship to imaginative freedom. Standing between Coverdale and literary greatness is his tepidness and his conventionality, his allegiance to that which is known and approved, and his inability to get beyond his own cultural understandings. The casting of Coverdale's problem, the artist's problem, in terms of his reading of a woman, and an exotic woman, is entirely conventional: woman is traditionally the Muse, and Coverdale is an artist who stymies the Muse because he is closed to inspiration and locked into a system of a priori ideas. Further, a woman who is exotic most severely challenges the artist's imaginative power because as *The Blithedale Romance* demonstrates, the culture's assumptions about woman are so strong that a leap beyond them is proof of marked imaginative gifts. To depart from conventional ideas of woman is, after all, to abandon Victorian culture's tripartite anchor of security: hearth, home, and motherhood. To swing free from this idea and its ramifications is to fly into perhaps as yet uncharted, and hence frightening, imaginative realms. Thus the most stringent test of an artist's (in this case, Coverdale's) powers of imagination may be the test posed by his relationship to notions about woman and his ability to transcend their limits in his art. The artist's imaginative reach is proven in his ability to follow and be faithful to his imaginative projections, his Hester Prynnes, rather than to succumb to the projections of his society, the community and its values and norms. Miles Coverdale fails the test.

Such, at least, are the implications of *The Blithedale Romance* if Coverdale's predispositions are counted as prejudice, if Coverdale's bias can be legitimately associated with misreadings of Zenobia that incriminate Coverdale but allow Zenobia to go scot free. The question before us, however, is whether or not such meanings, although they can be construed from the text, can be ascribed to Hawthorne's romance. Did the implied author anticipate, intend, and, in effect, engineer such a reading? I think not. Confronted with a narrative like *Blithedale*, the critical framework offered by the culture's horizon of expectations legitimately elicits the significance of Hawthorne's romance in our time, an undertaking that is an aspect of the literary history and continuing life of a literary work. But it proposes, as well, necessary restraints if we wish to recover the probable understandings of the text in its own time. Matters of genre already suggest, of course, certain restraints; Zenobia, within a romance design, is placed in a structural position from which we can infer that she is intended to be a woman of questionable character with questionable ideas. When genre expectations are supplemented by cultural expectations that the critical framework of woman's nature brings into focus, the gap between intended meaning and later significance widens. What is more, when Hawthorne's conservative characterization of heroines in other works is joined with his entirely conventional attachment to his wife and his imputed attitudes toward Margaret Fuller,[21] it seems even less likely that the implied author intended to undercut Coverdale's assessment of Zenobia.

But finally, the text itself does not question the narrator's reliability on the subject of woman. Rather, the implied author creates a narrator who never apologizes, never equivocates, and never explains but simply assumes that his audience respects his assessments and those values whose reasonableness depends on unarticulated assumptions about woman's nature and sphere. The text assumes Coverdale's reliability about "woman," although to us he may seem indisputably narrow and painfully sexist. At this juncture, the critical framework offered by woman's nature makes its final contribution to the hermeneutic and semiotic enterprise: recognition of the fact that one century's truth is another's prejudice. Setting significance aside and attempting to recover intended meanings, we must in the case of this romance read from the culture to the text rather than from the text to the culture. From his own and his culture's point of view,

Hawthorne knew only that Victorian genteel understandings, including the concept of woman's nature, were as near an approximation of truth as the human race had yet achieved. From our contemporary point of view, such an understanding of "truth" makes Hawthorne's romance a reactionary one, a flight into the safety of received attitudes toward woman. Hawthorne was able to imagine heroines more magnificent and multidimensional than the heroines of conventional romance, as his conception of Hester Prynne suggests. Yet even the presentation of Hester is at points hobbled by gender-inflected problems; the full implications of her character are resisted by a narrator speaking for an implied author behind whom stands Hawthorne, unable finally to let *The Scarlet Letter* break free of ideological shackles. The culture's horizon of expectations for woman was powerful enough to impede the imagination even of an artist of Hawthorne's stature. In fact, Hawthorne did not sustain the remarkable imaginative feat begun in Hester Prynne. Rather, he returned to more typical romance heroines in *The House of the Seven Gables* and *The Marble Faun*, and he brought Zenobia, as potentially remarkable a character as Hester Prynne, before a tribunal that ratifies conservative views of woman. He was finally unable to sustain the battle against cultural imperialism on the subject of woman that he had begun in *The Scarlet Letter*. Hawthorne's voyage out from the culture's horizon of expectations, from the notions that governed Cooper's craft, come to not much more than a gentleman's pilgrimage to a fair-haired heroine in a dovecote.

3. WILLIAM DEAN HOWELLS
The Male Imagination at the Crossroads

Bemused by gallantry, we hear
our mediocrities over-praised,
indolence read as abnegation,
slattern thought styled intuition,
every lapse forgiven.
                    —Adrienne Rich

The problem of woman that engaged the imagination of William Dean Howells is the problem of woman's sphere. In his *Suburban Sketches*, Howells calls American society "a hospital for invalid woman," a culture in which woman's place is reduced to a domesticity so narrow, so isolated, so trivialized[1] that the genteel American woman is left idle and aimless. Vast social and economic changes in post–Civil War America associated with the rise of wealth, industry, technology, and business, also brought affluence, leisure, and a further compartmentalization of the sexes, men on Wall Street and women at home, that cast genteel and nouveau riche women into inactivity or purposeless busyness. Women of this class were ensconced in an environment that, far from challenging them, gave them little to do and patronizingly reinforced their doing it poorly. The novels of Howells appeared in those decades following the Civil War when women, having discovered a range of abilities in themselves through their work in temperance unions, abolitionist societies, and later in hospitals and other arenas associated with the war effort, were demanding suffrage, access to birth control information, greater educational opportunities, and political power. In short, they demanded the amelioration of their lot and the expansion of the arena to which the culture assigned them. The fiction of Howells treats women's issues seriously, portraying heroines who are doctors, artists, and society women, single women and wives, but all constricted by prejudicial notions of woman's place and competence. Seeking to reconcile the historical expansion of woman's sphere with an ongoing idea of womanliness, the imagination of Howells is receptive to new initiatives on woman's part and is marked by a boldness with which it is usually not credited. Despite the conscious intent of Howells to expand woman's lot, however, there is also present a conservatism that attests to the unconscious constraints imposed by the culture's notions of gender.

The intervention of a conservative notion of woman's nature in Howells's texts, despite his receptivity to change, confirms the culture's ideology of woman and its power. Cooper, never questioning the culture's ideas of woman, constructed his texts from the materials of the culture's horizon of expectations. Hawthorne, consciously content with the culture's ideology, although subconsciously restless with it, marshaled the same materials to greater artistic effect than Cooper and constructed imaginative possibilities for female characters that he then deconstructed and denied. Howells, discontent with the culture's limitations on woman's sphere, set out to examine the problem and to promote new attitudes, but unwittingly fell back into the old dispensations for women.

Nonetheless it is legitimate to claim for Howells a more inclusive imagination of woman than that of many other male writers.[2] Ironically, the very gentility for which Howells has often been criticized may have allowed him to cast heroines in a less usual and therefore more innovative light than did, say, a Theodore Dreiser. In *Sister Carrie* a woman's virtue is as much the issue as it was for Cooper in *The Deerslayer*, but the norms of Dreiser's novel are infinitely more liberal than Cooper could have imagined. Howells, on the other hand, avoiding the subject of sexuality, created heroines as heroes are most often imagined, as fictional human beings with a range of aspirations and difficulties, with marriage and sexuality being but two. Howells attempted to think outside the culture's gender terms, but his texts confirm that the powerful idea of woman's nature can abort an artistic realization of that effort. As a consequence, the appeal in Howells's fiction to an expanded notion of woman's sphere proves to be conservative in its intent, serving the interests of an older idea of woman's nature from which Howells perceived his culture to have strayed.

In *Dr. Breen's Practice*, Howells establishes three categories of women: the mannish, the womanish, and the womanly. The mannish are those women who behave like men, perhaps the feminists of whom the novel's narrator disapproves. The womanish are frivolous, silly females. The womanly are those who conform to a concept of sexual dualism, those who know as Grace Breen does that "a woman isn't something else first, and a woman afterwards."[3] As his study entitled *The Heroines of Fiction* confirms, Howells favored changes in woman's education and sphere that once again would make womanly the vapid, womanish females of his genteel society. Evaluating the female characters of other writers and setting out his idea of the "Ever-Womanly," Howells praises Hawthorne for reinstating "a conception of entire womanhood in fiction" (2:190)[4] by his characterization of the womanly Hester and Zenobia. Howells rejects the womanish heroines of Cooper, Scott, and C.B. Brown because they are "of such an extremely conventional and ladylike deportment in all circumstances that you wish to kill them" (1:11). Asserting, perhaps patronizingly, that "a novel is great or not, as its women are important or unimportant" (1:113), Howells, a progenitor of realism, calls for the inclusion of faults as well as virtues in the characterization of heroines who are to be drawn from what Frank Norris called the observation of life in the brownstone on the corner. Thus Howells would include in portraits of heroines such conventional virtues as the "sudden and supreme self-sacrifice" (2:15) of which he thinks both coquettes and nuns capable, but also such willful and predatory traits as the "bad and indifferent" (2:168) that women may also possess.

Howells, however, subverts the very complexity he prefers in heroines by adopting a patronizing, sentimental tone each time he names a female fault. The implied authors of his fiction do this repeatedly and Howells does it himself in *The Heroines of Fiction*, where the clue to this tone is the word "charm." A girl's "potentialities of wrong have their charm" (1:214), he writes; strong and stubborn wills have "a peculiar charm" (2:178). He seems to feel some need to soften his mentioning a heroine's faults, to apologize for noticing them, succumbing to a decorum encouraged by that genteel understanding of woman's nature that identifies woman as a special, protected class exempt from the demands of the harsh world in which men operate. The chivalric, gallant Howells adopts an attitude toward heroines that serves to etherealize them once again, turning them back into the cute, inconsequential, diminutive creatures he laments finding in the works of other writers.[5] His fiction reflects an imagination where genteel combat takes place, a battleground where soldiers fight for the reeducation of females into a more substantial womanhood and where knights protect females from Howells's perceived truth that womankind has dwindled into inconsequence.

This combat in the fiction of Howells uncovers a difference between the male and the female imagination at work on the characterization of heroines. Howells would require of his heroines a more steady, serious, and responsible humanity, much as the women who created "woman's fiction" required their heroines to eschew emotion and to take responsibility for themselves and their lives. While female writers, however, wrote without chivalric compulsions, showing no need to cajole and patronize and protect their female characters, Howells seems never to forget, as he creates his heroines, that he is male. He is unable to take a gender-neutral, human view rather than a gender-inflected, male view of heroines. No male American writer more consciously sought to be expansive on the subject of woman's sphere, only to be unconsciously defeated by the agent that he could not perceive as his enemy, the idea of woman's nature and its complement—the idea of man's nature. The imagination of Howells, then, is an extraordinary indication of an insidious incursion of gender into the production of texts.

Howells saw that the conflict between the culture's gender expectations and new roles for women had dramatic possibilities, and he proceeded to make use of them in *Dr. Breen's Practice* (1881). This novel attests to Howells's boldness in dramatizing problems that besiege a woman who dares to enter a profession usually populated by men. Although the story of Grace is framed by her love interests, the drama of her fictional life is generated by her status as a "doctress." Through a series of twists and turns in the plot, Grace is led to feel she is an incompetent doctor, but she is rescued from self-doubt by the love of the understanding, respectful man she marries. She continues to practice medicine but only at her husband's suggestion, and only on the children of his factory hands.

To many feminists a plot such as this smacks of narrow, sexist attitudes. Intending to expand the authorial audience's sense of woman, however, the novel shows the imagination of Howells trying to come to terms with a representation of the professional woman. While much of Grace's "practice" is emotional, an equal amount of her "practice" is medical. The implied author joins characterization, narrative audience, and plot to create a complex statement about the problem of woman's sphere in the nineteenth century. The assumption that motivates the responses of characters to Dr. Grace Breen and that the implied author's artistic choices address is this: woman's nature unfits women for extra-domestic pursuits of any consequence, and the failures of individual women prove it. The intended meaning that counters this assumption and that emerges from the coalescence of the elements of the novel into an aesthetic whole is this: woman's nature is irrelevant to professional competence, neither fitting nor unfitting women for careers; women should be allowed to pursue careers; not all women possess the temperament to pursue careers. To dramatize this meaning, the implied author creates a heroine whose scrupulosity hobbles her in the practice of her profession. He surrounds her with characters who are right about her weaknesses, but for the wrong reasons, faulting her pursuits on grounds of gender while her problems are shown to stem from her particular temperament. Thus the novel discredits the idea that there is automatic virtue in either pursuing an extra-domestic career or remaining on the home front.

The characterization of Grace Breen and the plot of *Dr. Breen's Practice* are designed to reveal the relationship between a puritanical approach to life and the requirements of a successful career.[6] The narrator attributes to Grace a New England temperament—"a child's severe morality...an almost passionate desire to meet the consequences of her errors" (14)—that, particularly in its female incarnations, held no small interest for American writers. James took it up in Olive Chancellor of *The Bostonians*; Harriet Beecher Stowe developed it in the intensity and guilt of Mary Scudder of *The Minister's Wooing*; and Mary E. Wilkins Freeman's New England "nun" is built around it. The character of Grace Breen, however, outstrips all of them. According to the narrator, Grace's outlook on life is so strenuous that she contemplated returning home to practice medicine because there the "security and criticism would be hardest to bear, and therefore, as she fancied, the most useful to her in the formation of character" (12-13). Grace is placed in a situation guaranteed to activate her puritanical bent. Her first patient takes a boat ride and contracts pneumonia. Because Grace encouraged this expedition, she immediately feels that she acted irresponsibly. Although she initiates sensible measures to treat her patient, she too readily complies with his request that another physician be consulted.

The implied author ties Grace's quick decision to call in a second doctor to her scrupulosity, which is shown, in turn, to undermine her self-assurance. Grace claims that she called in Dr. Mulbridge because a patient's recovery depends on faith in the attending physician. The novel, however, shows this to be a rationalization on Grace's part. Rather than assert her competence and thus command her patient's respect and confidence, Grace is so shaken by her self-imposed guilt for approving the boat ride that she doubts her own abilities. Even the patient later points out to Grace that no male doctor would have so readily acquiesced to a request for another doctor. While the patient incorrectly attributes Grace's decision to her gender, the text ascribes it to her exaggerated sense of responsibility. Indeed, only Grace's temperament *can* account for her decision because the text offers no evidence of her being technically incompetent. Grace Breen is characterized as a doctor who, doubting her own abilities, sacrifices her first opportunity to prove herself—her temperament, rather than her gender, works against her pursuit of a career.[7]

Gender, however, aids and abets the temperamental insecurities from which Grace suffers. The imagination of Howells uses the hostile milieu which confronted a professional woman in the nineteenth century to undermine Grace, surrounding her with a narrative audience composed of characters fixated on the peculiarity of a woman who is a doctor. Because of preconceived ideas of woman's appropriate sphere, they doubt Grace's abilities before she has ever lifted a stethoscope. The narrative audience serves to heighten interest in Grace as a character, to catalog social attitudes toward women who transgress the law of woman's sphere, and to dramatize the

enormous odds against the success of even a confident woman—not to mention an insecure woman like Grace Breen,
whose competence is demeaned at every turn. Grace is subjected to a barrage of reactions from characters who, astonished at or uncomfortable with a woman who appears to
have exceeded their expectations, demonstrate the insight of
Howells into a career woman's situation in his world. A
mailman, for example, assumes that an envelope addressed to
an M.D. cannot be for Grace; the man whom Grace eventually marries blushes "when required to recognize Grace in
her professional quality" (74). Female characters repeatedly
speculate about Grace's love life and about her expertise in
medicine, discussing her private and professional life and the
latest hair styles in the same conversation. Dr. Mulbridge,
Grace's male colleague, treats Grace like a baby-sitter rather
than a peer, reducing her to an uncredentialed helpmate. The
cultural tyranny suffered by professional women is exercised
by all these people, unable to a person to consider doctoring
appropriate to a woman's sphere of activity.

The novel simultaneously indicts the narrative audience for
its narrow, prejudicial views and shows that a proper "womanliness" attaches to Grace despite her peculiar choice of
career. As Hawthorne attempted to move the hearts of his
assumed audience toward the adulterous Hester by drawing
out her "womanly" traits, so Howells tries to bring his authorial audience to sympathize with Grace Breen, prostituted
through professional training. While most attitudes and
motives ascribed to Grace are dismaying to late twentieth-
century readers, they are "womanly" nonetheless. The narrator explains that Grace entered medicine in the same spirit
as "other women enter convents, or go out to heathen lands"
(12), for a reason typically assigned to women—a broken
heart, suffered when her boyfriend married her best friend.
She has attempted to stay as close to woman's sphere as she
can, outside of marriage itself, by planning to treat children.
Moreover, Grace is made to dissociate herself from feminism

and the contemporary woman's movement by refusing quite sanely, according to the narrator, to "assume any duties or responsibilities toward it" (15). On top of this, Grace prefers to be called "Miss" rather than "Doctor," and she supports the traditional subservience of wives to husbands, telling her patient Louise to honor her husband's name "no matter how cruel and indifferent to you he has been" (31). Nonetheless, Grace is shown to be insightful rather than naive, knowingly suffering the slings and arrows of public opinion in becoming a doctor and pursuing conscience, rather than social approval, in her choice of career. She continues her work for a time in full knowledge of the prejudice against her, observing to her mother that there "isn't a woman in the house that wouldn't sooner trust herself in the hands of the stupidest boy that got his diploma with me than she would in mine" (44). Grace's awareness of the world's attitude makes her pursuit of medicine courageous—while at the same time it reinforces her self-sacrificial nature and stringent conscience.

Having rendered Grace palatable to his authorial audience by drawing attention to her "womanly" dimensions, the implied author creates a climax that serves two ends: it demonstrates the benefits of Grace's brief extra-domestic experience, and it shows the usefulness of marriage to a woman of her temperament. In facing obstacles, Grace has increased her self-esteem; yet her confidence is rooted finally in the love of a man rather than in the core of her own being. It is not until the novel's climax that Grace musters enough self-assurance to assert herself in the face of the brutal, misogynist Dr. Mulbridge. Earlier, though aware that Mulbridge treats her as a joke, she "felt that she could not openly resent it" (95). Now, when Mulbridge has the audacity to propose marriage to her, not once but twice, Grace rebuffs him with considerable force and with an accurate assessment of his character: "I think you are a tyrant, and that you want a slave, not a wife. You wish to be obeyed. You despise women" (254). She tells him, further, that he's now simply playing "the baffled tyrant" and is treating her "like a child that does n't know its own mind, or has none to know" (256). Unfortunately, from a late twentieth-century perspective, this scene, in which Grace's sense of self seemingly triumphs over prejudice, concludes with her delivering to Mulbridge what she considers the real "blow": that she has accepted the marriage proposal of Walter Libby (who earlier had blushed to call her Doctor), after which she "whirled about and vanished through the door" (256). Grace's courage and confidence, the traits required to stand up to difficult patients and to a cad like Mulbridge, are shown to come not from assurance of her competence but from the sense of self her decision to marry provides. A small portion of the world, however, the children of her husband's factory hands, will profit from her training. The case of Grace Breen demonstrates that character, not gender, accounts for professional success or failure.

The same proposition governs the fictional worlds of two other novels in which career women and their plight again provide the stimulus for Howells's imagination. As if forming a trilogy with *Dr. Breen's Practice* to demonstrate the range of women's options, *A Hazard of New Fortunes* (1890) includes a woman artist who remains single because she thinks career and marriage are incompatible, and *The Coast of Bohemia* (1893) treats a woman artist who combines marriage and career. In each novel, the implied author deploys a narrative audience that presupposes that a woman belongs at home, a narrator who identifies such presuppositions as prejudice, and a heroine who conforms to a conventional sense of woman's nature, which allows the authorial audience to feel comfortable with her. Alma Leighton of *A Hazard of New Fortunes*, for example, is shown to subscribe to a reduced but conventional notion of woman's sphere when she declares to an artist friend that were she to marry him, she would play "second fiddle. Do you suppose I shouldn't be woman enough to wish my work always less and lower than yours? At least I've heart enough for that!"[8] At the same time, a palatable heroine like Alma is allowed to be independent, insisting that she may or may not be an old maid, but she will in any case "pick and choose, as a man does; I won't merely be picked and chosen....A girl can get any man she wants to, if she goes about it the right way" (16:477). Her spirit is engaging because some dimensions of it are iconoclastic, smashing the idols of the culture. In short, the drama of Howells's stories of career women depends on independent heroines extending the notion of woman's sphere, upsetting expectations, and thus becoming distinctive enough to elicit the interest of both author and audience. Whether they marry and whether they eventually abandon their careers, they are shown to be "womanly" and to be turned away from the "womanish" by broadened education and experience.

The culture's horizon of expectations for woman, generally, and woman's sphere, specifically, are magnets around which the imagination of Howells organizes otherwise disparate social phenomena and themes, gathering them into an artistic whole. Once the magnets attract these phenomena and themes, the imagination of Howells seems to be further activated; various ramifications begin to unfold in plot and characterization. A case in point is *The Rise of Silas Lapham*, which chronicles the financial success, the social failures, and the ethical dilemmas of a nouveau riche couple, the Laphams. Each of the novel's concerns is tied to gender expectations that are then enlisted as a major source of dramatic interest, the treatment of Silas's financial success being a good example.

The Rise of Silas Lapham associates money and business and success with women from its opening pages and uses women as a source of dramatic conflict thereafter. This is unlike other novels of the time, such as Dreiser's *The Financier*, in which Frank Cowperwood engineers his rise to wealth without the assistance of any of the novel's female characters. In the fashion of the realist, the implied author introduces Silas through the device of an interview, in which Silas praises his mother because, he says, she "cooked, swept, washed, ironed, made and mended from daylight till dark" (12:6). She also read the Bible, went to church, washed Silas's "poor, dirty little feet" (12:6) and patched his clothes. In short, to Silas she was a marvel rendered yet more wonderful by her diminutive size; Silas's eyes mist over as he details the trials of this "little, frail thing, not bigger than a good-sized intermediate school-girl" (12:6). Suddenly, Silas begins "jabbing the point of his penknife into the writing-pad on the desk before him," say-ing, "when I hear women complaining nowadays that their lives are stunted and empty, I want to tell 'em about my *mother's* life" (12:7). This violent gesture provoked by his thoughts on female complaints and idleness is an intense reaction to the changing activities (or inactivities) of women in the second half of the nineteenth century. Silas prefers that woman should suffer and be still, although he would insist that the women in his world did not suffer at all compared with his sainted mother.

The very success of the Laphams enables them to aspire to the class Silas scorns, the idle rich who have been relieved of back-breaking toil. Silas wishes to place his own wife and daughters in that class; if he succeeds, his own daughters will be the next generation of women bereft of a sense of purpose, women whom he will metaphorically jab with his penknife and moralistically condemn for their complaining.

Thus is the scene set for the social climbing of the Laphams through their daughters, Irene and Pen. The daughters are involved in a love triangle that Howells rescues from the thematically trivial and generically trite by embedding it not only in the large concerns of the rise of a new monied class but in the paradoxical effects of wealth on women. Early in her marriage, Persis, the wife of Silas, had plenty to do, just as the mother of Silas always had. She was the brains of the Lapham paint business, the source of their wealth, and the initiator of almost every move Silas ever made. Like Marmee in Louisa May Alcott's *Little Women*, she controls and creates her world, but in her case the husband is in rather than out of

town. Silas's saying, "No hang back about *her*. I tell you she
was a *woman*!...Most of us marry silly little girls grown up to
look like women" (2:14) voices one of Howells's main concerns: the immaturity encouraged in the American woman.[9]
Now, however, Persis has been elevated to idleness and that is
exactly where Silas wants her to stay. When Persis advises Silas
on business ethics, he marshals the ideology of domesticity
against Persis, blaming her for their financial difficulties and
accusing her of overstepping her bounds: "I'm sick of this....If
you'll tend to the house, I'll manage my business without your
help," Silas grumps (12:47). Although Persis reminds him
that he was once very glad of her help, Silas orders her not to
"meddle," a word which in common parlance implies the
entire phrase "do not meddle in my business." Business suddenly becomes to Silas the province of the male and Persis
becomes an Eve figure responsible for Silas's faults.[10]

Persis is supposedly freed for leisure by financial success,
but Silas would instead imprison her within it, restricting her
to an idea of woman's sphere that he honors at his convenience. Thus by reference to the culture's expectations for
woman and prescriptions for woman's sphere, Howells inter-
jects into the otherwise routine, dramatically unpromising
marriage of the Laphams a conflict that the ideology of woman makes possible. A notion of woman's sphere, to be
violated or affirmed at convenience, underpins the individuality of Persis and the plausibility of Silas's reactions.

Having begun to poke about in the problem of the nouveau
riche woman and her underemployment, the imagination of
Howells notices more and more reverberations of sexual differentiation. The culture foists on woman the characteristic of
ambitiousness for wealth and social status. Cultural my-
thology has it that men cannot make enough money fast
enough to keep up with the spending habits and ambitions of
women. Howells himself once quipped that a woman could
never be president because the salary is insufficient to a woman's wardrobe. But in keeping with Thorstein Veblen's

proposition that women in American society are used as testaments to male success, this novel shows that Silas, not Persis, is ambitious for wealth and status; yet Silas pretends otherwise, shifting the taint of ambition to Persis. Silas brags to young Tom Corey that architects suggest improvements and "they always manage to get you when your wife is around, and then you're helpless" (12:55). Women are always getting men to spend their money, it seems.

The fact of the matter, however, is that Persis always tries to put the brakes on Silas's spending, and Silas uses Persis to disguise his own desires from Tom Corey. Although Persis suggested they build a house, she is made uncomfortable by the pretentious extremes to which Silas insists on carrying the project. Persis is insightful enough to perceive the social chasm between the Laphams and the Boston Brahmins; she knows that money does not guarantee social status. Her social sense is, of course, an aspect of her womanly nature. One stereotype of woman is that she is a creature who lives for society, and that stereotype is an exaggeration of the culture's desire to charge woman with responsibility for human interactions. Persis is shown to be uninterested in suffering her way into society. In *The Rise of Silas Lapham*, the heroine serves as a front for the clandestine ambitions of the hero. Gender expectations provide Howells with imaginative insight into the dynamics governing the relationships of heroes and heroines.

A Modern Instance is perhaps the best exemplar in the Howells canon of woman's sphere and sexual differentiation attracting a variety of otherwise disparate elements. America's first divorce novel, it is the age-old story of a young woman who marries a man who proves to be a rogue. Marcia Gaylord marries Bartley Hubbard, moves to Boston with him, and bears his child; eventually she is deserted by him. A divorce follows, and Marcia returns to her old home in Equity, where she lives miserably ever after. Critics have observed that the chronicle of Marcia and Bartley is tied to the death of religious belief across America.[11] Marcia begins and ends in rural Equity, where religion "had largely ceased to be a fact of spiritual experience, and the visible church flourished on condition of providing for the social needs of the community" (10:18). Marcia's mother had abandoned her own religion for her husband's agnosticism. Brahmin Boston, that former seat of religious conviction where Bartley attempts to make a career, is equally bankrupt religiously. Its women expend their energies on society and philanthropy rather than prayer; young men like Ben Halleck become ministers to counter their own doubt rather than to preach faith; and only the elderly Hallecks are orthodox believers in any sense. Marcia and Bartley Hubbard have no faith, no religion, and no idea of what such convictions really are. The implied author sets this couple adrift in a fictional world that lacks substantial values. The doomed marriage of Marcia and Bartley is intended as a representative modern instance of a far-reaching societal malaise.

Projected against the culture's horizon of gender expectations, the societal malaise captured in the unfortunate union of the Hubbards takes on yet more specific contours. On one level, Marcia and Bartley simply reenact an aspect of Cooper's fiction—Bartley seeks adventure (but now in society rather than on the frontier) and Marcia seeks stability (but now in a city rather than in a frontier settlement). Marcia attempts to domesticate Bartley, and he resists her efforts. In this post-Civil War fictional America, unlike Cooper's world, divorce follows the conflict between male and female natures. Something in America had changed, and the imagination of Howells associates that "something" with the problem of woman, the core of society's general breakdown in values. Paul Eakin explains the problem of woman in this way: Marcia is a case of inverted morality; she turns feverishly "to a cult of domestic love in order to disguise the defeat of her womanhood from the world and from herself." Eakin observes that womanhood, in this novel, amounts to Marcia's ability to redeem Bartley, and that Howells traces the breakdown of the nineteenth-century ideal of domestic womanhood, reminding us that, in Eakin's words, "the redemptive possibilities of woman's love were played out already in Mrs. Gaylord's [Marcia Hubbard's mother's] day."[12]

Unfortunately, the demise of woman's redemptive possibilities is not accompanied by a readjustment of the culture's thinking about woman. Consequently, women continue to implement a role that, far from being viable, has in fact become problematic. The efficient cause of Marcia's behavior in this novel, and the core around which the novel is organized, is the ideology of woman that, far from being salvific, is shown to be destructive of Marcia's psyche and of society's basic institution of marriage. Exploiting the dramatic possibilities of this ideology, Howells traces, step by step, the irritants leading to divorce, a symptom of society's larger dislocation of values.

From the perspective of the cult of true womanhood, Marcia Hubbard is an ideal young wife. She is ambitious for her husband and encourages him to study law; she listens to him "submissively" and makes his interests her own. The narrator credits her with "the charm of a young wife who devotedly loves her husband, who lives in and for him, tests everything by him, refers everything to him" (10:208-09). Marcia attempts to buttress Bartley's self-esteem at every turn. Reiterating genteel notions of woman, Bartley tells her that with her faith in him he shall "get along" but without her he shall "go to the bad" (10:342). Thus Marcia is encouraged to take her wifely responsibility seriously, and she does.

Through the narrator and Bartley, however, the implied author exposes the underside of Marcia's behavior. Marcia's referring everything to Bartley, the narrator tells us, is contrary to the fact that "she had a good mind" (10:209); he points out that her reliance on her husband is not intelligent. The implied author allows his authorial audience to see Bartley as a rogue, yet Marcia's notion of her duties, inscribed in her in her youth, blinds her to seeing that Bartley. Putting Bartley on a pedestal, Marcia blames herself for every wrinkle in her marriage, her only interest in life. She apologizes to Bartley for worrying him with her silly concerns when he merits her rebuke for having behaved reprehensibly. If Bartley behaves well, Marcia thinks she has effectively used her womanly influence; if he behaves poorly, she blames herself for failing in her duty. Even when Bartley deserts her, Marcia claims it was because she did not have enough faith in him.

Marcia's burden of responsibility for Bartley's conduct reaches masochistic proportions. Bartley stays out all night, and Marcia thinks of it as "a just punishment for her wickedness" in being jealous of another woman (10:372). Bartley abandons her and their daughter, and Marcia tells her friend Atherton, "I was always the one in fault, but he was always the one to make up first" (10:380). To our astonishment Marcia reveals to her friend Halleck that her one comfort is that she "had the strength to come back to him [Bartley], and let him do anything he would to me, after I had treated him so" (10:399). Even during the divorce proceedings when Bartley's behavior is shown to be undeniably irresponsible, Marcia stretches out her arms toward him and cries, "I will not have it! I didn't understand! I never meant to harm him! Let him go!" (10:445). Marcia Hubbard's scrupulosity as a woman and wife takes on the proportions of a psychological illness.

The novel associates all of this with the demise of religious values, a matter of concern to other novelists of the period, as well. Harold Frederic, for example, chronicles in *The Damnation of Theron Ware* a young minister's loss of faith, influenced in part by a woman, Celia Madden, but attributed to a pseudo-intellectual "awakening" unrelated to gender roles. Howells, however, connects the culture's gender expectations with the decline in religious values. According to these expectations, wives are to obey husbands as hubsands obey God. In the fictional world of the Hubbards, however, belief in God is no longer a viable force. Therefore a husband does not simply speak for God; he *is* God, as the narrator's language connotes by having Marcia's attitude toward Bartley secularize St. Paul. When she fails Bartley, she feels that she fails God as well. Having sinned against Bartley, she must do penance and seek forgiveness, as she consistently does. She "meditated" on Bartley, "meditated painfully and, in her sort, prayerfully upon him" (10:341). Even after Bartley has done his worst to her and to their daughter Fulvia, Marcia keeps the child "in continual remembrance of him," the diction of the indirect discourse here echoing the liturgical language in which the Last Supper is celebrated. Marcia lets no misgiving "blaspheme" the possibility that Bartley may return to her at any moment. In short, as the narrator puts it, "She was beginning to canonize him" (10:391). The spiritual propensities of woman, one of the most salient traits within the ideology of woman, have only secular objects to devote themselves to when a culture's religious impulse has been progressively secularized. Howells read the changing face of America in the rise of wealth and business and industry and in the decline of religion and morality. His imagination seized upon the shifting importance of women and the decline in their stature as the moral guardians of the culture to dramatize a society perilously in flux. Woman's world must somehow be shored up, Marcia's tragedy suggests, if the culture's malaise is to be corrected.

Despite this relatively expansive approach to woman's sphere, Howells was as surely committed to a conservative idea of woman's nature as Cooper and Hawthorne were. His appeal to the "womanliness" of heroines is not only strategic, a device used to persuade the authorial audience, but substantive, an expression of his own preferences. Narrators who articulate generalizations about woman that range from simply descriptive to normative are proof of this allegiance in Howells's texts. Neither had other later nineteenth-century writers purged from their narrators the habit of deductive thinking on the subject of women. On the contrary, Louisa May Alcott's *Work*, for example, is rife with such generalizations as "being a woman, two great tears fell"; and even the narrator of Kate Chopin's *The Awakening* slips into this practice, claiming that Edna "liked money as well as most women." Howells continues the time-honored practice along with the others.

Grace Breen, for example, is said to "cast a woman's look at the other woman." Whatever this means, it is primarily descriptive, a device used for rapid, economical characterization. Expressing a normative virtue through an appeal to the idea of woman's nature, the narrator of *Dr. Breen's Practice* delivers a well-meaning but patronizing claim: "When a woman says she never will forgive a man, she always has a condition of forgiveness in her heart." This statement, presenting itself as praise, in fact diminishes the seriousness of Grace—unless, that is, its assumptions are valued. The narrator delivers this generalization at a moment when Grace is being quite unreasonable. It applies woman's presumed readiness to forgive to a matter that was not a sin in the first place. Therefore this womanly forgiveness is rendered "cute" rather than substantial, as when a child makes an adult statement ("life is confusing") about a matter of no adult consequence ("my toys are always in a mess"). Grace's petulance will provoke an amused response only if the authorial audience values a sense of woman as a diminutive, irrational creature, especially when she is in love. The positive charge of the narrator's statement, if it has one, derives as well from the assumption that it is flattering to claim a place for Grace among the ranks of woman as she is defined by the culture. It affirms Grace's identity as a woman despite her professional pretensions. In the context of the novel and in the particular scene in which it appears, the narrator's statement is clearly intended to be positive, and it just as clearly depends entirely on underlying assumptions about woman to do its work. Once these assumptions no longer pertain, once petulance and cuteness are no longer thought flattering and predictably "womanly" in certain situations, the narrator's claim becomes patronizing, a reduction of Grace to the very childishness that Howells lamented in the American women of his time.

Often the generalizations of narrators appeal to woman's nature to discredit or to blame heroines. In *Their Wedding Journey*, for example, the narrator patronizingly says of a nun who takes pride in her hospital's chapel: "When we renounce the pomps and vanities of this world, we are pretty sure to find them in some other,—if we are women" (5:150); in *The Quality of Mercy* the narrator claims that "when anything wrong happens, a woman always wants someone punished" (18:32); in *Dr. Breen's Practice*, the narrator asserts that "women are generous creatures, and there is hardly any offense which they are not willing another woman should forgive her husband, when once they have said that they do not see how she could ever forgive him" (209). Statements like these take away with the left hand what they give with the right, praising and blaming simultaneously. Yet more remarkable than this, they undercut the very "program" for an expansion of woman's sphere that the texts intend. If nurture rather than nature determines a woman's potential, it makes sense to educate women to competence, self-esteem, and other characteristics that facilitate the successful pursuit of meaningful goals, whether in or out of the home. But if virtues and vices, strengths and weaknesses are attributable to gender, as the generalizations of Howells's narrators suggest, then women are essentially uneducable. If heroines are generous or vain or silly or irrational because they are women, no amount of education can change them unless they can be somehow "unwomaned."

Howells in no way intends to foster an idea that women are not educable or that, perish the thought, they should be "unwomaned." On the contrary, his implied authors muster narrators and all other devices of fiction to serve "womanliness." It is precisely the discrepancy between the narrators' intentions, on the one hand, and the meaning that can be construed from their words, on the other, that demonstrates the power of gender over Howells's imagination. The notions of woman that narrators betray are so much a matter of course, so largely unexamined and presumptively accurate, that their subversion of the texts' intentions on the matter of woman's sphere is simply not perceived by implied authors. They fail to notice the contradiction between shaping new attitudes toward woman's work and reinforcing the foundation on which the old, limiting attitudes depend. They fail to see that while the logic of woman's nature remains intact, negative reactions to new arenas for women are unlikely to go away. Those traits of woman that are perceived as distinct from those of man constitute the premises from which conclusions about woman's sphere are drawn. Until the culture's sense of woman is expanded to include "masculine" traits such as rationality, there is little hope for a cure for the invalid women hospitalized in American society, apart from an occasional bandaid—an education in Greek or Latin here, the training of a doctor there. Thus a narrow concept of woman's nature impedes the vision of Howells and the strategies of his texts, causing them quite unwittingly to undermine the intended meanings they promote on other fronts.

Intended meanings are sometimes contradicted not only by the narrators but in those plots that turn on the actions and decisions of heroines. The treatment of Persis in *The Rise of Silas Lapham* is a prime instance of this phenomenon. On the road to fortune and with the prodding of Persis, Silas the entrepreneur takes Rogers as a partner but later edges him out of the business, an act Persis believes to have been unethical. Her conscience activated, Persis rides Silas about his treatment of Rogers. Later, when Rogers is threatened by bankruptcy and wants Silas to rescue him by participating in an unethical stock deal, he argues his case to Silas from a business angle, but he cleverly approaches Persis from an angle predicated on assumptions about woman and her maternal nature. Rogers goes to the Lapham home when Silas is absent and tells Persis that his wife and children will suffer severe hardship if Silas will not participate in the deal. The heart of Persis is touched; she cannot bear to think of the Rogers family suffering. The arguments Rogers presents to Persis to justify his proposition are emotionally persuasive. Silas, on the other hand, perceives that Rogers's proposition is essentially unethical, and he refuses to join in his scheme. Thus a gender difference emerges: men can see complex, ethical issues where women, emotional and simple, cannot.

The implications of this difference in insight between Silas and Persis would have no particular significance if the imperceptiveness of Persis followed from her previous characterization. It does not. Prior to this scene, the implied author has attributed to Persis both an acute business sense and a sharp, even scrupulous conscience. It was Persis who saw the potential of the paint mine and suggested to Silas that he develop it to the full; Persis who acted as the manager of their joint enterprise; and Persis who was particularly alert to the ethics of the partnership with Rogers, urging Silas to act out of humane values rather than a business ethic that gives priority to profits rather than people. How does it come about, then, that this woman is hoodwinked by Rogers? The "womanliness" of Persis accounts for it. She is taken in by Rogers because her heart rules her head. His appeal to her on the grounds of his family's need is more than Persis can withstand, and the cleverness of his arguments is more than her intellect can sort out. As notions of woman's nature predict, the soft heart and the insufficiently hard head of a woman allow the implied author to render her ineffective in a complex, challenging situation.

Two aspects of the text make it reasonably certain that Howells did not intend to diminish Persis in her interaction with Rogers but, rather, fell imperceptively into the insidious trap of the culture's ideology of woman. First, the moral rise of Silas, the novel's major concern, requires that Silas stand alone in the difficult decision that marks his peak of moral rectitude. The primary purpose served by the demise of Persis as Silas's conscience is the elevation of Silas. Persis is diminished only incidentally, as it were, as if an idea of woman slips in and offers itself as acceptable grounds on which to do what must be done, allow Silas to stand alone. To achieve this, Persis must somehow be eliminated in the interests of Silas's moment of moral grandeur. While this may change our sense of the text's intended meaning, it in no way changes the significance of the treatment of Persis. When acuteness of conscience is nonetheless transferred to the male, a man proves to be best not only in his own sphere but in woman's as well, in the arena of conscience.[13]

A benign intent on the part of Howells is suggested, particularly in light of the sympathetic treatment of Persis elsewhere in the text. She is shown to be the victim of a catch-22. Expected because of her gender to tend to ethical matters, she is supposed to ignore them when they occur in the arena of business. She is bound to be "unwomaned," either by failing to call her husband to the moral values she is to sustain or by presuming to meddle in the sphere of the male. Substantiating Edwin Cady's opinion that Howells wanted women "in every aspect of life, to be stimulated to give the very best of their gifts to a sorrowfully needy world,"[14] the treatment of Persis, far from intending to diminish her, suggests that the implied author was misguided by a preconceived idea of woman's nature. At a crucial moment that idea intervened between the craft and the imagination of Howells and caused him to portray as plausible and consistent a confusion that Persis's previous actions render implausible and inconsistent.

Despite Howells's intention to liberate heroines from a constricting domesticity honored ordinarily only in the breach, he relies so heavily and so frequently on traits the culture designates as "womanly" that finally his fiction is vulnerable to the charge of trivializing heroines.[15] This comes about through persistently ascribing irrational behavior to heroines and positive responses to the irrationality to male characters and narrators alike. Delmar Gross Cooke, in 1922, offered a spirited defense of Howells and his illogical, irrational heroines, crediting Howells with "a very remarkable insight into the feminine heart" and claiming that for Howells women are mystifying and incomprehensible but nonetheless inspire the men under their influence, often to deeds that turn out to be good and kind. Cooke says: "Kindness and goodness, of course, should not be allowed to happen that way; but that is the way in which they do...the progress of our country, or the happiness of any one of us, will not be along the beautiful lines of logic. Howells' own acceptance of his women is based very little on gallantry and still less on illusion."[16]

Cooke shows himself, here, to be subject to the same sentimentality as Howells on the subject of woman and her presumed influence and power. Such an attitude is sentimental not only because it would not hold if examined against reality, but because it is gender based, occurring in Howells's fiction only in connection with heroines and never in connection with heroes. In *A Modern Instance*, for example, "the divine Clara," as Clara Kingsbury is fondly designated by a male friend, is made the butt of comedy because of her charity work with indigent children. Characterized as inept, maddeningly muddled about her finances, and impervious to instruction in this masculine realm, her addlemindedness extends into her good works as well. Her friend Halleck responds to her foibles with "how charming women are!", thus attributing Clara's cute deficiencies to all women. Yet when Howells's implied authors characterize men involved in social causes, they do not make them comic. Reverend Peck and Dr. Morrell of *Annie Kilburn* (1889), for example, are enlisted as mentors to the ineffectual Annie, who must learn to translate her good intentions into authentically charitable, compassionate deeds.

If Cooke were correct and if Howells were simply transcribing life, then certainly an occasional male character would bring about goodness and kindness through irrational, illogical means. Yet this never occurs. The absence of irrational male characters conspires with an overabundance of illogical heroines to suggest that Howells, looking at his world through the preconceived idea that woman is irrational, saw what he expected to see. There were of course irrational women out there on whom Howells could legitimately build his heroines; Howells is entitled to his donnée. Yet when no male characters of like disposition appear, Howells can be charged with a vision clouded by the concept of woman's nature and the traits it assigns to women, and he can be charged as well with ascribing that same vision to his assumed audience. For example, the very title of one of his novels, *A Woman's Reason* (1883), appeals to woman's presumed intellectual vagaries. Woman and reason are understood to be oxymoronic. Quite expectedly, the heroine of the novel finds herself in a bind because she rejects a lover on the grounds of "a perfect chain of logic" that predictably proves to be perfectly illogical. Howells starts with the a priori idea that woman's "logic" is incomprehensible to the male, fondly observes the results of this in working out the plot, and then gives the novel a title that conveys sex bias to us but truth of gender to Howells's assumed audience.

The degree to which the imagination of Howells was captive to notions of woman's nature is particularly evident in *Their Wedding Journey* and *A Hazard of New Fortunes*. The heroine of these novels, Isabel March, first is characterized as inconsequential and then is adored for it. In *Their Wedding Journey*, the newly-wed Isabel is happily absorbed in a husband she tends to spoil. The implied author uses a woman's concern for her husband's well-being, in moderate amounts an entirely appropriate concern in the nineteenth-century world, to trivialize her, taking her from good wife to foolish child by a process characteristic of Howells's technique. Behaving true to female type, Isabel worries about what goes on a dinner table—but here the table is not in her own dining room but on a train. The food on the train causes her to reminisce about an earlier trip to Europe, and her reminiscence makes her trivial because of its focus. Isabel recalls the trip by what was ordered for dinner, and the lengthy, specific catalog of what her husband ate shows that she is secretly proud of his masculine appetite: "Yes, he ate terribly at Susa, when I was too full of the notion of getting to Italy to care for *bouillon* and cold roast chicken. At Rome, I thought I must break with him on account of the wild boar; and at Heidelberg, the sausage and the ham!—how could he, in my presence? But I took him with all his faults—and was glad to get him" (5:10). Isabel is made to play into the culture's idea of woman's delicacy by pretending to be shocked and to disapprove of her husband's appetite, and she even is made to elevate questions of menu to questions of character. Thus we have a delicate woman, a masculine man, a superficial memory of an important event—and the continent of Europe—reduced to a series of menus. Isabel March is portrayed as a silly goose.

The implied author, however, does not understand that in rendering Isabel he has belittled women. On the contrary, he admires the woman who is absorbed in her husband, as Isabel is in hers, and tells us so by criticizing those women who are not. When Isabel March meets with her lady friends, the narrator says, "their only talk was of husbands, whom they viewed in every light to which husbands could be turned, and still found an inexhaustible novelty in the theme" (5:25). Because these women have no subject but their husbands and because they are portrayed as gossiping away an afternoon, we might assume that an audience is expected to find them cute and superficial. But much to our surprise, this passage shows that the narrator is quite satisfied with these women, for he continues: "Thus, with immense profit and comfort, they reassured one another by every question and answer, and in their weak content lapsed far behind the representative women of our age, when husbands are at best a necessary evil, and the relation of wives to them is known to be one of pitiable subjection" (5:25). The narrator divides women into two groups: those who are devoted to husbands and those who are not. If one must choose, the narrator implies, then the devotees of men are preferable to the malcontents who do not accept their proper place. Finally, he prefers Isabel.[17]

Yet something in this statement trivializes both groups. The narrator's tone is comic rather than satiric, bemused rather than biting, suggesting a reductive attitude toward these characters. Comedy, after all, portrays human—in this case, female—foibles, while satire identifies faults in the interests of reform. Belief in reform, in turn, is an act of faith in the possibility of improvement. These female characters, the narrator's comic tone suggests, are as woman is and shall ever be, "thank God." All that is missing here is that diminishing praise—the "Ah! Woman!" or the "How charming!"—with which narrators in Howells's fiction often conclude their analyses of the presumed foibles of woman.

That *Their Wedding Journey* does not seek to demean its heroine is made evident, also, in the attitude of Isabel's husband toward her and their marriage. The good, representatively American Basil March appreciates Isabel's womanliness, particularly her dependency. Basil March is "affected by her [Isabel's] compassion and tenderness" and "likes well enough to think 'She loves me,' but still better, 'How kind and good she is!' " (5:12). When years later he and Isabel return to Niagara, the destination of their original wedding journey, Basil is touched by what amounts to Isabel's sentimentality: "for the years had tended to make her rather more seriously maternal toward him than towards *the other children*; and he recognized that these fond reminiscences were the expression of the girlhood still lurking deep within her heart" (5:193, my italics). Basil has willingly become Isabel's child. The maternal dimension of woman's nature is seriously distorted by converting adults into children, yet Basil finds this attractive and participates fully in it.

A *Hazard of New Fortunes* returns to Isabel and Basil March in middle age. Isabel is shown, in this phase of her life, to fulfill her womanly and wifely duties to near perfection, but the way in which the narrator focuses on her has the effect of trivializing her nonetheless. Isabel reinforces Basil in his decisions, she directs his life in all areas pertaining to the home, and she puts "heart into him when he had lost it altogether" (16:37). Further, Isabel runs Basil as a captain runs a ship: "Early in their married life she had taken charge of him in all matters which she considered practical. She did not include the business of bread-winning in these....But in such things as rehanging the pictures, deciding on a summer boarding-place, taking a sea-side cottage, repapering rooms, choosing seats at the theatre, seeing what the children ate... shutting the cat out...he had failed her so often that she felt she could not leave him the slightest discretion....Her total distrust of his judgment...consisted with the greatest admiration of his mind and respect for his character....She subjected him, therefore, to an iron code, but after proclaiming it she was apt to abandon him to the native lawlessness of his temperament" (16:78). Isabel alternately scolds Basil and ignores his behavior, creating a good deal of comedy and some tragedy in their lives, but in any case performing those wifely, domestic duties that the male, absorbed in more important business, is likely to let slip.

Competent in life's details, Isabel is shown to be irrational and conventional in very unattractive ways. Characteristic of females in Howells' fiction, Isabel is assigned a certain tendency to act whimsically, unreflectively, and illogically. Thus when Isabel and Basil seek an apartment whose appointments she has detailed, she turns back on her own requirements for a preposterous reason: her fascination with a janitor. He is "one of those colored men" about whom Isabel then philosophizes: "I don't wonder they wanted to own them....If I had such a creature, nothing but death should part us, and I should no more think of giving him his *freedom*—" (16:46). Isabel's statement of course does not flatter her social conscience. But the implied author uses her statement for ends other than racism to demean women: to dramatize woman's crazy sentimentality. Having encountered this man, Isabel is willing to take an apartment that lacks a number of the features she required only an hour earlier.

Further, Isabel is made to be painfully and unattractively conventional, an ardent advocate of the status quo. Since other characters who oppose the status quo are sympathetically portrayed, the implied author again makes Isabel seem insignificant. She is not evil, not sainted. She is at best prudent and complacent and inconsequential. She tells Basil, for example, that neither he nor anyone else should involve himself with laborers on strike—although theirs is the cause of the hour. Isabel does not quite approve, either, of women who are too active in social causes. Margaret Vance, a wealthy young woman who works in behalf of laborers, is characterized by Basil as Christlike. Yet Isabel says, " ' Oh, Christ came into the world to teach us how to live rightly in it, too. If we were all to spend our time in hospitals, it would be rather dismal for the homes. But perhaps you don't think the homes are worth minding?' she suggested, with a certain note in her voice that he knew" (16:452). Isabel uses the tactic of appealing to extremes, pitting one good against another, social activism against home life, as if assigning value to social action belittles domestic activity. Reinforcing her conventionality and her defensiveness, Basil "got up and kissed her" (16:452). The implied author and his male protagonists, presuming woman's frailty, are much too genteel to tell a woman the truth and much too comfortable with woman in the role of Vesta to challenge her social conscience.[18]

Thus the heart of Howells, active in his implied authors, is captive to the traits subsumed within a genteel concept of woman's nature, while his head perceives a need to expand the education and sphere of women and to change society's perceptions. The intended meanings of Howells's novels undercut prejudicial notions of the incompetence of heroines but reinforce the very sense of heroines as acceptably delicate and irrational "girls" from which such notions originate. Despite his including an occasional career woman in his fiction, and despite his clear but often frustrated intent to demonstrate their potential, Howells is finally unable to imagine new possibilities for his heroines, except in the vaguest terms. Even in his Altrurian romances, when deploying the vehicle of a utopia that not only allows, but by definition encourages, a writer to push imagination to its limits, he was unable to see beyond woman as woman's nature would have her. Part of the Altrurian romance cycle (*Letters to an Altrurian Traveller* [1893], *A Traveller from Altruria* [1894], and *Through the Eye of the Needle* [1907]) treats its American female characters much as Howells's other fiction does: as foolish women consumed by the same sort of trivial activities that absorb Isabel March.

Yet is is revealing that when it comes to Altrurian women, Howells's implied author avoids consequential characterization. The hero, Homos, merely registers shock that wealthy American women are busily idle ladies who play no public role. When Homos and his new American wife return to Altruria, Altrurian women are still not described by the implied author. He only suggests that Altrurian women do their own housework and participate in public affairs and that, like Altrurian men, they are extremely egalitarian, serving people in all walks of life and eating at table with those for whom they have cooked. Exactly how or in what public affairs the women participate remains unspecified. It seems, therefore, that Howells could only vaguely imagine some indefinite public role for women. The only specific alternate of which he could conceive, evidently, was returning "ladies" to the drudgery at which Silas Lapham's mother suffered and from which Silas and Persis worked to relieve Persis and the Lapham daughters. The degree to which this constitutes a failure of imagination is suggested by the some 150 utopian fictions written in the later nineteenth century, sixteen of which were female utopias, ranging from Mary Lane's *Mizora, A Prophecy* (1889) to Charlotte Perkins Gilman's *Herland* (1915).[19] Although these utopias proposed all manner of startling arrangements in a genre that allows relatively unlimited possibilities, Howells used the Altrurian romances to send the message to women that, if they have been so foolish as to leave their homes, they should return to them at once.

On balance, the imagination and the craft of William Dean Howells were finally limited by notions of woman's nature. While the implied authors of Howells's fiction work to expand the culture's sense of woman, their intentions are far from realized. Problems interfere that attach to the ideology of gender, promoting strategies and statements in Howells's craft that undermine his better insights. Paradoxically, Howells failed to see that the very idea of a woman's nature to which he himself subscribed delineated those gender distinctions that in turn separate women from the world, provoke a sentimental attitude toward them, and finally render them insubstantial. He failed to see, as well, the insidious incursions of woman's nature into his imaginative enterprise.

4. HENRY JAMES
The Summit of the Male Imagination

> It is art that *makes* life, makes interest, makes importance, for our consideration and application of these things, and I know of no substitute whatever for the force and beauty of its process.
>
> —Henry James

In *The Tragic Muse*, Henry James creates a dialogue that is among the most instructive on the subject of male-female relationships in nineteenth-century American literature. Peter Sherringham, a connoisseur of theater, is in conversation with Miriam Rooth, an actress whom Peter both patronizes and loves. A man with fixed ideas about women, Peter can accommodate an actress within his sublime category of "woman" only because, as he says, "It's as the actress that the woman produces the most complete and satisfactory artistic results.... There's another art in which she's not bad....That of being charming and good, that of being indispensable to man."[1] A man whose greatest pleasure is the theater and whose most recent theatrical pleasure has been the progress of Miriam Rooth, Sherringham recognizes Miriam as an actress of exceptional talent. Yet when he comes to propose marriage to her, he says, "Give it up and live with *me*." Astonished at first, Miriam says sarcastically, "I'm much obliged, but that's not my choice," to which Peter then replies, "You shall be anything you like except this." Miriam can hardly believe his words: "Except what I most want to be? I *am* much obliged" (7:360).

It is indeed astonishing that a man who has perceived such talent as Miriam's would ask that she give up the very thing at which she excels. Yet Peter is even more outrageous. When Miriam refuses to sacrifice the theater for him, he woundedly responds, "Don't you care for me? Haven't you any gratitude?" Peter wants Miriam to show her gratitude for his patronage by abandoning the very talent that his patronage was intended to develop. He even threatens Miriam with rejection and alienation, pointing out to her that, if she is not careful, she will take on the undesirably "hard polish" associated with another successful actress reputed to be cold. Success, that is, will ruin her lovableness, her womanliness. Finally, Peter irrationally says to her, "What I want is you yourself" (7:370-71). He seems to think that, in the case of a woman, professional abilities and talents are something glued to the exterior and unattached to the inner person, which is apparently some indefinable substance that will be uncovered once she is stripped of her talents.

On the evening of Miriam's greatest success, Peter again asks Miriam to renounce her career to marry him. He offers to "manage" Miriam—and he doesn't mean her theatrical career, but her career as wife to a minor diplomat assigned in a minor capacity to a foreign embassy. This, he claims, will put Miriam, now a major actress in the capital of London, in "a bigger theatre than any of those places in the Strand" (8:340). On this occasion, Miriam articulates the precise paradox of Peter's request that she renounce the theatre: her talent is exactly what attracts Peter to her. Without it, she points out, "I should be a dull, empty, third-rate woman, and yet that's the fate you ask me to face and insanely pretend you're ready to face yourself." At this, finally putting his cards on the table, Peter tells Miriam: "You were made to charm and console, to represent beauty and harmony and variety to miserable human beings; and the daily life of man is the theatre for that—not a vulgar shop with a turnstile that's open only once in the twenty-four hours" (8:341). Peter's idea of Miriam's ultimate talent is her God-given womanly nature, a nature designed to serve men twenty-four hours a day. Miriam turns the tables on Peter at this juncture and suggests that he sacrifice *his* career for *hers*, which horrifies him. Would she see him throw up his work and his prospects and "simply become your appendage?" Clear-sighted as usual, Miriam responds coolly, "My dear fellow, you invite me with the best conscience in the world to become yours" (8:342). Inviting her to play out her career on the stage appropriate for woman, the domestic stage, Peter Sherringham, in 1890, is every bit as presumptuous before Miriam Rooth as Natty Bumppo, in 1841, was before Judith Hutter in Cooper's *The Deerslayer*.

While assumptions of male superiority and the idea of sexual differentiation on which they stand remain constant across nineteenth-century America, the imaginations of those who dramatize such assumptions have changed. Cooper did not recognize as presumptuous the words and attitudes of Natty Bumppo; rather, Natty was made to think and preach as was appropriate within the divinely ordained, hierarchical ordering of the sexes. Henry James, on the other hand, recognized behavior such as Peter Sherringham's for what it was and made use of it. The imagination of James often was superior to the culture's ideology of gender. His fiction confirms the continued ascendancy of sexual differentiation in American culture and shows the power of his imagination to bend the culture's myopia to his own artistic purposes. In the fiction of Howells, the text frequently proves more powerful than the writer as an ideology of woman creeps in and dictates, as it were, words and phrases whose connotations undermine the writer's intentions. In the fiction of James, the craftsman continually struggles with the text—with the conventions of language, literature, genre, and society, the raw materials and the intertexts from which a text is fashioned—and forces it to do his will.

Henry James saw artistic opportunity in the liabilities of the culture on the subject of sex, and he seized the culture's limitations to amplify the dramatic interest of his heroines. In fact, the culture's horizon of expectations plays a major role in the artistic achievements with which James is most often credited. Perhaps James's greatest interest is to create a central intelligence and record the drama of the mind. One way he does this is to set the constricted vision of an observer against a complex female character to record the movements of the observing intelligence. His complicated heroines move well beyond the categories of fair and dark ladies, and their potential is augmented by the traditions of popular fiction and the romance. Provoked rather than subdued by the ideology of gender, the imagination of James crafted female characters into magnificent and prodigious heroines; by manipulating women's limiting circumstances, he provided aesthetic solutions to questions raised by the culture's horizon of expectations for woman.

In his retrospective preface to *The Portrait of a Lady*, Henry James sets forth the artistic challenge he perceived in the subject of an engaging young female figure who had long preoccupied his imagination. The character of Isabel Archer fascinated James as a potential "subject" of fiction precisely because he believed that her character, while of great interest to him, had nothing in particular to recommend it as a fictional subject, since "millions of presumptuous girls, intelligent or not intelligent, daily affront their destiny, and what is it open to their destiny to *be*, at the most, that we should make an ado about it?" (3:xiii). Late in his career, having already examined the problems of female characters who, like Christina Light and Isabel Archer, are severely limited by their culture's ideology of woman, James calls the desire to make a subject of Isabel an "extravagance," and he asks by what "process of logical accretion" this "slight 'personality,' the mere slim shade of an intelligent but presumptuous girl" could be "endowed with the high attributes of a subject" (3:xii-xiii). James goes on to claim that the wonder is "how absolutely, how inordinately, the Isabel Archers, and even much smaller female fry, insist on mattering" (3:xiii). The artistic challenge James recalls having accepted with such pleasure grows, in effect, out of cultural preconceptions about woman. "Female fry" are by definition small, though they "insist on mattering." The trick for the artist, James believes, is to magnify them. When James wrote, in a letter to H.G. Wells, that "it is art that *makes* life, makes interest, makes importance, for our consideration...and I know of no substitute whatever for the force and beauty of its process," he might have been describing the process of creating Isabel Archer.

James decided that the problem of Isabel Archer, the difficulty to be "braved," admitted a double solution. He must dramatize both Isabel's importance to other characters and her relation to herself, placing the weight on the side of Isabel's consciousness. Again taking the culture's view as his own, James remembers telling himself, as he began to create Isabel, that this was "as interesting and as beautiful a difficulty as you could wish....To depend upon her and her little concerns wholly to see you through will necessitate, remember, your really 'doing' her" (3:xv-xvi). Convinced that Isabel has no status to speak of, James seems to select her as a dare, a test of his craft. Whereas Hawthorne's dramatic impetus for *The Scarlet Letter* is an adulteress made to mount a scaffold to do public penance for a crime of passion, James starts with what he believes to be much less promising material: an inconspicuous girl from Albany, New York, for whom the equivalent of a scaffold must be devised if she is to be made into something. The donnée is exceptional for the romancer Hawthorne but apparently unexceptional for the realist James. Hawthorne's selection of Hester Prynne is a bold philosophical decision because of attitudes toward woman; James's selection of Isabel Archer is an audacious artistic choice because woman's nature and place, presumed by James and his projected audience to be of relatively little consequence, make Isabel a potentially uninteresting subject that only a bold imaginative leap and a consummate handling of craft can rescue for the high purposes of art.

A narrow idea of woman having supplied James with his beautiful difficulty, he extends the culture's problem to solve the artistic problem it presents. James's implied author utilizes Isabel's difference from other women as one of his major devices to enlarge her importance. The setting for the novel's beginning is Gardencourt, an English country estate. Amidst talk of an ambiguously "independent" American girl, Isabel arrives provoking further speculation, and her cousin Ralph Touchett poses the question out of which the entire novel grows: what was [Isabel] going to do with herself? (3:87). The narrator points out that "this question was irregular, for with most women one had no occasion to ask it. Most women did with themselves nothing at all; they waited, in attitudes more or less gracefully passive, for a man to come that way and furnish them with a destiny. Isabel's originality was that she gave one an impression of having intentions of her own" (3:87). The implied author immediately establishes through the narrator the context within which Isabel is to be viewed and from which stems her originality and interest as a fictional subject: the context of a young woman outstanding among women—a young woman on whom marriage and the future are unlikely to be simply imposed because she is likely to choose her own course.

Having magnified Isabel by distinguishing her from other women, the implied author then invests Isabel with a sense of self different from other women. Back in Albany, the narrator claims, Isabel judged that unlike herself most girls are "horribly ignorant" (3:62) and that she needs no man to tell her how to live. Once in England, she is aware that, as her cousin Ralph tells her, nineteen out of twenty women would have married Lord Warburton, the man who first proposes to

Isabel. Later, when she inherits money, the narrator claims that Isabel, casting her good fortune in comparative terms, reflected that "to be rich was a virtue because it was to be able to *do*, and that to do could only be sweet. It was the graceful contrary of the stupid side of weakness—especially the feminine variety" (3:301). Isabel is shown to fancy herself a person superior to most of her sex and therefore a woman who will make enlightened, exceptional use of her life and her fortunes.

James deploys female satellite characters to emphasize and amplify Isabel's uniqueness, to teach Isabel about the world, and to embody the options open to women. Mrs. Touchett, Isabel's aunt, provides Isabel with a negative example of a wife; Madame Merle, Isabel's admired acquaintance, is a cool, polished cosmopolite; and Henrietta Stackpole, Isabel's American friend, is a career woman. These female characters dramatically embody contrasting character traits that serve not only to highlight Isabel's distinctiveness but also to illustrate the proportions of her difference. Compared with these other female characters, Isabel proves to be not only different from other women, but different from other women who are themselves different from other women. Mrs Touchett is an entirely eccentric wife, wishing to be simultaneously single and married, living apart from her husband all but one month of each year. Serena Merle, the unmarried mother of an illegitimate child, wanders from one country house to another as a means of "earning" her living. Henrietta Stackpole is a terrifyingly American journalist in hot pursuit of a "masculine" career. Thus James calls on both the expectations of ordinary women and the violation of expectations by extraordinary women to carve out a highly foreign, and thus interesting, territory for the character of Isabel Archer. Isabel stands out even among other exceptions to the rule of women's lives.

The degree of James's imaginative audacity is further indicated by the basically conventional plot of *The Portrait of a*

Lady: a young woman visits Europe, inherits a fortune, marries, comes painfully to recognize that her choice for a husband is a disaster, and decides to live with her mistake. James noted in the novel's preface that a young woman going off to Europe in his time was but a "mild adventure." Isabel's perception of her circumstances is the vehicle James selects to convert the ordinary into something sufficiently extraordinary to fulfill his special "obligation to be amusing," as he calls it in his preface. Isabel's vision, in turn, is provocative because her potential, which appears to exceed usual expectations, draws the authorial audience suspensefully into its orbit. Whether Isabel will prove to be as different from other women as she appears to be is the basic question that the plot must answer. Thus even the plot of *The Portrait* turns on an idea of woman's nature, but Isabel's character seems to controvert it rather than conform to it.

What James then does, however, with what he calls initially unpromising materials is impressive indeed. First, Isabel's character is depicted, not as iconoclastic in any simple, straightforward way, but as engagingly complex. The drama of her self-perception, awareness, and life choices is heightened by a conventional streak that conflicts with her desire to be different from other women. Isabel is shown, for example, to behave conventionally with each of her suitors; she takes pleasure in the rituals of courtship that express gender distinctions and prerogatives.[2] When courted by the man she will eventually marry, she pretends that "there was less of her than there really was" (4:191), not unlike the female who loses at tennis in order to flatter her male partner. She is also shown to harbor "in the depths of her nature" an "unquenchable desire to please" (3:45) which is in tune with cultural definitions of femininity. Isabel's character contains two selves: the conventional is drawn to woman's usual place and role, and the unconventional longs for the power and control not usually granted her sex.[3]

To understand Isabel's decisions and the intentions of *The*

Portrait of a Lady, it is crucial to recognize this conflict in Isabel's character and the concept of woman's nature that makes this conflict plausible and predictable. For readers in our time, *The Portrait* consistently provokes three major questions: why is a woman of Isabel's pretensions to independence made to marry; why is she made to marry Gilbert Osmond; and why is she made to return to Osmond rather than choose the more humane Caspar Goodwood, who promises her the independence she supposedly seeks? The answer to each of these questions is in Isabel's conflicting selves, which in turn result from the gender expectations of the culture in which James, the realist, embeds her. Isabel's decisions must be viewed within the framework of the culture's ideology of woman, if the implied author's intended meanings are to be accessible and persuasive to us.

A reputedly bright, exceptional young woman inherits a fortune but does not seize the opportunities for freedom and experimentation it offers. Instead, she is set off on a year's travels by the implied author and then married off. Dorothea Krook explains that, given the historical and dramatic context of *The Portrait of a Lady*, "Isabel could not have done something other than marry; she could not have taken a degree or become a pioneer in women's education."[4] Krook correctly observes that marriage is part of James's donnée primarily because it is virtually the only option open to a woman of Isabel's circumstances. It is equally correct to observe that it is virtually the sole option the novel tradition offers to Isabels. Therefore, the interesting aspect of Isabel's decision to marry is not the decision itself, which is to be expected for both mimetic and literary reasons, but the psychological impetus that propels her toward marriage. In keeping with her complex character, Isabel is made to seek two things in life: "unlimited expansion" and "some private duty that might gather one's energies to a point" (4:82). Pursuing expansion, Isabel travels and finds herself unimpressed with expatriates, whose lives she sees as inane and pointless. Isabel seeks a meaningful life with duties and responsibilities, but by cultural fiat, the structuring duties available to her are tied to marriage.

Granting that Isabel must marry, her remarkably uninsightful choice of Gilbert Osmond, a heartless esthete in need of money, certainly seems to diminish Isabel's intelligence. Yet if we project Isabel against the culture's horizon of expectations, this, too, is a matter of how cultural predispositions affect Isabel's character and what conflict results. On the one hand, Osmond appears to Isabel to offer an opportunity to express her conventional self. The narrator couches Isabel's desire to marry Osmond entirely in "womanly" terms. She thought that she would "surrender" to him with "humility," yet "marry him with a kind of pride; she was not only taking, she was giving" (4:82). Isabel's inner self corresponds perfectly in this respect with her culture's ideals. As is proper, she has found a man seemingly superior to herself, a man whose position enables her to exercise her culturally approved, womanly traits of humility and generosity. On the other hand, Isabel's other, "different" half sees in Osmond a unique opportunity. Having proposed to Isabel, Gilbert Osmond gives her seemingly unlimited time and space for a response, advising her to travel and to do exactly as she pleases. He appears to her to be a man one could marry without suffering the more stringent restrictions of the institution of marriage that more insistent husbands might impose. Furthermore, Osmond seems to Isabel, before their marriage, to be "helpless and ineffectual"; in him "she had found her occasion." She would use her money to "launch his boat for him; she would be his providence....The finest—in the sense of being the subtlest—manly organism she had ever known had become her property" (4:192-94). When a girl is initiated into womanhood in the Victorian novel and culture, marriage launches the woman and a husband launches a wife. In marrying Osmond, Isabel thinks she creates a reversal of expectations: she will launch her marriage, she thinks, and the wife will launch the husband. Isabel usurps the usual power of the male in choosing Osmond.

Isabel discovers the destructive dimensions of having chosen to marry Osmond, but nonetheless returns to him as the novel concludes. This decision provokes more debate than any other aspect of the novel. Yet it is entirely consistent with the implied author's development of Isabel's character and circumstances. Isabel's conventional self, like the fictional Victorian world she inhabits, is shown to subscribe to the idea of a hierarchy of the sexes. Despite a heinous relationship with her husband, Isabel's decision to return to him is consistent with her declared dedication to notions of wifely duties that emanate from woman's nature and its correlate, man's nature. She wants to do her "duty" and "play the part of a good wife" (4:174), she tells Ralph Touchett. Recognizing that Osmond "expected his wife to feel with him and for him, to enter into his opinions, his ambitions, his preferences," Isabel sees this as "no great insolence" on the part of "a husband originally at least so tender" (4:200). She goes so far as to judge it her duty to be afraid of her husband and claims "that's what women are expected to be" (4:306). To her, marriage means that "when one had to choose, one chose as a matter of course for one's husband" (4:361). Given the intellectual superiority attributed to Isabel, it is tempting to assume a degree of cynicism in the indirect discourse which reveals this to us. However, because the implied author also attributes to Isabel a strong attraction to the norms for Victorian womanhood, we must assume that she believes what she thinks.

Isabel's returning to Osmond satisfies the unconventional half of her nature, that part of her self that earlier enjoyed the power to refuse suitors and later enjoyed launching Osmond's ship. Remaining married to Osmond, Isabel retains her power over him. While we must remember that no woman could blithely walk out on a marriage in the 1870s and the 1880s,[5] it is nevertheless true that Isabel can control Osmond to some extent by returning to Rome, a motive of which she is not incapable. At his side, she can obstruct his plans for his daughter, and she can threaten the social embarrassment that, more than anything else in life, is abhorred by the conventional Osmond, the worshipper of propriety. Married, Isabel holds the most elevated position available to the Victorian woman, and she retains the only power granted a woman in her world: the power to influence or to thwart a husband. Isabel will wrest from convention and its sexual hierarchy as much power as a woman can obtain and will pursue thereby the independent life she always desired, a life more limited than she originally anticipated but as free as a woman's life can realistically be. At the same time, she will appear to be a lady, a married woman exercising the lady's role of wife and benevolent stepmother.

The contemporary reader may still wonder, however, why Isabel is not made to marry the worthy Caspar Goodwood, no matter the motives supplied for her unfortunate choice of Gilbert Osmond and her decision to return to him. Isabel's resistance to Caspar's advances has been cast by many critics as a mark of frigidity,[6] a misreading that stems from a failure to take into account the conflict in Isabel's character between the conventional and the unconventional. Isabel's acceptance of the prerogatives of husbands joins James's characterization of Caspar to motivate her rejection of this wealthy American who so loves her that he pursues her across continents. Two of Caspar's most prominent traits, his insistence and his persistence, throw Osmond into relief and make him seem a paragon of liberality when he is courting Isabel; they also account for Isabel's response to Caspar. Characterized as a man who, in Isabel's view, takes control of all he touches, Caspar asks in a "slightly peremptory tone" (3:216) why Isabel did not answer his letter to her; he presses her to explain her decision to marry; he says he would prefer a dead Isabel to an Isabel married to someone else; he follows Isabel to Europe despite her request that he not do so. When Isabel receives from Caspar the lightning kiss which concludes the novel, she feels it as an "act of possession" (4:436), which it is, as any woman has reason to know. Exercising the prerogatives the culture grants a man in pursuit of the woman he wishes to marry, Caspar suffocates Isabel; he deprives her of "the sense of freedom" (3:162). She dislikes his air of "knowing better what was good for her than she knew herself" (3:219), his co-opting her. Since Isabel accepts the prerogatives of husbands, she would understandably be very cautious of the nature of the man with whom she contracts a marriage. The part of her that appreciates freedom would reject Caspar's preemptory temperament and would find Osmond's manner a welcome contrast.

Isabel's rejection of Caspar and her return to Osmond result from the novel's consistently developing those facets of her character established in the beginning of the novel. The authorial audience would not be unprepared for Isabel's decisions. Buttressing Isabel's predicament are the culture's attitudes toward marriage, men, and power that are made clear in the attitudes of other characters. One or another of them throughout the novel is shown to assume, for example, that Isabel is somehow an over-reacher if she doesn't accept now Warburton's offer, now Caspar's. Except in the case of a male, like Osmond, who is thought to be downright reprehensible, it is presumed that Isabel should feel honored rather than oppressed by male advances. Even Isabel's greatest admirer, Ralph Touchett, reminds her that Lord Warburton's proposal is a great honor, a simultaneous tribute to Isabel and recognition of the glory that male attentions and desires shed on women. Given the degree to which the ideology of woman and its ramifications saturate the world of *The Portrait*, it is remarkable not that Isabel honors male rights but that she retains any spirit of independence whatsoever. The idea of woman's nature is the foundation on which the implied author builds to establish Isabel's difference from other women and her conventional streak. The conflict of these two aspects of self accounts for Isabel's decisions and creates the dramatic interest of the fictional life of a "female fry."

Cultural expections of woman are brought into the service of James's art on another front: creating the drama of consciousness. Choosing from among the ranks of the well-bred and the well-dressed, James elects characters who are, as Dorothea Krook writes, "endowed in an extraordinary degree with the gifts of intelligence, imagination, sensibility, and a rare delicacy of moral insight," an "inordinate capacity for *being* and *seeing*: for life, that is, and for consciousness; for living and for understanding."[7] The experience of life is made to work on the consciousness and understanding of these characters, causing them either to develop their potential or to retreat into the safe and familiar. The drama of the mind requires, of course, a point of departure against which to measure the distance traveled, whether toward or away from a fuller apprehension of life. In James's fiction, observer figures begin with a defect of vision, a gap between their perception and the reality they confront, or which confronts them. Often the differences between Europe and America, the poles from which James's international theme emerges, are used to capture the evolution of a mind. Frequently, however, the gap between perception and reality is dramatized by placing on one side an observer whose mind is a repository of preconceptions of woman, a manifestation of fixed ideas and stasis, and on the other a female character whose very existence calls such preconceptions into question. The mind of the observer is challenged to bridge that gap; the drama of consciousness is rendered palpable through the agency of ideas about woman. Female characters enlisted to this end are a realist's version of the Muse; they are vehicles of inspiration or its refusal. James also uses such characters to turn the Sleeping Beauty myth on its head, so that the metaphorical kiss of a female character awakens a male observer to a new and fuller life. James offers these female characters as a telling measure, as well, of flexibility and insight, a test of the powers of imagination in observer figures whose weight of a priori ideas must be lifted if their vision is to expand.

In his early novel *Roderick Hudson*, James already shows himself to be cognizant of the use cultural assumptions about woman can be to the drama of consciousness. The observer figure, Rowland Mallet, finances the adventures of a young artist, Roderick Hudson, giving him the opportunity to develop his artistic talents in the stimulating ambiance of Rome. Roderick's story, which is also the drama of Rowland Mallet observing him, involves two important female characters, Roderick's American fiancé, Mary Garland, and his European acquaintance, Christina Light. Mary Garland speaks to Roderick's American pole, his innocence, and Christina Light to his European pole, experience with all its ramifications and risks. Rowland Mallet, the prototype of James's Lambert Strether of *The Ambassadors*, submits to the allure of the more comprehensive but less rigid vision of life that Europe and Christina Light offer.

Rowland Mallet is deployed, unsteadily, as the novel's center of consciousness. Most of the story is filtered through his eyes, which means that Mary and Christina are subject to his preconceptions of woman. Rowland is shown to have a single but divided imagination of woman: one hemisphere for fair ladies and another for dark; one that attracts him to the familiar, to stasis, and another that draws him to the unknown, to freedom; one that is reassuring and one that is threatening.

Rowland Mallet first meets Mary Garland when she is seated "at the table, near the candles, busy with a substantial piece of needlework" (1:51), wearing, all too predictably, a white dress. To Rowland's mind she is "tall and straight" with "an air of maidenly strength and decision" (1:54). Surely James was amusing himself, here, with the type of the fair lady. When Mary Garland comes to Rome to be with her fiancé, we learn through Rowland that all her activities—her interest in art and her quest for knowledge—are motivated by her desire to shape herself into a proper wife for Roderick Hudson. As Rowland sees it, Mary is simply completing her hope chest in Rome, expanding her knowledge so "that she might noiselessly lay [it] away, piece by piece, in the fragant darkness of her serious mind, so that under this head at least she should not be a perfectly portionless bride" (1:342). Rowland also attributes Mary's fastidiousness, thoroughness, and circumspection before the wonders of Rome not only to her provincialism and inexperience but to her devotion to Roderick. Her interests expand and her self-respect increases because "she has a sense of devoting her consciousness not to her own ends, but to those of another whose career would be high and splendid" (1:343). Rowland persistently construes Mary's behavior to coincide with expectations for female deportment from fair heroines in fiction and good women in handbooks; he assigns to Mary's actions a single meaning: devotion to the man she loves.

That Rowland's reading of Mary coincides with the culture's concept of woman's nature does not of itself prove any deficiency in Rowland's vision; Mary Garland may be as Rowland perceives her to be. As the novel unfolds, Mary does in fact behave like the stereotypical "woman in love," sticking to Roderick through thick and thin and tolerating a good bit of offensive treatment from both Roderick and his mother. Yet Rowland's image of Mary consistently is constrictive rather than expansive, immediately confining Mary on the assumption that she is simple, rather than seeking to unlock her character on the assumption that she is complex. For example, her pursuit of knowledge and culture while abroad is, first of all, a straightforward, neutral fact, admitting of more than one gloss. Mary may, after all, be interested in art for its own sake or for her own sake. She may seek knowledge to satisfy her own curiosity. Early in the novel while still in Northampton, Mary tells Rowland that the hardest part of her work as a minister's daughter in West Nazareth is "not doing anything" (1:79). Knowing, therefore, that Mary dislikes minding appearances and apparently likes activity, Rowland might wonder what she would find to do in Rome if she did not visit galleries and attempt to increase her knowledge. Rowland might ask why Mary from time to time utters "a deep full murmur of gratification" (1:452) when she sees a Titian or a Raphael. But he doesn't ask such questions. Rather, he immediately attributes all that Mary does to the influence of Roderick Hudson rather than to her own imperatives. Without ever entertaining any other possibilities, he assumes that, fair creature as he finds her to be, her entire existence is hostage to the man she loves and that the label of "woman in love" completely captures her character. He betrays a habit of mind that tends to construe the world in a priori rather than exploratory terms.

The implied author reinforces this tendency by showing Rowland's willingness to generalize about woman. Expatiating to Roderick on the subject of woman, Rowland, a bachelor, asserts that "no woman who *cares*...is ever more of a moralist than she is of a partisan. If she becomes that, it's a sign she has ceased to care" (1:87). Rowland holds that a woman's heart rules her head and her judgment. Further, the implied author shows that Rowland's assessments of behavior are driven by considerations of gender. For instance, he is taken with one of Mary's letters on the grounds of its "shortness," its "dryness," and its "exquisite modesty in its saying nothing from the girl herself" (1:134). The letter corresponds with a common notion that woman should be self-effacing and reticent. He is as delighted with Mary's letter "as he had been pleased by the angular gesture of some maiden-saint in a primitive painting. The whole thing quickened that impression of fine feeling combined with an almost rigid simplicity....Its homely stiffness showed as the direct reflection of a life concentrated...in a single devoted idea" (1:134). This same Rowland Mallet insists that Roderick Hudson visit Italy to expand his knowledge, sharpen his skills, complicate his vision, and render him more cosmopolitan and complex. Yet Rowland is charmed to find in a young woman the opposite characteristics: rigidity, simplicity, homely uneasiness, single-mindedness—and the inexperience of a maiden-saint in a primitive painting. An observer who notes and praises such characteristics as these in a woman and seeks to develop their opposite in a young man is an observer who subscribes to his culture's notions of sexual differentiation and to a prescription for the ideal woman and wife. An observer who is in love, as Rowland is with Mary, and who prefers fair maidens is likely to be a man who will discover in the behavior of his beloved not an unusual and unexpected personality but the character and motives that meet his fondest expectations.[8]

Does James intend, however, that the reader understand Rowland's habit of mind as a limitation or simply as a way of perceiving the world? Does the implied author anticipate that the authorial audience will construe Rowland's perception as an angle of vision or as a prejudice that works against insight and understanding? When Rowland's vision of Christina Light joins his vision of Mary Garland, the intended meaning of the text becomes clear: Rowland's perceptions are fixed rather than free, limited rather than expansive. James here rejuvenates the tired categories of fair and dark ladies by enlarging their importance, by making them agents in the drama of consciousness. The dark lady of *Roderick Hudson*, ironically named Christina Light, is beautiful and captivating to Rowland. When she first appears, Rowland sees a tall, slender, elegant twenty year old, with dark blue eyes and "a mass of dusky hair," who "led by a cord a large poodle of the most fantastic aspect...a tired princess—these were the general features of his vision....She left a vague sweet perfume behind her as she passed" (1:94-95). Christina's beauty fascinates Rowland. Whatever his opinion of her character, he consistently admires her looks. Whatever his opinion of her motives, he is a careful observer of her strengths. He recognizes, for example, her "easy use of her imagination...energy

was there, audacity, the restless questioning soul" (1:278-79).
Rowland knows, too, that Christina is intelligent, and he is
touched by her humility on the subject of Roderick Hudson,
whom Rowland presumes she loves. In fact, Rowland is quite
willing to be Christina's friend. He honestly believes what he
tells her, that she belongs by destiny to the great, dangerous,
and delightful world, being "made to ornament it magnifi-
cently...to charm it irresistibly" (1:287).

At the same time, Rowland Mallet is shown to fear Christina Light. She is a dangerous woman despite her intelligence
and charms—or perhaps because of them. As Rowland in-
structs Roderick, "There are two kinds of women—you ought
to know by this time—the safe and the unsafe" (1:160). Thus
Rowland consistently divides the world of women, and thus
Christina falls on one side of an imaginary line while Mary
Garland falls on the other. Christina is the dark lady of
Rowland's imagination, a "dangerous woman" as he says; her
magnetism and vitality give her the power to draw a man into
her orbit, even if he prefers to remain judiciously in his own.

Rowland Mallet is portrayed as fancying that he knows the
motives of dark and fair ladies before he ever encounters any
individual woman. He is shown to be wrong. Rowland assumes that Christina is in love with Roderick, and so she must
be jealous of Mary Garland, his intended. Still presupposing
that love, Rowland construes as base Christina's decision to
break her engagement to the wealthy Prince Casamassima,
positing a motive traditionally associated with women in love
and particularly with women who fear that they are losing in
the game of love: he thinks Christina wants to hurt Mary.

Rowland's reading of Christina's motives is shown to be
insupportable on at least two counts. First, Christina has
given Rowland information that amply accounts for a broken
engagement without recourse to further, more subliminal
motives; she tells him that she is discontent because her mother is trying to marry her to the Prince against her will. Nevertheless, Rowland overlooks this information when assessing

Christina's act. Second, Rowland's own reflections should deter his negative conclusions about Christina—if he would consult them. He is vaguely conscious of some possible distortion in his reading of Christina; he reflects that it was "monstrous" to think she sacrificed a fortune to jealousy. Yet he ignores his own intuitions and attaches a petty motive to Christina's act. Rowland calls up certain checks and balances on his judgment, only to set them aside in order to find against Christina Light. So blind is he to the real situation of Roderick, Mary, and Christina that, when Christina correctly points out to him that Roderick doesn't care for Mary and therefore there is no cause for jealousy, Rowland dismisses her view. Reminiscent of Hawthorne's Coverdale in *The Blithedale Romance*, Rowland is characterized as an observer whose perceptions are at least limited and sometimes even distorted by his culture's horizon of expectations.[9] James sets this horizon, this abstract mental construct, against female characters, fictionally concrete constructs, to capture the limitations of vision and the drama of growth in the mind of Rowland.

James also uses literary traditions and codes and their reverberations to complicate the characterization of heroines. As William Veeder demonstrates in his instructive study of James's relationship to the popular fiction of his time, James uses the stereotypes of fair and dark ladies provided by popular fiction, but he always complicates them.[10] Thus the fair Mary Garland and the dark Christina Light prefigure James's later, more complex heroines. Mary foreshadows Gertrude Wentworth, Isabel Archer, Maria Gostrey, Milly Theale, and Maggie Verver; Christina heralds Eugenia, Madame Merle, Madame de Vionnet, Kate Croy, and Charlotte Stant.

Christina Light is an early instance of a female character who exceeds the boundaries of the dark lady of popular fiction. In her characterization, intertextuality is implicitly at work as the dark lady of literature hovers behind Christina and silently draws attention to Christina's complexity. Christina is shown to labor at every turn under the preconceptions that color both Rowland's vision and the fictional world. In characterizing her, James delved into the predicament of an unorthodox female in an orthodox world. Even Rowland Mallet understands all too well that Christina has a fertile and iconoclastic imagination of life and an irreverent attitude toward convention. Rowland warns Roderick that Christina is "altogether a singular type of young lady....It may be a charm, but it's certainly not the orthodox charm of marriageable maidenhood, the charm of the 'nice girl' or the 'dear girl' as we have been accustomed to know those blest creatures....Young unmarried women should be careful not to have too much [atmosphere]" (1:188). The implied author designs Christina's actions to prove that she does not fit into the category of nice and dear girls. Reminiscent of Hester Prynne in her boldness, Christina dares visit Rowland unchaperoned; she breaks an engagement to marry; she unabashedly reports her unconventional activities to others; and she expresses opinions that are unorthodox for a woman to hold, never mind to reveal. Christina even dares to suggest new patterns of behavior between the sexes.

The implied author exploits Christina's possibilities, making her into much more than a simple vixen or rebel by granting her two features that complicate her character and render it affecting. Christina is allowed to be aware of her situation and its cause, and she is made to judge herself against the very norms she theoretically rejects. Christina recognizes that her world is small and vulgar and understands that her confinement to it stems from her gender and her beauty. Mary Monson, in Cooper's *The Ways of the Hour*, is shown to be mentally unstable when she is granted a similar insight. The implied author of James, however, finds Christina Light to be sane and her world to be insane. Christina understands that her womanliness and her physical gifts stand between her and the good life as she would define it: a life of

love, truth, friendship, activity. She knows that her exceptional beauty makes her a salable commodity to the highest
bidder in the marriage market, causes others to respond to her
appearance rather than her person, and cuts her off from male
friendship by causing others always to cast her as the bride or
the femme fatale rather than the companion. Finally, Christina knows that her gender and her beauty limit her activity
and dictate a role insufficient to her energies. As she says, "I
can't loll all the morning on a sofa and sit perched all the
afternoon in a carriage. I get horribly restless; I must move; I
must do something and see something" (1:276). Because she
is a woman, however, she cannot do the something she
pleases.

Despite such insight, Christina is shown to assess her own
value against the conventional norms that arbitrarily constrict a spirit like hers, and to find herself wanting. She
accuses herself of vanity, folly, ignorance, affectation, and
falsity; she calls herself "the fruit of a horrible education sown
on a worthless soil" (1:260) and "egotistical" (1:208). The
implied author shows her to be her own worst critic, turning
against herself the weapons of a culture whose ideas of woman her life expands upon. Further, Christina is shown to try
to please the man she loves—Rowland Mallet—by attempting
to bend herself into the shape of womanhood that he prefers.
Upon Rowland's request, for example, Christina totally re-
moves herself from Roderick Hudson's life in order to clear
the way for Mary Garland. To compound Christina's dilemma, the implied author shows Rowland's failure to credit her
generosity and decency; Rowland denies her the recognition
that his conventional values should grant her for an unselfish
act.

Thus Christina suffers both from her world's imposing
conventional norms on her and from the seemingly inescapable reverberations of these norms in her own soul. While all
this demonstrates the shallowness of Rowland Mallet's vision,
it also lifts Christina's characterization well beyond the dark

lady of popular fiction and makes her an arresting and sympathetic character.[11]

Perhaps the most comprehensive instance in James's fiction of the complication of a female character and her elevation beyond the formula for the dark lady is Charlotte Stant of *The Golden Bowl*. In this novel, a priori ideas of all sorts are not simply exposed; they are overturned. *The Golden Bowl* is the drama of the consciousness of a young and innocent American woman, Maggie Verver. Married to the Italian Prince Amerigo, Maggie becomes aware of his adulterous relationship with her best friend, Charlotte Stant, who has become the wife of Maggie's beloved father, Adam Verver. The second half of the novel traces Maggie's response to the adultery and her calculated manipulation of manners and of her own temperament to win back her husband.

Superficially, the categories of fair and dark heroines and virtue and vice seem clear. In all good faith, Maggie and her father have entered marriages with beautiful but impecunious people and, in their way, have treated them generously. Furthermore, Maggie is absolutely devoted to Charlotte. On the surface, it would seem that, if ever in American fiction there was a betrayed innocent, it is Maggie Verver; and if ever there was a culpable adultress who, according to all standards of propriety and decency, should be condemned, it is Charlotte Stant. Yet Maggie and Charlotte are manipulated in a way that reverses the usual categories of moral judgment. Maggie's unwitting complicity in evil and Charlotte's efforts to do good are dramatized in such a way that finally the underpinnings of fair and dark ladies and virtue and vice have been dismantled and reconstructed.[12] There is evil in good and good in evil far beyond the wildest nightmares of conventional thinkers. This intended meaning of *The Golden Bowl* is conveyed to the authorial audience by the drama of the conditions under which a character like Charlotte Stant labors, conditions used by the intrepid implied author to complicate her character and her culpability.

Charlotte is characterized as an exceptional woman who lacks a field for expressing her talents because she is both financially insecure and unmarried. Far from being a vulgar fortune hunter, Charlotte married the wealthy Adam Verver on grounds close to impeccable. Charlotte offers her former lover Amerigo (who, comically, will be her stepson when she marries Adam) and Maggie the opportunity to advise against her marriage. Her efforts to be certain that the ground beneath her feet is solid from all points of view, that she has fulfilled the letter of the law, leads her to judge that "her position, in the matter of responsibility, was therefore inattackably straight" (23:290-91). The implied author takes care to show Charlotte as a character with tact, taste, and talent who deserves the life that, given her world, only a fortunate marriage can provide; she behaves correctly in procuring this life.

The implied author weaves through this picture the innocent Maggie, as devoted to her father's happiness as he is to hers. Maggie spends as much time as possible with her father, leaving Amerigo and Charlotte to their own devices.[13] The exemplary daughter unwittingly creates the space in which adultery can take place; she naively sends Amerigo and Charlotte on country weekends together. As Amerigo reflects in Book I of the novel, Maggie (like her father) proceeds as if there had been no fall from Paradise. It is in this context that Charlotte and Amerigo resume their affair and Charlotte asks Amerigo, "What do they [Maggie and her father] really suppose...becomes of one?—not so much sentimentally or morally, so to call it...but even just physically, materially, as a mere wandering woman: as a decent harmless wife, after all" (23:305). The blame for Amerigo and Charlotte's affair begins to shift from the adulteress to the "innocent" who fabricate the occasion for sin.

The implied author seems to anticipate a rather simple attitude on the part of the inscribed audience toward adultery and an adulteress, as Hawthorne did in the process of writing

The Scarlet Letter, and sets out to complicate that attitude, still characterizing Charlotte's behavior as impeccable, even after the resumption of her affair with Amerigo. Charlotte is aware of the reasons for which Adam Verver hired her into marriage, and she does all she can to make life perfect for him and Maggie. Their continued devotion to one another, even after each marries, is read by Charlotte as an expression of their desire to be together. As Charlotte puts it, "What could be more simple than one's going through with everything... when it's so plain a part of one's contract? I've got so much, by my marriage...that I should deserve no charity if I stinted my return. Not to do that, to give back on the contrary all one can, are just one's decency and one's honour and one's virtue" (23:318). Charlotte will hold up her end of the business of marriage to Adam. It is a situation she must accept and even appreciate, given her financial circumstances, and she therefore deals "from day to day and from one occasion to the other, with the duties of a remunerated office. Her perfect, her brilliant efficiency had doubtless all the while, contributed immensely to the pleasant ease in which her husband and her husband's daughter were lapped" (23:318).

Charlotte's multidimensionality is the implied author's occasion to bring Maggie Verver to expanded awareness and understanding. Quite remarkably, Charlotte's character is rendered sufficiently imposing to complicate not only the inscribed audience's preconceptions of the adulterous woman but the perceptions of her victim, Maggie Verver, as well. As the novel begins, Charlotte looms in Maggie's mind as a model woman, and she retains this position, even in defeat, as the novel ends. The character of Charlotte is a tool utilized to dramatize Maggie's developing consciousness while also a subject of great interest in its own right. Here we see the craft of James at its consummate best, working each fictional device until it gives to the artist everything it can conceivably yield. The dark lady has been complicated, audience assumptions have been challenged, and now the myth of Sleeping Beauty is given a double turn. First, as in *Roderick Hudson* many years earlier, a female character rather than a male character offers the kiss that awakens another; and, second, she is made to offer it to another female character, whose awakening requires recognition of and assimilation in a world heretofore unimagined by her.

Observing Charlotte, Maggie is instructed in the deportment that will enable her to satisfy her passion for her husband and win him back. Eschewing the role of "outraged wife" that would in no way suffice and in no way impress the Prince,[14] Maggie never complains and never stoops to vulgar accusations and recriminations. Rather she slowly takes possession of the Prince in much the way Charlotte had: through attentiveness and bonding.[15] Whereas Amerigo and Charlotte had been joined together in the secret of their adultery, Maggie and Amerigo are united in the secret of Maggie's knowledge of that adultery. Ironically, with Charlotte as her guide, Maggie is brought from innocent girlhood into mature womanhood, a process that requires Maggie to manipulate manners as she expands her awareness. Thus the gap between perception and reality is closed for Maggie as her innocent ideas of friends and marriage fall away. This is accomplished by the implied author's bold depiction of the "evil" female genius of the household as a model woman who, finally commanding Maggie's admiration, is intended to command that of the authorial audience as well.

The amplification of heroines, the drama of consciousness, and the complication of fair and dark ladies with the complexity of characterization it enables are artistic effects that James achieves by referring his texts to the culture's literary, social, and ideological horizons. James was entirely able, as well, to take the culture's frame of reference as his subject and to satirize it. In *The Portrait of a Lady*, James begins with a subject presumed to be insignificant and amplifies it. In *The Bostonians*, James begins with a subject presumed to be significant and cuts it down to size. The text of *The Bostonians* argues, in effect, that American culture has magnified to the point of distortion, as in a fun house mirror, that which is at best a subject and in any case a mere mental construct that bears little resemblance to reality. That mental construct is sexual differentiation and its ramifications.

The Bostonians, a novel of James's middle period, grew out of his visit to the United States between 1881 and 1883. James found in American culture a confusion of the private and public realms, a nest of questionable reform movements, and, most peculiarly and saliently, as he wrote in his notebooks, "the decline in the sentiment of sex."[16] The common denominator in all this, in James's perception, was woman. Prior to the Civil War, she was primarily a private and domestic creature, respected by her culture in her womanly role. In the 1880s, she sought a place in the public arena. The shifts in her place in society and in her attitudes provoked a countermovement, anti-feminism, that amplified the din of reform, with everyone seeking to change woman in some way. Thus the feminist cause offered itself to James's imagination as a timely paradigm of what he perceived to be society's confusion of the public and private and the loud vacuousness of reform movements. It is not only the feminist reform movement that is held up to ridicule. Rather, it is the frame of reference, the mental outlook that has generated the poles of feminism on the one hand and conservative attitudes toward "woman" on the other, that is the object of James's satire.

The ideology of woman functioned in the imagination of Howells as a magnet that attracted and shaped various phenomena. In *The Bostonians*, James uses the ideology of woman as the magnet around which *characters* order their lives and seek meaning. These notions drive their actions, account for the conflicts in the plot, and mark their identity. Olive Chancellor is a spinster of old Boston reform stock who, in stark contrast with Constance Fenimore Woolson's Madam Carroll, who devotes herself utterly to her husband and to her genteel, wifely role in *For the Major*, spends her energies trying to mold Verena Tarrant, a young woman she loves, into a feminist. Basil Ransom is a conservative southern gentleman who spends his energies trying to cast Verena in a domestic, traditional mold. Verena Tarrant is the clay in Ransom's potter's wheel. She finally marries Basil Ransom. The story of these three characters, and of a nest of other reformers, is told by an omniscient narrator who has little respect for the craft these characters practice. Thus all parties to the feminist issue are satirized, both those who insist on the culture's traditional definition of woman's nature and those who rebel against it. *The Bostonians*, driven by the imagination of James that stands above all this, is critical of making an issue of woman in the first place, of treating her as a class apart, as a subject for oratory or manipulation, as an item for public display, as a pawn rather than a human being.

The management of the love triangle of Olive Chancellor, Verena Tarrant, and Basil Ransom suggests that the division of gender characteristics into exclusive categories, the source of all arguments about woman's place, is itself a distortion of reality. The implied author of *The Bostonians* ascribes to Olive Chancellor and to Basil Ransom similar motives and similar deeds, until finally they are distinguished from one another only by anatomy. Each falls in love with the wispy Verena, and each seeks to possess her totally. Olive wants to rescue Verena from her culturally inferior background, bring her to live with her, support her, and educate her in women's rights. Basil Ransom wants to rescue Verena from Olive Chancellor and bring her to live with him. In their home, Basil will educate her into his version of women's rights. Both wish to usher Verena into "correct" thinking about woman, but the fact that each defines such thinking differently does not alter the principle to which each adheres: the absolute truth of his or her view and the desire to impose it on Verena.[17] The implied author, emphasizing the similarity of these two, ascribes parallel gestures to each: Olive flings her cloak over

Verena as she drags her away from a group of young men, and Basil covers Verena's face when he steals her from Olive. Thus the implied author of *The Bostonians* collapses that compartmentalizing of the sexes into extreme camps for which both feminist and conservative ideologues are responsible because they turn sexual differentiation into caricature.

Basil Ransom is characterized as party to this exaggeration of sexual differences. The narrator introduces him as a "lean, pale, sallow, shabby, striking young man, with his superior head, his sedentary shoulders, his expression of bright grimness and hard enthusiasm, his provincial, distinguished appearance" who is, "as a representative of his sex, the most important personage in my narrative."[18] One cannot resist noting the irony that a southern man is the most important person in a novel about the women's movement entitled *The Bostonians*. Whether deliberately or not, the implied author suggests that a man, an outsider geographically and generically, is the most important catalytic agent in women's lives. The implied author uses Ransom as a handbook of conservative ideas about woman. Ransom likes women who do not think too much, who are private and passive, and who understand their quiet power, the power to set men in motion. He believes that women want to please men and that a good man will make any woman forget feminism. Further, he believes women are inferior to men and tiresome when they claim otherwise.

Ransom's assumptions about woman undergird his interaction with women. To the patronizing Ransom is attributed a set of strategies that frustrates women's attempts to be taken seriously, to change the view of them that Ransom's ideas express. Ransom's methods include flattery, trivializing, and scoffing. When a female reformer tells him he clearly disapproves of the feminist struggle, he claims that his gallant offer to escort her home is proof of sympathy. He substitutes flattery, that is, for discussion of the issue. Also, he trivializes serious matters. When Verena tries to convince him that the

number of women without homes and husbands renders a
domestic model for women inadequate, he replies that he is
willing to have a dozen wives.[19] Finally, the narrator declares
Ransom "a scoffer of scoffers" (325).

Believing woman to be inferior and thinking he is superior,
Basil consistently treats women like children and never so
much as listens to their ideas. Verena is trained in oratory in
the interests of feminism. Hearing one of Verena's speeches,
Ransom "took it for granted the matter of her speech was
ridiculous; how could it help being....She was none the less
charming for that" (271). The degree to which Ransom is
captive to ideas of woman is patent in the fact that he does not
merely reject women's ideas, he rejects the idea that women
could have ideas. Whether the feminists are right or wrong is
therefore a nonquestion for Ransom.

On the grounds that woman is inferior Ransom assumes
his right to exercise authority over her. Conceiving of woman
as a helpless and charming child and believing in definitions
of the sexes that cast men as protectors of the weaker sex, Basil
imagines himself a kind of knight called to rescue the woman
he loves from the opposition. The implied author signals
Ransom's bad faith by the narrator's rendering of what Basil is
thinking as he attempts to make Verena come away with him.
He enjoys her hesitation, and he is "slightly conscious of a
man's brutality—of being pushed by an impulse to test her
good nature, which seemed to have no limit" (250). Verena
challenges a statement of his in a tone that seems mocking and
defiant, so he draws her to him and gives her "a concise
account of his situation in the form of a deliberate kiss" (340).
A woman can be silenced and controlled more effectively by a
kiss than by argument, a strategy also used by Caspar Goodwood on Isabel Archer in *The Portrait of a Lady* and by
Prince Amerigo on Maggie Verver in *The Golden Bowl*.[20]
Ransom substitutes sex for rational argument and then enjoys
his role as sexual aggressor, as the male who, "by muscular
force," would "wrest" Verena, the woman "open to attack,"

from his rival. In the sexual poetics of *The Bostonians*, sexual politics are characterized as the politics of physical power that, because exercised somewhat subtly, have become not simply acceptable but are not even recognized as exercise of power—the logical outgrowth of the idea of the physical and intellectual superiority of the male, of his duty to protect woman, and of his right to possess her. Thus the decline in the sentiment of sex in America is captured in the exaggeration of cultural presuppositions about woman into an ideology that, in its implementation, finally denies women any intellect and importance whatsoever. The extremity of this situation, lest it is not apparent to the authorial audience from Basil's words and manner, is capped by Basil's being a writer of no consequence and by the narrator's attitude toward the marriage of Basil and Verena: a union "far from brilliant," he says, in which Verena is destined to shed many tears.

That Basil Ransom is a fool and Olive Chancellor is foolish are made indisputably clear in the characterization of Verena Tarrant—the prize these people seek so desperately to win is of little value. The material on which both Ransom and Olive wish to work is insubstantial, and yet it is, ironically, the version of womanhood that the culture claims to prefer. To Verena are ascribed the "womanly" traits of a sentimental heroine and the semes of woman valued within a genteel definition of woman's nature. Verena is pale (if not anemic), submissive, pliable, adaptable, pleasing, and blushing. Predictably, when she speaks in public she dresses in white and wears flowers on her bosom, reminiscent of Hawthorne's Priscilla. And just as the arch-reformer Hollingsworth of *The Blithedale Romance* prefers Priscilla, so Verena is the girl of men's and of reformers' dreams.[21] Rolling out a pedestal and elevating Verena to heights on which she is incapable of standing, Olive sees her as the perfect spokesperson for the feminist cause; a seedy journalist thinks it foolish that Verena carefully prepares her speeches because her girlishness is her trump card anyway; and Basil Ransom sees that Verena draws an audience because she is "unspeakably attractive." A female character whom the implied author sees as an effeminate woman, Verena seems to the characters in *The Bostonians* to be the perfect vessel for feminist ideas.

The extravagant ridiculousness of Verena and of her admirers is captured in Verena's speeches, which are so vacuous that there would be little reason to attend her lectures outside of an attraction to curiosities. Her oratory is a hodge-podge of tired metaphors, like "painful earthly pilgrimage" and "the gulf that yawns" and "the garden of life," that demean the very ideas she intends to champion.[22] Olive and Basil do not perceive that Verena's rhetoric makes it impossible to determine whether the feminist ideas she expresses have substantial merit. Waxing eloquently about the cold heart that only "the touch of woman can warm," Verena is certainly no intellectual giant—but then, "womanly" women are not expected to be.

Verena's undisciplined mind is incapable of making discriminations and is subject to massive shifts in opinion. The implied author makes the private Verena deploy the same vacuous rhetoric that characterizes her public person; she totally confuses the private and public spheres. Further, when Verena is intense about feminism, she is feminist; when intense about Basil Ransom, she behaves like the stereotypical "woman in love." As the narrator says, "the truth had changed sides" and Verena goes where the fires of passion burn for her in a given moment.

Thus *The Bostonians* manifests little respect for walking embodiments of a genteel idea of woman's nature, even less for platform reformers, and none at all for conservatives like Basil Ransom who reduce pliable women to clay, ready for the molding and firing. Reformers and conservatives lack substantial humanity and also the human interconnectedness that makes a healthy society; they display no "convivial movement" toward one another nor any "mutual recognition," the narrator claims. This is particularly ironic, given that the culture assigns to woman, whom this novel is in a sense all about, the task of building warm, nurturing human communities. Dehumanized, these characters display what the narrator calls "the terror of the American heart": finding oneself face to face with another human being. To avoid this terror, they lose and excuse themselves in ideology, as the characterization of all the satellite figures in *The Bostonians* suggests. Miss Birdseye of the "Short-Skirts League" belonged to "every league that had been founded for almost any purpose whatever" (27). Miss Farrinder is a worker for the cause who is thought to "embody the domestic virtues...to be a shining proof, in short, that the forum, for ladies, is not necessarily hostile to the fireside" (31). She tells Olive that when she works for the cause, she feels like Napoleon on the eve of his great victories, energized by "unfriendly elements—I like to win them over" (46). Dr. Prance, a career woman who wants nothing to do with the feminist movement, is "plain and spare," "tough and technical." Adeline Luna "would rather be trampled upon by men than by women" (163) and grants her own sex no more dignity than does her southern counterpart, Basil Ransom. In *The Bostonians*, stupidity freely crosses gender lines and the sentiment of sex has run amok. The culture's attachment to the ideology of woman is James's major device to make tangible and dramatic the nation's state of mind and soul; it is also a major critique of the ideology itself.

While James's imagination is whetted by the culture's horizon of expectations, his texts on rare occasions manifest gender-inflected problems, an example of which occurs in *The Portrait of a Lady*. Lydia Touchett is characterized as abrasive, independent, and determined never to please. Her character violates all expectations of woman's proper demeanor and duty. She is seldom at Gardencourt, her husband's home, but she does return there to nurse her dying husband and later her dying son. Because the narrator makes it perfectly clear

that Mrs. Touchett never undertakes an action for appearances' sake, her presence at these deathbeds can be assumed to mark some feeling for her husband and her son.
However, she attends upon her husband's death with "no
tears, no sighs, no exaggeration," causing Isabel to charge her
with emotional sterility. Moreover, as Mrs. Touchett never
disguised the nature of her marriage nor was she ever sentimental, it would be dishonest, sentimental, and entirely contrary to her character for Lydia now to assume the mask of the
bereaved widow. Lydia Touchett attends her dying son with
some care and is with him, holding his hand, when he dies.
Even though she submits on this occasion to Isabel's caress,
the only mark of affection she accepts in the course of the
novel, she remains "stiff and dry-eyed."

The narrator, like Isabel, seems unable to recognize grief
and emotion in any form save the predictable one of tears and
calls into question Mrs. Touchett's human qualities, accusing
her of taking consolation in the fact that death "happened to
other people and not to herself. Death was disagreeable, but in
this case it was her son's death, not her own" (4:422). As if
offering evidence for this devastating judgment, the narrator
then tells us that Mrs. Touchett, as soon after her son's death
as possible, gathered herself together in order to proceed with
her life. Against what implicit norm is it being judged that
Mrs. Touchett should not do exactly as she does? She is
characterized as a pragmatist, after all, and the definitive
nature of death can certainly prompt a pragmatist to get on
with life with all due haste. Nor does doing so necessarily
signal an absence of feeling. One wonders whether the narrator would evaluate with the same severity a dry-eyed male
character returning to the relief of routine after a death in the
family.

Mrs. Touchett is of course a difficult, even a brittle, character. Nevertheless, her behavior seems to be judged sim-
plistically by gender-related expectations. In the culture's
view, sentiment and a soft manner are major touchstones of a

proper woman's character. In the absence of these tokens, Lydia Touchett is subjected to disproportionate recrimination. An idea of woman's nature and the manner it dictates works against Isabel's and the narrator's valuation of Lydia to obscure the implications of certain of her deeds.

Another instance in which the idea of woman's nature interferes with James's judgment occurs in *The Tragic Muse*, the only novel in which James cast a major female character as an artist. Miriam Rooth is an artist figure—albeit an actress, a role not uncommon for women in James's day and a profession in which James was especially interested in the 1890s, when he was writing for the theater. Miriam is imbued with remarkable acting talent and an indomitable drive to use that talent to succeed in her chosen field. As the plot of *The Tragic Muse* unfolds, Miriam becomes enamored of Nick Dormer in much the same way Christina Light is captivated by Rowland Mallet in *Roderick Hudson*. Like Christina with Roderick, Miriam understands that Nick will never be attracted to her as a spouse, although her face inspires him to paint, just as Christina's beauty motivates Roderick Hudson to sculpt. Miriam is Nick's muse,[23] but she never believes she will be his flesh and blood interest, and there is no indication that she would sacrifice her career for Nick Dormer or anyone else. Nick asks practically nothing of Miriam and certainly does not ask her to abandon her career.

In a preface written years after *The Tragic Muse*, however, James claims that Miriam would sacrifice her career for Nick. He asserts that because Miriam can see Nick's career and hers as a single artistic endeavor,

she has no fear of not being able to satisfy him, even to the point of "chucking" for him, if need be, that artistic identity of her own which she has begun to build up. It will all be to the glory therefore of their common infatuation with "art": she will doubtless be no less willing to serve his than she was eager to serve her own, purged now of the too great shrillness....I must have had it well before me that she was all aware of the small strain a great sacrifice to Nick would cost her—by reason of the strong effect on her of his own superior logic, in which the very intensity of concentration was so to find its account. [7:xviii-xx]

James's statement is simply astounding. He says in the preface that he does not at all go "behind" Miriam in the novel, and he does not. Yet we see in the preface a portion of what he does think to be "behind" her—and it is sheer projection on James's part.[24] James's thoughts of what Miriam *would* do if Nick *had* asked her to "chuck" her career express a purely conventional thought unsubstantiated by the novel he actually wrote. The preface imposes on Miriam a self-sacrificial mode that belongs to an ideal of woman's nature but in no way pertains to the character James portrays in *The Tragic Muse*.

In the light of the *The Tragic Muse*'s extraordinary insight into the problems that assail a professional woman, how does one account for James's misconstruction of his own achievement? It is as though he did not realize that he had created a serious artist figure who is a woman. In fact, James's fiction generally *is* notable for the absence of such figures. For instance, in his short fiction James creates comic, shamefully popular women writers, such as Jane Highmore of "The Next Time," who, try as she might, is always a vulgar success. In all his short stories, he portrays only one respectable woman artist, Mrs. Harvey of "Broken Wings."

The absence of female artist figures who are successful in James's terms is doubly notable because of James's admiration for George Eliot, Constance Fenimore Woolson, and Edith Wharton. While it would be comforting to think that a mind and imagination as powerful as James's would operate without gender bias in assessing artistic achievement, such, unfortunately, is not clearly the case. Giving Henry James advance notice, as it were, of Virginia Woolf's later observation that men had presumed through history and, quite literally, volu-

minously to expatiate on the subject of woman, Constance
Fenimore Woolson wrote the following to James: "How did
you ever dare write a portrait of a lady? Fancy any woman attempting the portrait of a gentleman! Wouldn't there be a
storm of ridicule! Every clerk on the Maumee river would
know more about it than a George Eliot."[25] Although we are
fortunate that James did dare his portraits, the implications of
Woolson's statement are well worth drawing out.

James and all his male colleagues did indeed presume to
know the souls and minds of women—the sentimental attitudes of a Howells on the supposed "mystery" of woman
notwithstanding. Furthermore, James apparently did believe
that gender bore on art, that what he perceived to be the
preponderance of the Jane Highmores over the Mrs. Harveys
was more than an accident of the marketplace as his comments suggest on the subject of Woolson's *East Angels:*

It is a characteristic of the feminine, as distinguished from the
masculine hand, that in any portrait of a corner of human affairs...
what we used to call the love-story, will be the dominant one....In
novels by men other things are there to a greater or less degree, and I
therefore doubt whether a man may be said ever to have produced a
work belonging exactly to the class in question. In men's novels, even
of the simplest strain, there are still other references and other
explanations; in women's, when they are of the category to which I
allude, there are none but that one. And there is certainly much to be
said for it.[26]

Patronizingly allowing that what he takes to be woman's
foremost subject has something to be said for it, James also
sets up an invidious distinction between the masculine and
the feminine "hand." Gender is not irrelevant to James in
matters of art.

Having remarked on the "daring" of James in writing a
portrait of a lady, Woolson continues in the same letter to
him: "For my own part, in my small writings, I never dare put
down what men are thinking, but confine myself simply to

what they do and say. For, long experience has taught me that whatever I suppose them to be thinking at any especial time, that is sure to be exactly what they are *not* thinking. What they *are* thinking, however, nobody but a ghost could know."[27] Unlike James, Constance Fenimore Woolson did create serious female artist figures. The inspired Miss Grief, in the story of the same name, is recognized by a male writer to have gifts superior to his; Miss Macks of "The Street of the Hyacinth" achieves in Rome a wisdom and sophistication that, while it includes a recognition of the limitations of her talent, brings with it a maturity considerably greater than James allows Roderick Hudson in similar circumstances. Like the creators of "woman's fiction" before her, Woolson neither presumed to write admonitory fiction for men nor, unfortunately, dared publicly to declare herself a serious artist, whatever her private wishes may have been. Rather, assuming the pose that her sister writers most often adopted, she wrote to the forbidding James: "I do not come in as a literary woman at all, but as a sort of—of admiring aunt."[28]

The contrast between James, on the one hand, and women writers like Woolson, on the other, reminds us as starkly as possible of the degree to which nineteenth-century men and women perceived themselves as different beings and then constructed their lives on the basis of that perception; the men writers took the world and everyone in it as their province while the women eschewed such global views. It is no surprise, therefore, that James did not recall the seriousness he had himself attributed to the artistic talents and ambitions of his own creation, Miriam Rooth. His ideas of the woman artist, as well as the cultural ambiance that he lived in and helped to sustain, would have encouraged little else. The surprise is not that James misconstrued his design for Miriam Rooth but, rather, that he rose to the occasion of her in the first place.

A final speculation is in order about James and his treatment not only of Miriam Rooth but of female artists generally, and that is his enormous interest in what was essentially woman's sphere in his time. In *The American Scene*, he accuses the American male of a blunder he considers more colossal than any conceivable error in business or government. He asserts that the American male, absorbed in the world of business, has abdicated to women every human occupation except business. According to James, the American male has surrendered "all the *other* so numerous relations with the world he lives in that are imputable to the civilized being." The male's default, writes James, has become "the unexampled opportunity of the woman—which she would have been an incredible fool not to pounce upon."[29] James describes a milieu in which woman's sphere remains in principle what it had always been: the domestic and social arena, the affective areas of human life. To James, the territory men abdicated is simply the whole of the world that is of any intrinsic interest. Far from imagining woman's sphere as a limitation, a realm to which woman is relegated while real life proceeds elsewhere, James thought that the arena assigned to woman was that incomparable world where the interaction occurs that provides psychological revelations of endless fascination. Far from lamenting woman's assignment to a single sphere, James counts her assignment an enviable privilege, an assignment to an arena much more capacious than men realized. This may explain James's failure to appreciate the fictional terms of Miriam's life and her dedication to art rather than to marriage, ordinarily a woman's passport to the best of worlds.

The discrepancy between James's preface and his characterization of Miriam Rooth may reveal the difference between his conscious perception of social reality and his imaginative capability. Like Howells, James was an insightful observer of the human scene. Unlike Howells, James was exceptionally alert to the ideology adduced to justify limitations placed on women. Perhaps because of this, the ideology of woman informed his art only at his invitation, and only as his art's servant. It provided him the materials to render palpable the drama of consciousness, the complexity of the human being, and the value of female characters who, exceeding the assumptions of their fictional world, become engrossing and indeed extraordinary subjects of fiction.

5. EDITH WHARTON
The Female Imagination and the Territory Within

There's a certain Slant of light,
Winter Afternoons—
That oppresses, like the Heft
Of Cathedral Tunes—

Heavenly Hurt, it gives us—
We can find no scar,
But internal difference,
Where the Meanings, are—
                    —Emily Dickinson

In *The Madwoman in the Attic,* Sandra Gilbert and Susan Gubar discuss the place of women writers in a patriarchal culture, where models of literary authority are male and where, therefore, the use of authoritative models may involve dangerous forms of self-denial and create severe forms of self-doubt. To overcome their situation, women writers adopt different strategies; they may write in "lesser" genres, mimic men, create submerged meanings behind the public and more accessible ones, or deal with central female experiences from a female perspective.[1] Edith Wharton's first thirty-five years of life were marked by forms of self-denial so dangerous that she suffered a mental illness and by self-doubt of such serious proportions that not until 1899, with the publication of *The Greater Inclination*, her first volume of short stories, was she at all confident in herself. She writes in her autobiography that with her recognition as a writer she was "called to life," she discovered "that soul of mine."[2] Wharton's experience fits Gilbert and Gubar's description on other counts, as well. Suggestive of her responsiveness to female literary models, in *A Motor-Flight Through France* her tribute to George Sand, upon visiting Nohant, is more extended and emotionally charged than her reaction to any other site.[3] Writing in a culture dominated by male literary authorities, she nevertheless chose to write primarily in "major" rather than "lesser" genres. Significantly, her imagination joins her experience of being a woman to create a different perspective on the same world also fictionalized by Howells and James—a female perspective that deconstructs that world and gives access to regions beyond the imagination of the male writer.

Howells and James stand apart from their heroines, the one fondly observing the charm of their foibles and the other accepting their "beautiful difficulties" as the artist's challenge. Edith Wharton was denied such luxury. A woman as well as an artist, she stood in that "certain Slant of light... that oppresses," as Emily Dickinson wrote, and makes "internal difference, where the meanings, are—." That internal difference shows itself in Wharton's wielding of the instrument of gender. In virtually every area of importance for heroines, Wharton imagines more fully and deeply than her male counterparts the consequences of the culture's ideology of woman. The pursuit of marriage and the conventions that test and mature James's Isabel Archer ruin Wharton's Lily Bart. The benign, conventional postures of the courted Isabel are escalated into the venal manipulations of convention by Wharton's Undine Spragg. The charm of Howells's Isabel March, as she hangs pictures and tends Basil's diet, becomes the aimlessness of Wharton's Pauline Manford. The scrupulosity of Howell's New England-bred Grace Breen, propelling her out of a profession and into marriage, emerges in Wharton's Anna Leath as a fear of frigidity that leads to a fractured life. The decline in the sentiment of sex in James's Olive Chancellor is transposed into the asexuality of Wharton's Undine

Spragg. The cute irrationality of Howells's Clara Kingsbury assumes the form of intellectual dessication in Wharton's Halo Spear.

Obviously, the culture's ideology of woman had a radical impact on the imagination of Edith Wharton and the texts which resulted. Compared with Wharton, writers like Howells and James sought answers to predictable, relatively obvious questions about woman to which the culture's horizon of expectations gave rise. To ask about the consequences of a woman becoming a doctor, and then use ideas of woman to formulate an aesthetic answer, as Howells did in *Dr. Breen's Practice,* is to ask a question handed to the writer on the platter of then-current events. To seek dramatic material in the situation of a young American woman in Europe is to capitalize, as James did, on an obvious cultural phenomenon. But to ask questions and to create dramatic situations that turn the culture's ideology of woman on its head, that controvert the culture's frame of reference, is to be revolutionary and imaginative rather than predictable and derivative.

The fiction of Edith Wharton seeks aesthetic solutions to startling, even shocking, questions posed by the culture's expectations. For example, given the culture's patriarchal assumption that marriage is hierarchical and that partners constrain one another's freedom by right of contract and by right of sacred Scripture, what would happen if a man and a woman attempted to live as equal partners and without imposing any formal constraints whatsoever on one another? *The Gods Arrive* seeks an aesthetic solution to this question. Or given that within the culture's system of sexual differentiation the male is deemed intellectually superior, what would happen if a woman of superior intelligence were to love a man of inferior intelligence, and the man recognized his inferiority? *The Touchstone* and *Twilight Sleep* and *Hudson River Bracketed* dramatize the consequences of such a situation.

What would be the result if a woman took at face value the sexual proscriptions with which the culture's ideology surrounds her? Not necessarily a rebellious sexual seductiveness, as male novelists casting woman as temptress have feared, and not necessarily a modest but warm response from a maiden who comes to love at the proper, culturally assigned moment. Rather, the result might well be a sexually crippling fear of frigidity, as in the case of Anna Leath in *The Reef*, or, even worse, an absolute indifference to sex, as in the case of Undine Spragg in *The Custom of the Country*. The culture's horizon of expectations joins Wharton's imagination to pose unthinkable, unsettling questions and to craft aesthetic solutions that disclose as self-fulfilling prophecies the very rules a patriarchy designs to defend itself against its own worst fears. Wharton treats aspects of women's lives, particularly their intellects and their sexuality, at a depth and with a complexity that a woman's perspective made possible.

Marriage and the ideology of domesticity that informs it are the framework within which Wharton most often places her heroines. The extent to which Wharton relies on the laws of gender and their rule that a woman marry is made strikingly clear in *The House of Mirth* and the fate of its twenty-nine year old heroine, Lily Bart, who is intelligent, attractive, talented, and unmarried. Like James's *Portrait of a Lady*, which answers the question of what a singular young woman like Isabel Archer will do with herself, *The House of Mirth* answers the question of what a singular woman like Lily Bart, who cannot bring herself to marry, will do with herself. A half century earlier, in 1857, Catherine Maria Sedgwick had taken up the same problem in a novel entitled *Married or Single?* Like Lily Bart, the heroine, Grace, leads an idle life at first and refuses a venal marriage, but unlike Lily, Grace learns to support herself and eventually marries a worthy gentleman. Lily Bart, on the other hand, formed into a "futile shape" to be an "ornament," in the words of one of her prospects, Lawrence Selden, develops no means to support herself independently, as her abortive attempts at the craft of millinery and at secretarial work indicate, and never marries.

The implied author takes pains to draw the connection between Lily's problem and gender: Lily notes that a girl must marry while "a man may if he chooses,"[4] and Lawrence Selden does remain a bachelor, leading a comfortably shabby life, and, with the approval of society, is allowed indiscretions and liaisons that in no way compromise his future or his place in the house of mirth.[5] Thus the ramifications of Lily Bart's early lament, "What a miserable thing it is to be a woman"(9), become perfectly clear as the novel unfolds. Her experience echoes that of antebellum American women who, according to Ann Douglas, were told by ministers: "Stay within your proper confines and you will be worshipped...step outside and you will cease to exist."[6] The imagination of Wharton builds Lily Bart's case entirely on gender, claiming it is essentially Lily's gender that accounts for her descent from the heights to the depths of society, and positing that such a fall is highly unlikely for a male, using the comparative fate of Lawrence Selden as example. The novel holds the culture's horizon of expectations responsible for the death of Lily Bart.

It is also that horizon against which practices that run counter to expectations stand in bold and significant relief. Wharton imagines nonhierarchical, unrestrictive agreements between men and women that are, in effect, marriages on new terms. Her predecessor sister novelists earlier had identified the constrictions and constraints placed on women within the patriarchal construct of marriage. Elizabeth Stoddard, for example, in *The Morgesons* in 1862, had set young Cassandra on a road that brought her into contact with characters like Alice Morgeson, who says that "marriage puts an end to the wisdom of women" and that men "require the souls and bodies of women, without having the trouble of knowing the difference between the one and other!" Taking up where other female writers left off, Wharton tries out fictional, nonpatriarchal arrangements. In an early short story, "The Reckoning," she explores the possibility of nonbinding agreements between characters satirized as vulgar and enamored of every passing fad. With sympathy for those who experiment with new life styles for sincere, generous, and unselfish reasons, she returns late in her life to the theme of marriage on new terms in *Hudson River Bracketed* and *The Gods Arrive*. The plots of these two novels, which Wharton unaccountably listed among her five favorites, chart the lives of an aspiring male novelist, Vance, and his muse, Halo. Halo educates Vance, inspires him, encourages him, and wrecks her life on him as he struggles with a sick and dependent wife, an unappreciative public, and a lack of self-discipline, sophistication, and formal education. Having already contracted a marriage of economic convenience, when Halo meets Vance she divorces her husband and runs off to Europe with Vance. To protect his ego and to please him, she suppresses her talents and grants him a freedom that Vance, in his infidelity and immaturity, transforms into license. At the conclusion of *The Gods Arrive*, a pregnant Halo Spear welcomes Vance back after he has cast her aside. She wastes her life on a man who treats her abominably while laboriously turning out one artistic success and two popular but flawed novels.

Among the several reasons offered to account for the troubles between Vance and Halo is Halo's attempt to conduct their partnership on the basis of a spiritual rather than a legal contract, a radical commitment to freedom in relationships, considering the culture's frame of reference for male-female relationships. Halo is led to discover that freedom is not what men really want. Ironically, in this novel it drives men and women apart rather than draws them together. Halo Spear gives Vance all manner of latitude to ensure that he will not feel suffocated, including hiding her pregnancy from him lest he feel constrained to marry her. Yet the more freedom Halo grants Vance, the more he suspects the quality of her love. As he reflects on the subject of his first marriage and the previously unwanted devotion of his uneducated, suffocating, and therefore exasperating first wife, Vance arrives at what seems a chilling conclusion: a scrupulous respect for the

freedom of another causes the tie between two people to wear
thin rather than to grow strong, while "the irritating friction
of familiarity" between him and his first wife "had made
separation unthinkable."[7] The captive of a priori ideas of
woman, Vance supposes that when a woman genuinely loves
a man, she worshipfully stands at his side, hoping to possess
rather than to free him. Vance cannot understand an unconventional woman like Halo as a loving woman.[8] Halo cannot
have a free and equal relationship with a man. Attitudes
toward woman and toward marriage are used by Wharton to
chart the tragedy of Halo Spear and to put her, plausibly, in
her place.

The instability of Halo and Vance's partnership is connected by the implied author of these novels with yet another
radical, peculiar departure from conventional norms: a
"marriage" between fully free and equal partners who are
intellectual peers. The imagination of Wharton explored dramatic questions and touched areas of a woman's self within
male-female relationships that were largely uncharted, if recognized at all, by male writers. Cooper, Hawthorne, and
Dreiser could make imaginative use of the sexual norms governing women; Howells could deploy the culture's attitudes
toward women and careers to create his dramas; James
was able to seize society's myopia to make palpable the
movements of consciousness. It remained for a woman like
Edith Wharton, following other women like Elizabeth Oaks
Smith, to make imaginative capital out of a territory that
women entered at their peril, the territory of the mind, and its
suburb, women's talents and their expression. Halo Spear
assumes intellectual parity in not just one but two relationships with men, and suffers the consequences. Introduced in
Hudson River Bracketed on the verge of marrying to support
her parents in the manner to which they are accustomed, and
having assessed her prospects and talents in painting and
writing, Halo has decided that her real gift "was for appreciat-
ing the gifts of others....She had measured herself and knew

it—and what else was there for her but marriage?"⁹ Thus
Halo marries Lewis Tarrant, who relies on Halo's talent and
uses her as a scout for his literary magazine. Halo naively
believes their marriage will be a partnership until she is
brought to the realization that, her husband's pride allowing
no vigorous intellectual exchange and brooking no disagreement, a woman's intellectual power is not only unappreciated
by a husband but irritating to him. Halo is then patronizingly
treated by Lewis, who "had fitted up a rather jolly room on
the roof—a sort of workshop-study, in which he had reserved
a corner for her modelling and painting. He always encouraged her in the practice of the arts he had himself abandoned,
and while gently disparaging her writing was increasingly
disposed to think there was 'something in' her experiments
with paint and clay" (223). Reacting to this depreciation of
her potential, Halo infrequently tries her hand at the arts; she
"rummaged among canvases, fussed with her easel, and got
out a bunch of paper flowers which she had manufactured
after reading somewhere that Cézanne's flowers were always
done from paper models. 'Now for a Cézanne!' she mocked"
(223).

In *Hudson River Bracketed*, Halo Spear is temporarily
saved from dessication by Vance Weston's entering her life.
Starved for appreciation and for intellectual exchange, Halo
plays muse to Vance; introducing this backwoods boy to
books, she revels in his companionship, throws herself into his
artistic aspirations, and enables his rare accomplishments in
his craft by her fine critical eye. Yet Vance, like Lewis Tarrant,
is made to reject Halo's inspiration and intelligence at the first
sign of success. In *Hudson River Bracketed*, Vance is launched
by Halo; in *The Gods Arrive* he withdraws from their intellectual companionship.

The grounds enlisted in *The Gods Arrive* to explain
Vance's refusing Halo's full participation in his life are those
the culture's ideology of woman readily offers. Vance, an
egomaniac who wants woman in her place but not his, is so

irritated by Halo's expertise that at times he prefers that she not type his manuscripts rather than subject them to her critical eye. Vance is also shown to prefer the company of his pseudo-intellectual male companions to that of the far more perceptive Halo, upon which Halo commits a damaging error: she makes herself small before Vance, behaving like his servant rather than his peer, in order to bolster his ego. Rendered defensive and insecure by Vance's attitude toward her mind and threatened in her femininity, Halo tries to "show Vance that she understood his heart as well as his brain....She would prove to him that her only happiness was in knowing that he was happy" (58). She abstains from criticizing work of his that is decidedly flawed, although she knows that his pseudo-intellectual friends read her silence as a mark of an inferior mind. A destructive dynamic ensues. The more Halo effaces herself before Vance, the more he takes up with his coterie of male companions, causing Halo to suppress further any expression of her artistic insights. She does this despite her understanding "that he ascribed her own lukewarm share in their talks to feminine inferiority. 'Of course general ideas always bore women to death,' he said in a tone of apology" (45). Vance and Halo share ideas with one another less and less, and Halo progressively wastes away intellectually, in large part because of the assumptions about woman on which Vance acts, which inflate his sense of worth by offering someone in his world to whom he can feel superior.

Indeed, Vance Weston is essentially the type of male character, not infrequent in Wharton's fiction, who wheels out the culture's ideology of woman when it serves his needs. Woman's nature and sphere, an article of faith in Cooper's fiction, is shown in Wharton's to have become a tool to be manipulated by the venal. Vance is shown to use Halo's critical acumen when it promises to forward his success and then to blame Halo for her intellectual strengths when it suits him. Anything but a god but nonetheless the director of Halo's life, it is Vance who formulates the thought that judges Halo guilty of disobedience to woman's nature. In the company of the disreputable Floss Delaney, Vance dares to reflect, "Ah, this was what women were for—to feel the way to one's heart" (287). The narrator later tells us that Vance believes his talent is better sustained by a "strong emotional stimulant....Intellectual comradeship between lovers was unattainable; that was not the service women could render to men" (382-83).

The devaluation of woman's mind haunted Wharton from the beginning to the end of her career. She had originally taken up the presumed intellectual disparity between men and women thirty years before *Hudson River Bracketed* (1929) and *The Gods Arrive* (1932) in the novella *The Touchstone* (1900). Here, too, the imagination of Wharton tallies the wages extracted from a woman for the sin of intellect. No good mental deed on the part of a Wharton heroine is allowed to go unpunished, a particularly poignant fact because of what it suggests about Edith Wharton's personal experience as a woman of exceptional mind.[10] Margaret Aubyn, the only serious female artist figure whom Wharton dared to commit to paper, is already dead when the novella opens, but even in death she plays antagonist to the novella's protagonist, Glennard, who foreshadows Vance Weston. Margaret is characterized as an exceptional novelist who achieves extraordinary success; she is shown to displease Glennard precisely because she is talented and despite her self-effacement. The narrator states the problem in no uncertain terms: Glennard could not love Margaret because he had "an ambitious man's impatience of distinguished women....It was not that she bored him; she did what was infinitely worse—she made him feel his inferiority....if a man is at times indirectly flattered by the moral superiority of woman, her mental ascendency is extenuated by no such oblique tribute to his powers."[11]

Glennard reacts to Margaret in terms of gender rather than in terms of Margaret Aubyn, the individual, who by no means flaunts and in fact underplays her superiority. The implied author thus sets out clearly and undeniably society's expectation—indeed, its insistence—that woman and intellect are incompatible. Shown to recognize that Margaret's intelligence and gifts outstrip the categories prepared for them by the concept of woman's nature, Glennard becomes angry with Margaret and tells himself that no man need suffer such a woman. He enlists cultural assumptions about woman to justify his reaction to Margaret, making her wrong to be intelligent in order to make himself right in his lesser gifts. Despite her love for Glennard, Margaret does not win him— she is made to suffer for exceptional intellectual and creative abilities.

In 1927 Wharton's imagination turned again to the matter of a woman's intellect and gifts in *Twilight Sleep,* an artistically disappointing but nonetheless unmistakable indictment of the America of the twenties. The most memorable character in the novel is Pauline Manford, who, as Blake Nevius points out, is "a type of the invading race for which Edith Wharton has small regard."[12] *Twilight Sleep* does satirize Pauline Manford, a woman busy about incessant, pointless activities, but the causes of Pauline's frenzy, and the motives attributed to her, moderate the novel's judgment against her. Here, the withering of a woman's intellect and gifts is associated with the emptiness of the sphere to which woman is assigned—the domestic sphere that threatens atrophy of the mind rather than promises the mental stimulation James thought ideally possible there.

Pauline Manford is shown to have fulfilled the culture's design in her early married life, having no business save marriage and its subsidiaries, clubs and charities. Perhaps for lack of other purpose in life, Pauline treats her marriage with the same earnestness with which a man conducts his career; she conceives of her responsibilities to husband and children as "management," the narrator says, and of herself as laden with significant duties, which less responsible women avoid. She frenetically pursues the extensions of woman's sphere; she exaggerates woman's role and stupidly exercises it, speaking one day on motherhood, for example, and another on abortion; she jams her calendar with teas, gurus, hairdressers, pop lectures, and redecorating. She is characterized as rattled, inconsistent, and foolish.

For all her unintelligent behavior, Pauline is intelligent. When newly married for the second time, she shows herself to be competent as well as clever, efficient, sagacious, and serene, as her husband, Manford, notes. She is the wonderful new wife, consulted by an admiring new husband. When he senses her superiority to him, however, he withdraws his admiration, as Lewis Tarrant was later to do with Halo Spear, and becomes bored with her. As his own "sense of power" in his profession grows, "his awe" of her diminishes, and he begins to "feel himself first her equal, then ever so little her superior."[13] Finally, Manford excludes her from his life: "As his professional authority grew he had become more jealous of interference with it" (67). Manford will not be cast in Pauline's shadow.

From this point a vicious cycle is set in motion, with Manford holding Pauline at a distance and Pauline throwing herself ever more passionately into various and ever more trivial activities, such as purchasing and coordinating the services of a fire brigade to protect her new mansion. Manford observes that Pauline enjoys this "as much as other women do love-making" (297). Increasingly desperate to please her husband, Pauline, echoing the activities of Howells's Isabel March, orders muffins with meticulous care and gives herself over to the most minor of Manford's comforts. Unlike Howells's attitude toward Isabel March, however, Wharton does not find Pauline "cute" or "charming." She does, however, present Pauline from a female perspective in which it is not Pauline who is trivial but, rather, the world to which society assigns her. The narrator's language indicates the novel's attitude toward woman's sphere. The narrator says that Pauline pursues her domestic duties "as eagerly as her husband, in the early days of his legal career, used to study the documents of a new case" (181). She goes about her gardening as a man goes about the expansion of a business enterprise. She exults in planting 25,000 more bulbs this year than last; she is exhilarated to spend more money each year to enlarge and improve her garden; she faces "unexpected demands with promptness and energy"; she beats down "exorbitant charges" and struggles "through difficult moments" and comes out "at the end of the year tired but victorious....To Pauline that was 'life' " (253).

This exaggerated language is of course satiric, but it reveals the model Pauline adopts to render her activity meaningful: she is hard at work in the female version of the free enterprise system. Manford unwittingly puts his finger on Pauline's situation when he reflects that had Pauline been a lawyer, "she might have worked off her steam in office hours" (121-22). Exactly. Pauline has no office to go to, no outlet for her abundant energies save the home and its suburbs, the garden and benevolent societies. Pauline's spirits droop when she is inactive and rise "with the invigorating sense of being once more in a hurry" because busy, hurried people are purposeful people (279). She is elated when her daughter consults her and makes her feel needed.[14] Clearly, Pauline's sphere of activity is inadequate for her ability and energy, so limiting her that she must scratch like a bird for some small sense of power, authority, duty, or purpose.

The simple truth of *Twilight Sleep* is that the objects to which women are to devote themselves are inherently incommensurate with the energy brought to them. Where William Dean Howells trivialized women in the process of intending to expose the emptiness of their work, Wharton saw that the by-product of the vacuousness of the work was the waste of women's talent and energy and imagination. Rumors of the triviality of woman's work appear in *The Age of Innocence*, where the responsibilities of May Welland's mother, for example, are summarized in an incongruous list that includes keeping track of her husband's hairbrushes, providing stamps for his letters, and attending to the morality and traditions of American culture. The consequences of having no important work to do appear in *The Custom of the Country*, where metaphors of "business" and "pioneer blood" applied to profitable deals in the marriage market suggest the distortions that idleness spawns. Believing that women are full human beings, Wharton's implied authors respect heroines like Pauline Manford by holding them to standards rather than patronizing them; they insist that excesses are stupid, not charming. Describing the genesis of *The House of Mirth*, Wharton wrote that "a frivolous society can acquire dramatic significance only through what its frivolity destroys."[15] This describes, as well, the case of Pauline Manford, a character whose mind and energies are shown to be potentially more and better than her fictional world allows.

Wharton's female perspective on Pauline Manford offers a further insight into Pauline's situation. Woman's sphere is not only full of trivialities, it is empty of intellectual give and take. *Twilight Sleep* blames Pauline's husband for this. He withdraws from her not only physically but intellectually as well, until finally he purposely avoids any serious discussion with her. While it is true that Pauline's definition of serious matters is ludicrous, it is equally true that her husband relegates her to life's playroom and treats her opinions like so many disposable toys. Men do not desire intellectual parity with women, but, rather, they insist on the superiority that the culture's horizon of expectations leads them to believe is naturally theirs.

The imagination of Wharton was equally bold in its treatment of female sexuality. As she had done with questions of intellect, Wharton explores in sexuality another area that was inaccessible or unimaginable, or both, to male writers. In the imaginations of nineteenth-century male novelists, female characters often take on either the contours of dark temptress figures, charged like Hawthorne's Zenobia with a threatening

sexuality, or fair virginal figures, charged like Hawthorne's
Phoebe with a responsible, temperate handling of "womanliness." By the culture's definition—that is, male definition—
"womanliness" includes sexual desire, either to be elicited by
the proper man in due time (Phoebe) or used seductively out
of due time (Hester Prynne) or perhaps entirely displaced and
offered to another woman (James's Olive Chancellor). Edith
Wharton even dared to imagine the consequences of another
female response to sexuality—frigidity, or fear of it. Where
James in *The Bostonians* created a society that substitutes
ideology for the sentiment of sex, Wharton dissects the inner
life of a heroine of New England background and associates it
with neither ideology nor sentiment but frigidity.

Wharton's most Jamesian novel, *The Reef,* recalls not only
The Bostonians in its concern with the New England mentality but *The Golden Bowl* in its sharply delimited cast of
characters. James's Fawns becomes Wharton's Givré, where
four characters work out their individual destinies in the light
of an affair between two of them. A middle-aged widow, Anna
Leath, plans to marry a beau out of her past, George Darrow.
Before marrying him, however, she learns of a recent escapade
of his: a brief affair with a young woman, Sophy Viner, who is
about to become, coincidentally, governess to Anna's daughter and fiancé to Anna's stepson, Owen. Try as she might to
understand Darrow's circumstance, and loving him as she
does, Anna simply cannot shake his affair from her mind. She
becomes suspicious of all he says; she worries that he will
again be unfaithful; she suffers an insatiable desire to learn
every last detail of Darrow and Sophy's relationship, from the
theaters they visited to the restaurants they frequented. Anna
seems to become obsessed, in short, with Darrow's affair.

The reasons for Anna's seeming obsession are made perfectly clear. She is sexually insecure. As a girl, she was "a
model of ladylike repression" who, talking of books and
pictures while the young Darrow tried to kiss her, would then
accuse herself of being "cold...a prude and an idiot" and

question "if any man could really care for her."[16] Later, when she met and married Fraser Leath, "his kiss dropped on her like a cold smooth pebble" (91), and Anna arrives at middle age with her sexual responsiveness essentially untested; she has known physical love, but, as Shug observes about Celie in Alice Walker's *Color Purple,* she is a virgin according to a woman's definition of virginity, an initiate whom George Darrow would introduce into the mysteries of love.[17] Anna reflects that "she had always known that she should not be afraid of [strong or full emotion]" (83); she does not believe she is a frigid woman.

Yet Darrow's dalliance with Sophy Viner becomes déjà vu for Anna, the reliving of a nightmare. She fears that Sophy has known love and passion with an intensity that she, Anna, will never experience, and asks herself: "Don't I feel things as other women do?" (343). As in her youth Anna feared "that other girls...were yet possessed of some vital secret which escaped her" (85-86), so in maturity Anna suffers that same fear, that she is not as womanly as other women but is some-how too cold, too intellectual, too given to talking about books rather than making love. She begins to convert every-thing into evidence of her insufficiency as a woman, musing, for example, that she is "not more than half a woman" for wanting to be gentle rather than punishing with Sophy be-cause of her affair with Darrow (286). She seems to assume that a vicious manifestation of jealousy would somehow prove that she is passionate and thus normal. The implied author slowly transforms Anna's obsession with Darrow's affair, su-perficially a puritanical reaction to sexual conduct, into evi-dence of Anna's obsession with questions of her own sexual adequacy and her own womanliness. Ironically, the very ideal of woman to which Anna was so successfully trained as a girl is shown to initiate her insecurity and to come back to haunt her as a woman. The novel offers no proof that Anna *is* frigid; rather, it shows the consequences of a woman fearing that she may be so.

To reinforce this intended meaning of Anna's history, quite apart from any concern with physical infidelity, Darrow's affair takes place when he is en route to propose to Anna. Although Anna has previously put off her rendezvous with Darrow, throwing him into self-pity and insecurity, this timing nonetheless raises questions about the character of a man who engages in a sexual pecadillo at such a time. Moreover, the implied author characterizes Darrow's later interactions with Sophy as selfish rather than concerned, as if to ensure that the reader will understand the affair as a pecadillo. Knowing that both he and Sophy cannot remain at the Leath household, Darrow sets out to eliminate Sophy from the foursome, encouraging her among other things to pursue the very career in the theater against which he had warned her earlier, when it had suited his convenience. Darrow repeatedly exercises a kind of right of ownership over Sophy, as if his brief sexual possession of her legitimizes his efforts to control and direct her in ways that suit him. As he says to her, their supposed friendship gives him "the right to intervene for what I believe to be your benefit" (172). The novel's treatment of George Darrow and the turning of Anna's obsessiveness away from Darrow toward Anna's own insecurities are calculated not simply to reveal and explain Anna's character but to justify her reactions to Darrow's affair. Anna is intended to be seen not as a stereotypical prude but as a woman who has cause to doubt George Darrow.

Despite all this, *The Reef* has the unintended effect of working against the very meanings that its attention to Anna's background and Darrow's character would suggest by somehow diminishing the reader's sympathy for Anna and creating instead sympathy for Darrow. As Blake Nevius observes, the novel seems to load the dice "in favor of Darrow," who then "comes off better than he deserves." Nevius attributes this phenomenon to Wharton's uncertain handling of Darrow's character, to "certain questions posed insistently by her private experience," and "moral conventions whose force is to a large degree lost upon the present-day audience."[18] As Nevius says, Darrow's character is seen somewhat sympathetically because it is seen by Anna, who is too kind to him. But why, apart from loving him, Anna is so careful of Darrow and why she can seem so obsessed by the affair can be answered if the culture's ideology of woman and her nature is enlisted as a critical frame of reference. The laws of gender include a double standard that divides the characteristics of men and women in all arenas including the sexual. The proper woman is often defined as sexually reserved, at least until awakened, granting man a corner on sexual passion. A woman's *pudeur* simply expresses her nature, while a man's honorable conduct with proper women is understood to be a pose of sorts, a necessary check on his sexually passionate nature. Consequently, for a woman to have a sexual fling is a violation of her God-given nature; for a man it is an expression of nature. A woman who has an affair is blamable; a man is not, or at least not in the same degree.

This double standard is tacitly at work on two fronts in *The Reef*. First, it accounts for the intensity of Anna's cross-examination of her response to Darrow's affair. Given Anna's milieu, she must wonder if she is not making too much over a minor sexual escapade, so she must examine and reexamine herself, as if the real issues, Darrow's fidelity and loyalty, are perhaps bogus or are considerations to be set aside because he is a man. The double standard that Anna can be presumed to have assimilated joins her sexual insecurity, causing her to doubt her judgment and the legitimacy of questions about Darrow's character that, in fact, his conduct justifiably raises. Second, the double standard may lurk in the mind of the audience as well, diverting it from the implications of Darrow's conduct to questions about Anna's reasonableness. A man's affair is of small consequence by cultural definition. Men simply do these things. Hence, a woman who does more than simply observe them and perhaps complain mildly or sadly is quite possibly unreasonable, perhaps obsessed, and certainly a bit prudish. As Lawrence Selden is allowed his liaisons but Lily Bart is not in *The House of Mirth*, and as Lawrence Lefferts is tolerated at the very dinner table at which Ellen Olenska is an object of gossip in *The Age of Innocence*, so George Darrow should be permitted an "indiscretion" without having to suffer Anna Leath's condemnation. Ironically, the same idea of woman's nature which contributed to the formation of Anna's character and the sexual insecurity that marks her life now encourages the reader's withdrawing sympathy for Anna as she attempts to come to terms with her own psyche. Wharton builds this novel around the ideology of woman and its effects, and that same ideology becomes, ironically, the reef from which Wharton's craft was unable to protect her audience.

As bold and insightful as Wharton was to take up the subject of a woman's fear of frigidity, its causes and consequences, she performed a still more outrageous imaginative act in the characterization of Undine Spragg in *The Custom of the Country*. The very concept of frigidity that informs the history of Anna Leath depends on the culture's terms for female sexuality; frigidity locates itself at one extreme of the territory that those terms carve out, with the other extreme being nymphomania, and the "healthy" middle ground being the "normal" sexual responsiveness that men presumably long for in women. In the characterization of Undine Spragg, Edith Wharton imagines a female character whose inner self operates outside this sexual frame of reference, outside the sexual desire, or its rejection, that patriarchy projects on women, and renders it meaningless. Undine Spragg is more boldly characterized than is Edna Pontellier in Kate Chopin's *The Awakening*. Edna's awakenings include the discovery of her own sexual passion, a passion whose meaning, and whose legitimacy or illegitimacy, depend on the conventional frame of reference for female sexuality. Edna discovers within herself a broader spectrum of sexual drives than she had previously imagined, only to recognize that the range of acceptable behavior on that spectrum is suffocatingly narrow. Her interest in sex is awakened, only to find itself without an arena in which to be practiced. Undine Spragg, on the other hand, is invested with an intelligence that understands the uses of sex but is divested of any physical or emotional interest in the practice of sex. Where Kate Chopin chronicles a woman's awakening to sexual passion and her movement from asexuality to sexuality, and where Henry James sees a "decline" in the sentiment of sex, Edith Wharton sees a total absence of sexual passion or even sentiment of sex.

Undine Spragg's "sexual" conduct is associated with her upbringing as a girl, her consignment to a protected class as a woman, and her participation in a culture fixated on business. These three factors interlock in the creation of an asexual being. The implied author sets Undine on the road to a sexuality in her childhood, when her training to perpetual immaturity began. Undine grows into biological adulthood, but she remains a psychological child, believing that the world owes a woman a living. As if interested in men as sexual beings, she ironically marries three times and is treated chivalrously in each case, each husband caring for her as she expects to be cared for, "like the lilies of the field."[19]

This petted child-woman who has no duties or responsibilities is shown to be nonetheless a bundle of energy, none of which she has any interest in spending sexually. When Ralph Marvell takes her in his arms, for example, "he felt her resign herself like a tired child" (152). Undine's only use for her sexuality is a physically asexual one: to achieve power and material pleasures. She rebuffs Ralph's advances until he lets her have her own way, upon which she allows him to "take her to his breast" (154). Articulating an American attitude toward sex, a character in *The Custom of the Country* claims that in effete societies love is the emotional center of gravity while "in our new one it's business. In America the real *crime passionnel* is a 'big steal'—there's more excitement in wrecking railways than homes" (207). Although the character who speaks these words speaks about the American male, he describes Undine as well. As Elizabeth Ammons has insightfully pointed out, those energies that might be poured into love-making are poured by Undine into a woman's business—managing society.[20] Not puritanism but business has snuffed out sex in America. To be puritanical about sex, after all, one must think to avoid it. But in Undine's case, sex is so inconsequential that she never so much as thinks of it.

In Undine Spragg, Wharton not only recorded the common observation that a woman may barter one interest, sex, for another interest, money and what it can buy; she made the uncommon observation that the sex to be used as barter may be of no interest whatsoever; a woman may trade what is, to her, nothing in exchange for something. Undine's absolute sexual indifference deconstructs the culture's frame of sexual reference, rendering it meaningless. In characterizing Undine, Wharton joins the ranks of women writers who, according to Gilbert and Gubar, not only deal with female experience from a female perspective but also subvert patriarchal standards— in this case, the standards according to which a woman's sexuality is her pearl beyond price.

Even Wharton's career, however, and particularly its conclusion in *Hudson River Bracketed* and *The Gods Arrive*, raises questions about how powerful the culture's ideology of woman is. Most often, Wharton is in control of the text where it involves gender, but in her later novels gender differentiations seem to cloud her vision in complicated ways. First, despite her years as a novelist, her devotion to her craft, and her recognition of its role in her identity and happiness, Wharton chose to make the artist of *Hudson River Bracketed* and *The Gods Arrive* male. Could it be that, as Susan Gubar explains about George Eliot's analysis of female creativity, Wharton remained to some extent a character in search of an author, even at the age of seventy, and therefore imagined that a character confident in a vocation to art required a male

identity for reasons of verisimilitude? Or did Wharton, like
George Eliot, suffer the "conviction that female creativity has
been perverted (here as female narcissism and elsewhere…as
enthrallment to male authority)," and therefore never wrote a
female *kunstlerroman?*[21] Whatever the case, as already noted,
Wharton only crafted one female artist figure, Margaret
Aubyn in *The Touchstone.* The absence of such a figure in
Wharton's fiction is made more perplexing because Wharton
was an admirer of George Eliot and George Sand and a friend
of Vernon Lee and Mrs. Humphrey Ward. Edith Wharton was
not the sole female artist in Edith Wharton's life.

Perhaps the reticence of Wharton's autobiography, completed in 1934, two years after *The Gods Arrive,* provides a
clue. A female artist figure cast as a protagonist would likely
invite all manner of critical speculation and roman à clef
readings that Wharton would have abhorred. Certainly Wharton would not care to be credited with the attitudes ascribed
to Vance Weston, the artist figure she did create. Although he
is occasionally allowed to wax poetic about prose, Vance is
characterized as undisciplined, foolish, vain, unrealistic, and
unproductive—none of which resembles Edith Wharton in
the least.

Wharton's decision to make this artist male may be wiser
than it appears on the surface. Clearly she intended to satirize
American novelists of the twenties, many of whom she felt
could have come from Vance Weston's Euphoria, Illinois.
Perhaps the unsteady hand with which she conducts her
satire, seeming at times to take Vance seriously and at other
times to take him to be a fool, is related in a perverse way to
the culture's horizon of expectations for woman. The twentieth-century history of American women novelists, prior to
Wharton's death, runs something like this: at the turn of the
century, women novelists were suspect even in their artistic
prime; after World War I, women novelists were over-
shadowed by masculinists, writers of war stories and chron-
iclers of modern male alienation; in the thirties, women

novelists were overlooked for those whom the immature and uncultured Vance Weston fictionally represents. The younger Edith Wharton was not secure enough in her vocation to draw out of her foundering self a female protagonist who is an artist; the older Edith Wharton, realizing that women novelists were ignored by the culture, purposely did not assign her own gender to an artist, choosing instead to satirize the state of the arts as governed by men. Perhaps quite significantly, Wharton sets Vance Weston to writing a novel set in Spain, reminiscent of Hemingway, and she includes in *The Gods Arrive* two minor characters, Jane and Kate, who operate a bookstore in Paris that brings to mind Shakespeare and Company, Sylvia Beach, and perhaps Gertrude Stein and Alice B. Toklas. Vance and his coterie are representative of the state of the art of fiction in America, a state for which women novelists were in no way responsible.

The culture's commitment to sexual differentiation influenced Wharton's artistic decisions in *The Gods Arrive* on a second front. She was apparently so persuaded that males are the sexually-charged half of the culture's gender dichotomies, and perhaps so offended by the sexual escapades of the post–World War I generation, that she allowed the implied author to motivate Vance Weston implausibly. The attraction of Vance to Halo Spear is sufficiently accounted for (although Halo's continued allegiance to Vance is not). But his attraction to, indeed his complete absorption in, Floss Delaney, a floozy from his youth, is handled implausibly at best; Vance feels an "irresistible longing for her" while she shows no commensurate interest and, moreover, no interest whatsoever in anything that has become important to Vance—whether art, history, or culture, in the course of two long novels. The characterization of Vance breaks down and becomes inconsistent. Without adequate preparation he is made the victim of his own sexual drives, as if Wharton imagined an exaggerated version of the sexually-aroused male that worked in favor of George Darrow in *The Reef*. Nothing in *The Gods Arrive* accounts for the depths of Vance's foolishness. To account for Vance the novel implicitly leaves the field to the culture's and the reader's horizon of expectations on the subject of gender.

Although it would be comforting to believe that, having herself chafed under the limitations of cultural assumptions, Wharton surely must have rejected the notion that human talents are determined by gender, this simple conclusion is unwarranted. For all that Edith Wharton experienced and for all that she perceived in the condition of women, she did not necessarily reason from that condition back to sexual differentiation, with its notion of a distinct woman's nature, as the culprit. On the contrary, she apparently held, in her conscious mind, that the sexes differ from one another in ways far more profound than mere anatomy. She condemned not the notion of the complementarity of the sexes and its ramifications but, rather, the failure of American society to build intelligently around the givens of male and female differences.

Wharton's *French Ways and Their Meaning* includes a chapter entitled "The New Frenchwoman" in which is stated explicitly opinions about the American woman which the fiction implies. She asserts that the American woman is "still in the kindergarten. The world she lives in is exactly like the most improved and advanced and scientifically equipped Montessori-method baby-school,"[22] an opinion that the characterization of Undine Spragg captures. She attributes the feebleness of the American woman to her exclusion from extra-domestic concerns and from a "splendid and a decisive part" in history, war, politics, literature, art, and religion that French society has granted women. The characterization of Pauline Manford, in particular, with her trivial occupations, dramatizes this. Wharton even associates the narrowness of woman's sphere with the problems that plague the relationships of men and women in America, asserting that men will find more stimulating the companionship of intelligent wives.

These opinions, however, stand on Wharton's apparent conviction that the complementarity of the sexes, with its

assignment of traits on the basis of gender, is an accurate description of nature rather than an arbitrary cultural construct.
American women are immature, she claims, because they
develop their individuality "in the void, without the checks,
the stimulus, and the discipline that comes of contact with the
stronger masculine individuality. And it is not only because
the man is the stronger and the closer to reality that his
influence is necessary to develop woman to real womanhood;
it is because the two sexes complete each other mentally as
well as physiologically that no modern civilization has been
really rich or deep, or stimulating to other civilisations, which
has not been based on the recognised interaction of influences
between men and women" (102-03). And what is it, according to Wharton, that makes a woman more intelligent and
therefore more stimulating to the man who comes home to
her? The fact that such a woman has not

spent all her time with other women. No matter how intelligent
women are individually, they tend, collectively, to narrow down their
interests, and take a feminine, or even a female, rather than a
broadly human view of things. The woman whose mind is attuned
to men's minds has a much larger view of the world, and attaches
much less importance to trifles, because men, being usually brought
by circumstances into closer contact with reality, insensibly communicate their breadth of view to women. A "man's woman" is
never fussy and seldom spiteful, because she breathes too free an air,
and is having too good a time. [119].

One might argue that Wharton's repeated association of
men's breadth of mind with their experience of a wider world
saves Wharton from the charge of devaluing her own sex.
Comforting as such reasoning would be, Wharton's over-all
point is that French women *do* participate in that wider world,
they *are* included in business and in arts and politics, and still
it is contact with men that brings them to maturity and "a
broadly human view of things." In Wharton's view, it is
contact with men as well as worldly experience that women

need. We can be sure, it seems, that Edith Wharton would have been as unhappy to be relegated to Charlotte Perkins Gilman's Herland as would Twain to John Bunyan's heaven.

Finally, even this woman artist, who suffered the boredom of a husband who was her intellectual inferior and the murmurs that accompanied being a divorcee, did not identify the division of the sexes into polar extremes as the cause of the problems that plague her fictional heroines and that colored her own life. Like the mind of Henry James in his prefaces, the conscious mind of Edith Wharton did not break free entirely from her culture's ideology of woman. Her imagination, however, the driving force behind her fiction, saw well into it and beyond.

AFTERWORD

A radical critique of literature, feminist in its
impulse, would take the work first of all as a clue to
how we live, how we have been living, how we have
been led to imagine ourselves, how our language has
trapped as well as liberated us, how the very act of
naming has been till now a male prerogative, and
how we can begin to see and name—and therefore
live—afresh.

—Adrienne Rich

While cultural presuppositions are not necessarily false-
hoods, nineteenth-century notions of sexual differentiation
and hence of woman's nature are inaccurate descriptions of
human reality and therefore dangerous if invested with power.
The nineteenth century could not see, it seems, that in nature
there is only male and female and that "masculine" and
"feminine" are ideas about the male and the female, mental
constructs rather than facts. The nineteenth century seemed
to confuse a frame of reference with the facts which that frame
was designed to illuminate. Thus flesh and blood women were
coerced to replicate abstractions rather than abstractions like
"feminine" being drawn complexly and inclusively enough to
take in the whole of the reality they presumed to describe.

Because frames of reference are useful only in the service of
life, eliciting meaning and creating knowledge, they should be
jettisoned, I believe, when they misconstrue more than they
construe, when they diminish rather than expand our understanding, when they no longer serve but subvert life. Nineteenth-century ideas about gender and sexual differentiation
are misconstruing, diminishing, and subverting. The history

of the century shows us the dangers of these ideas, the conflicts they created and the human potential, particularly female potential, that they effectively denied. The fiction of the century shows us that, while writers often exploited the culture's horizon of expectations to excellent purpose, they also succumbed to it on occasion and allowed it to constrain their imaginations, to reduce their creative freedom. Although it is impossible to be "outside" culture and although the creative process necessarily includes interaction between imagination and culture, there may come a point in the life of art, as in the lives of human beings, when some aspect of a cultural horizon becomes more obstructing than useful.

If the concept of woman's nature and sphere were simply a historical phenomenon that our culture had left behind, the interest of this study would be purely, blessedly academic. Unfortunately, this notion pursues us, even well into the 1980s. It thrives among radical feminists as well as among the moral majority. We make claims and recommend programs on grounds that are, ironically, Victorian. With the best of intentions and with women's interests at heart, we claim that more women in Congress will lead to more humane government—an echo of Hawthorne's "The New Adam and Eve." We contend that women are more opposed to war than men—despite the evidence of such novels as Edith Wharton's *A Son at the Front* and Willa Cather's *One of Ours*. Avant-garde theologians claim that the admission of women to the priesthood would make the church more nurturing, less concerned with power, less competitive. Even if the source of difference is taken to be experience and conditioning rather than God, such thinking assumes that however it has come about, woman's nature is distinct from man's, and proceeds to reinforce and perpetuate that assumption. Such thinking fails to note that women should be in Congress and in pulpits not because of their specific gender but because of their shared humanity. Such thinking, once again, sets the trap in which the Victorian woman was caught.

Whereas contemporary dichotomous thinking about the sexes tends to value traits the culture has labeled "feminine" and to place them at least on a par with those cast as "masculine," they in fact propose a doctrine of separate but equal that proved a failure in the education of blacks and is likely to prove a failure in the liberation of women. In the course of human history, parallel structures have had a way of rearranging themselves into hierarchies. Certainly the history of patriarchy demonstrates this by its rhetoric which supports the view that men and women have different but equally important gifts (if women's are not said to be yet more valuable than men's), while its practice assigns superior value and power to presumably "masculine" traits such as assertiveness and competitiveness.

French feminists such as Luce Irigaray and Helene Cixous are probing the very axis of thinking in an effort to free our minds from the binary oppositions that structure our thought and thus our thinking about women, and men as well. If we were able, in the here and now, to abandon dichotomous thought patterns, to restructure totally our conceptual habits, then Victorian ideas would indeed be merely academic. But as Jane Gallop points out, thinkers and writers continually fall back into the very modes of thinking that they set out to critique.[1] We are still a long way from the millennium. Therefore we do well to recall what Carolyn Heilbrun wrote in 1973: "Our future salvation lies in a movement away from sexual polarization and the prison of gender toward a world in which individual roles and the modes of personal behavior can be freely chosen."[2] While feminist theory undertakes what is perhaps the most exciting intellectual initiative of our time, the effort to rethink the act of thinking itself, with "woman" as the keystone in the project, nineteenth-century sexual poetics may serve to alert us to some of the more subtle and as yet uncataloged inroads of sexual differentiation and binary thinking.

Examination of the workings of sexual poetics in the fiction of writers like Cooper and Hawthorne, Howells and James may serve to alert more of us to the pitfalls of binary thinking because, although one might prefer otherwise, the fiction of these writers is still more widely taught, presumably respected, and available for classroom use and bookstore display than that of their female contemporaries. Their works, therefore, remain among our most accessible and convenient literary reminders that the moment we find ourselves claiming something for women that we would not claim for men, or vice versa, we are perpetuating the ideological structure that first apportioned and then confined human potential within the straitjacket of gender. As nineteenth-century American fiction shows us, the Grace Breens and Margaret Aubyns of our world will not be granted both their womanhood and their competence as doctors and artists while limiting ideas of "woman" pervade their culture's horizon of expectations and shape women's lives.

NOTES

PROLOGUE

Epigraph: Sandra M. Gilbert, "What Do Feminist Critics Want? A Postcard from the Volcano," *ADE Bulletin* 66 (1980). Rpt. in *The New Feminist Criticism: Essays on Women, Literature and Theory,* ed. Elaine Showalter (New York: Pantheon, 1985) 31.

1. "Literary History as a Challenge to Literary Theory," trans. Elizabeth Benzinger, *New Literary History* 2 (1970): 18-19. An expanded version of this appears as Thesis 4 in the opening chapter of Jauss's *Toward an Aesthetic of Reception,* trans. Timothy Bahti (Minneapolis: U. of Minnesota, 1982) 28.

2. E.D. Hirsch, Jr., *Validity in Interpretation* (New Haven: Yale UP, 1967) 8. Hirsch draws a very useful distinction between intended meaning and significance, defining meaning as that which a writer had reason to believe that an assumed audience would construe from a text, and significance as that which future readers, necessarily unforeseen by a writer, may construe from a text.

3. Nina Baym, *Woman's Fiction: A Guide to Novels by and about Women in America, 1820-1870* (Ithaca: Cornell UP, 1978) 14. Baym comments that even the women who wrote "woman's fiction" subscribed to the culture's concept of woman's nature, woman's sphere.

4. In *Art and Illusion: A Study in the Psychology of Pictorial Representation* (London: Phaidon, 1959) 20, E.H. Gombrich reminds us that "the more we become aware of the enormous pull in man to repeat what he has learned, the greater will be our admiration for those exceptional beings who could break this spell and make a significant advance on which others could build."

5. Baym 19.

6. New York: Pantheon, 1985, 3-17. For excellent annotated bibli-

ographies of studies in this burgeoning field of reader response, see
Susan R. Suleiman and Inge Crosman, eds., *The Reader in the Text:
Essays on Audience and Interpretation* (Princeton: Princeton UP, 1980)
and Jane Tompkins, ed., *Reader-Response Criticism: From Formalism
to Post-Structuralism* (Baltimore: Johns Hopkins UP, 1980). See also
Gender and Reading: Essays on Readers, Texts, and Contexts, ed.
Elizabeth A. Flynn and Patroscinio P. Schweickart (Baltimore: Johns
Hopkins UP, 1986).

7. *Manners: Or Happy Homes and Good Society All the Year
Around* (Boston: J.E. Tilton & Co., 1868) 20. Quoted in Robert E.
Riegel, *American Women: A Story of Social Change* (Rutherford:
Fairleigh Dickinson UP, 1970), 35.

8. Riegel, 34. My discussion of ideas of woman in nineteenth-
century America draws on Ruth H. Bloch, "Untangling the Roots of
Modern Sex Roles: A Survey of Four Centuries of Change," *Signs* 4
(Winter, 1978): 237-52; Nancy Cott, *The Bonds of Womanhood:
"Woman's Sphere" in New England, 1780-1835* (New Haven: Yale UP,
1977); Ernest Earnest, *The American Eve in Fact and Fiction,
1775-1914* (Urbana: U of Illinois P, 1974); Eleanor Flexnor, *Century of
Struggle* (Cambridge: Harvard UP, 1959); Margaret S. Marsh, "The
Anarchist-Feminist Response to the 'Woman Question' in Late Nine-
teenth-Century America," *American Quarterly* 30 (Fall, 1978):
533-47; William L. O'Neill, *Everyone Was Brave* (Chicago: Quad-
ragle, 1969); Andrew Sinclair, *The Emancipation of the American
Woman* (New York: Harper, 1975); Page Smith, *Daughters of the
Promised Land: Women in American History* (Boston: Little, 1970);
Barbara Welter, "The Cult of True Womanhood, 1820-1860," *Dimity
Convictions: The American Woman in the Nineteenth Century*
(Athens: Ohio UP, 1976) 21-41; Barbara J. Berg, *The Remembered
Gate: Origins of American Feminism* (New York: Oxford UP, 1978);
Judith Fryer, *The Faces of Eve: Women in the Nineteenth Century
American Novel* (New York: Oxford UP, 1976); *Clio's Consciousness
Raised: New Perspectives on the History of Women*, ed. Mary
Hartman and Lois W. Banner (New York: Harper, 1974); *What Man-
ner of Woman: Essays on English and American Life and Literature*
(New York: New York UP, 1977); Ronald W. Hogeland, "The Female
Appendage: Feminine Lifestyle in America 1820-1860," *Civil War
History* 17 (1971): 101-14; Ann Douglas, *The Feminization of Amer-
ican Culture* (New York: Knopf, 1977); Paul Eakin, *The New England
Girl: Cultural Ideals in Hawthorne, Stowe, Howells, and James*

(Athens: U of Georgia P, 1976); Leslie Fiedler, *Love and Death in the American Novel* (New York: Criterion, 1960). Useful studies of the way in which female writers and readers handle the commonplaces of the culture are Baym, *Woman's Fiction;* Nancy K. Miller, "Emphasis Added: Plots and Plausibilities in Women's Fiction," *PMLA* 96 (January 1981): 36-48; Helen Papashvily, *All the Happy Endings* (New York: Harper, 1956); Josephine Donovan, *New England Local Color Literature: A Women's Tradition* (New York: Ungar, 1983); Sandra M. Gilbert and Susan Gubar, *The Madwoman in the Attic: The Woman Writer and the Nineteenth-Century Literary Imagination* (New Haven: Yale UP, 1979).

9. Marshall Brown writes that "realism developed into a central issue in mid-century precisely because the conception of reality had become increasingly problematic" ("The Logic of Realism: A Hegelian Approach," *PMLA* 96 [March 1981]: 225).

10. "The Modern Novel," *North American Review* 159 (November 1894): 598; *Atlantic* 51 (April 1883): 471. Quoted in Harold H. Kolb, *The Illusion of Life: American Realism as a Literary Form* (Charlottesville: UP of Virginia, 1969) 46-47. Fredric Jameson writes that the romance genre "expresses a nostalgia for a social order in the process of being undermined and destroyed by nascent capitalism, yet still for the moment coexisting side by side with the latter" ("Magical Narratives: Romance as Genre," *New Literary History* 7 [1975]: 158).

11. *The Resisting Reader: A Feminist Approach to American Fiction* (Bloomington: Indiana UP, 1978) xii. Ruth Yeazell, in "Fictional Heroines and Feminist Critics" (*Novel* 8 [Fall 1974]: 29-38), warns against the critical pitfalls of blaming novelists for their choice of heroines, their donnée, and notes that, if women have been betrayed, the fault lies not with the novelist for chronicling it but with society and institutions.

CHAPTER 1. JAMES FENIMORE COOPER

Epigraph: Ralph Waldo Emerson, "Woman," *Miscellanies* (Boston: Houghton, 1904) 409.

1. "The Stylistic Approach to Literary History," *New Literary History* 2 (1970): 40.

2. Jonathan Culler, *Structuralist Poetics* (Ithaca: Cornell UP, 1975) 113.

3. *The Works of James Fenimore Cooper,* 32 vols. (New York: Putnam's, 1896-1897), 17: 56-57. All references to Cooper's novels are to this edition and are cited in the text by volume.

4. Kay Seymour House notes that Cooper set out to show Americans the values and models available to them (*Cooper's Americans* [Columbus: Ohio State UP, 1965] 9).

5. This method of distinguishing fiction from reality by attention to audiences inscribed in texts is developed by Rabinowitz in "Assertion and Assumption: Fictional Patterns and the External World," *PMLA* 96 (May 1981): 408-19.

6. On assertions, see Rabinowitz 414-16.

7. Jameson, 160.

8. This is not to deny Joel Porte's contention that Natty flees Judith because of her sexuality. Rather, the idea of woman neutralizes woman's sexuality if the heroine conforms to its notion of woman before she falls, before she mixes good and evil, and while she still meets God's design and initial plan (*The Romance in America* [Middletown, Conn.: Wesleyan UP, 1969] 10). A.N. Kaul contends that in *The Deerslayer,* marriage is linked to the social order and that to reject marriage is to reject the social order (*The American Vision: Actual and Ideal Society in Nineteenth-Century Fiction* [New Haven: Yale UP, 1963] 131-32). Donald Darnell contends that Judith is punished for her social presumption rather than for questionable virtue (*"The Deerslayer:* Cooper's Tragedy of Manners," *Studies in the Novel* 11 [Winter 1979]: 406-15).

9. Jauss, *Reception* 21-22.

10. In *The Family, Sex and Marriage in England, 1500-1800* (New York: Harper, 1977) 503, Lawrence Stone notes that in the sixteenth, seventeenth, and eighteenth centuries a man's honor depended on his word, a woman's on her reputation for chastity. Natty Bumppo conducts himself like an eighteenth-century man, operating out of gender presuppositions which would not insult Hist, if Indian and white civilization share the same system of gender divisions.

11. See Edwin Fussell, *Frontier: American Literature and the American West* (Princeton: Princeton UP, 1965) 65-67, on cultural relativism. See also Charles Boewe, "Cooper's Doctrine of Gifts," *Tulane Studies in English* 7 (1962): 27-35.

12. Kay Seymour House points out that in Cooper "the fact of femininity transcends and makes almost irrelevant race, environment or religion" (*Cooper's Americans* 18). In connection with *The Last of the*

Mohicans, David T. Haberly contends that on the frontier women ruin the harmony between whites and reds; it is the "nature" of white women to excite passion in men and hence to upset the balance between man and nature ("Women and Indians: *The Last of the Mohicans* and the Captivity Tradition," *American Quarterly* 28 [Fall 1976]: 440).

13. Nina Baym calls attention to Cooper's "adumbration of the 'American girl' " in "Women in American Literature, 1790-1870," in *What Manner of Woman,* ed. Marlene Springer (New York: New York UP, 1977) 217. Leslie Fiedler says Eve Effingham prefigures "James's American girl before the fact" (*Love and Death in the American Novel* [New York: Criterion, 1960] 185). See also Baym's "The Women of Cooper's Leatherstocking Tales," *American Quarterly* 23 (December 1971): 696-709.

14. "Fenimore Cooper's Heroines," *American Novelists Revisited: Essays in Feminist Criticism* (Boston: Hall, 1982) 42.

15. Mary Louise Pratt, *Toward a Speech Act Theory of Literary Discourse* (Bloomington: Indiana UP, 1977) 136.

16. "The Leatherstocking Tales Re-Examined," *South Atlantic Quarterly* 46 (1947): 536.

17. My discussion of Cooper's "American girl" appeared in "Toward Daisy Miller: Cooper's Idea of 'The American Girl,' " *Studies in the Novel* 14 (Fall 1981): 237-49.

18. Frank M. Collins comments on "the regenerative influence exercised by the homemaker upon the culture and the haven to which she allows her husband to retire ("Cooper and the American Dream," *PMLA* 81 [1966]: 89). Leslie Fiedler notes that "in Cooper's America, the attribution to the female of all moral authority had turned her into a super-ego figure, the embodiment of civilization itself" (*Love and Death in the American Novel* 208-09). Cooper himself, in *Notions of the Americans* (1828; New York: Ungar, 1963) 1:186-97, describes "the American girl" as natural, delicate, innocent, and revered because of her influence and moral ascendancy.

19. According to Thomas R. Lounsbury (*James Fenimore Cooper* [Boston: Houghton, 1882] 251, Lucy Hardinge is modeled on Cooper's wife.

20. On equity legislation, see Mary R. Beard, *Woman as a Force in History* (New York: Collier, 1962) 70-71. Kay Seymour House notes that Mrs. Cooper's family put her property in a trust "for her sole and separate use independent of her husband" (*Cooper's Americans* 39). Barbara Ann Bardes and Suzanne Gossett point out that "to Cooper,

the married woman's property act was a symbol of all the evils which were destroying American society"; that the law was not passed in response to feminist pressure but to eliminate loopholes that favored real estate holders; and that Cooper distorts the "facts" of the law in *The Ways of the Hour*. Bardes and Gossett contest John P. McWilliams's claim (*Political Justice in a Republic: James Fenimore Cooper's America* [Berkeley: U of California P, 1972] 389) that only Dunscomb talks about women's roles, and he is made to do so only for comic relief and not as an expression of Cooper's views ("Cooper and the 'Cup and Saucer' Law: A New Reading of *The Ways of the Hour*," *American Quarterly* 32 [1980]:499-518).

21. James Grossman, *James Fenimore Cooper* (New York: Sloane, 1949) 16. Steven Railton writes that Cooper appreciated his domestic felicity and found in his wife "a woman who could fill the role his mother had originally played in his life, and who could fulfill the needs his mother had created in him" (*Fenimore Cooper: A Study of His Life and Imagination* [Princeton: Princeton UP, 1978] 53).

CHAPTER 2. NATHANIEL HAWTHORNE

Epigraph: Patrocinio P. Schweickart, "Reading Ourselves: Toward a Feminist Theory of Reading," *Gender and Reading: Essays on Readers, Texts, and Contexts*, ed. Elizabeth A. Flynn and Patrocinio P. Schweickart (Baltimore: Johns Hopkins UP, 1986) 43-44.

1. *The Centenary Edition of the Works of Nathaniel Hawthorne*, ed. William Charvat et al., 16 vols. (Columbus: Ohio State UP, 1963-1985) 10:251. All references to Hawthorne's works are to this edition and are subsequently cited in the text by volume.

2. *Art and Illusion: A Study in the Psychology of Pictorial Representation* (London: Phaidon, 1959) 16.

3. R.P. Boas identifies Hester with the romantic lady: self-willed, beautiful, brunette, resolute, aggressively sexual, and un-American ("The Romantic Lady," *Romanticism in America*, ed. George Boas [Baltimore: Johns Hopkins UP, 1940] 66-67). Kristin Herzog notes the duality of Hester's characterization and the "dark woman" who becomes "a symbol of saving grace" (*Women, Ethnics, and Exotics* [Knoxville: U of Tennessee P, 1983] 12-13, 52).

4. Nina Baym charges critics with misunderstanding Hawthorne's comment that speculations vanish if a woman's heart comes uppermost

(*The Shape of Hawthorne's Career* [Ithaca: Cornell UP, 1976] 135). Baym and others apparently locate the passage in Hester's mind and take it to be *her* reflections on her own situation. Darrell Abel seems to accept Hawthorne as narrator when he writes that to Hawthorne woman's essential life consists in the right exercise of emotion. Unfitted by her intense femininity for intellectual speculations, Hester "unwomaned herself and deluded herself with mistaken notions" ("Hawthorne's Hester," *College English* 13 [March 1952]: 308). Richard Brodhead correctly observes Hester's "openness to all the varieties of experience—intellectual, imaginative, emotional—that the continuing emergency of her life brings to her" (*Hawthorne, Melville, and the Novel* [Chicago: U of Chicago P, 1976] 63). What the narrator finds "unwomanly" is what makes Hester a remarkable character, according to Brodhead. The narrator seems to wish to disown the most fascinating dimensions of Hester.

    5. See Stanislaw Elie, "The Novel as an Expression of the Writer's Vision of the World," trans. Teresa Halikowska-Smith, *New Literary History* 9 (1977): 120-21.

    6. Critics have alternately praised and blamed Hawthorne's handling of his narrators. In *Form and Fable in American Fiction* (New York: Oxford UP, 1961) 173-75, for example, Daniel Hoffman expatiates on what Yvor Winters called Hawthorne's "formula of alternative possibilities" and Hawthorne's ironies within ironies. Ernest Sandeen notes that the narrative voice of *The Scarlet Letter* delivers "pious lectures... so plainly out of key with what is going on that we may suspect they are pieces of calculated irony" (*"The Scarlet Letter* as a Love Story," *PMLA* 77 [September 1962]: 425-35). But Martin Green rejects the assumption that Hawthorne's narrator is calculatingly ironic; charging Hawthorne with meaningless equivocation, he contends that there is no a priori reason to accept any ambiguity in Hawthorne as meaningful: "It is usually a device of caution or a carelessness" (*Re-Appraisals: Some Commonsense Readings in American Literature* [New York: Norton, 1965] 83-84). Marshall VanDeusen, however, finds the narrator to be an urbane character who plays with paradox "as the only instrument adequate for controlling its own doubts, and which is yet a means of releasing them and giving them a dangerous license" ("Narrative Tone in 'The Custom House' and *The Scarlet Letter,*" *Nineteenth-Century Fiction* 21 [June 1966]: 69). Gloria Chasson Erlich perceptively credits the narrator's ambivalence to "Hawthorne's conflicting attitudes toward woman, the 'lurid intermixture' of two

incompatible emotions that cause the language to diverge from the manifest content of the narrative" ("Deadly Innocence: Hawthorne's Dark Women," *New England Quarterly* 41 [June 1968] 168). Ellen Tuttle Hansen claims that the narrator's "mistakes" are intentional and a means to admit all evidence and thus achieve a broader vision, a wider sympathy, and a fuller understanding of life's complexities ("Ambiguity and the Narrator in *The Scarlet Letter*," *Journal of Narrative Technique* 5 [September 1975]: 147-63).

7. *The Rhetoric of Fiction* (Chicago: U of Chicago P, 1961) 178, 388-89.

8. Certain theological arguments have been adduced to justify Hilda's words. In *Studies in Classic American Literature* (New York: Boni, 1930) 124, for example, D.H. Lawrence points out that the sin of Adam and Eve was one of knowledge, not of deed. If Lawrence is correct, then Hilda is quite right to take care in selecting her companions. Harold T. McCarthy, in "Hawthorne's Dialogue with Rome: *The Marble Faun*" (*Studi Americani* 14 [1968]: 107), writes that Hawthorne respected the principle on which Hilda acts; sound puritanism teaches that one's first duty is to personal salvation, in pursuit of which one "was to shut out all possible access to evil, whether it came from family, friends, or others." Hawthorne's fiction, however, holds that "there is no sin without action" (Nina Baym, "The Heart, the Head, and the Unpardonable Sin," *New England Quarterly* 40 [1967]: 33), and therefore Hilda is disturbingly fastidious if viewed from Hawthorne's usual perspective.

9. Even the genteel William Dean Howells confesses he dislikes Hilda because of her "cold spirit," and wonders if Hawthorne didn't "mean to let us see something ugly in the angelic Hilda's effort for self-protection and her ruthless self-pity for her own involuntary privity to Miriam's guilt" (*Heroines of Fiction*, 2 vols. [New York: Harper, 1901] 1:188). Samuel Coale contends that Hawthorne does not humanize Hilda because to do so would destroy a whole moral world ("*The Marble Faun*: 'A Frail Structure of Our Own Reading,' " *Essays in Literature* 7 [Spring 1980]: 63).

10. Both Hawthorne's relationship with his wife and his desire for success may have contributed to his allegiance to Hilda. Louisa Hall Tharp reports that over Sophia's loud protest, friends associated Sophia Hawthorne with Hilda of *The Marble Faun*, and that Hawthorne called Sophia his Dove. Like Hilda, Sophia was a copyist and, according to Tharp, Hawthorne was intensely proud of her work (*The Peabody Sisters of Salem* [Boston: Little, 1950] 258). Hawthorne's *American*

Notebooks (8:384) is filled with terms of endearment that suggest Hawthorne's dependence on Sophia: "dear little wife," "my naughty little wife," "my dearest spouse," he sings, "I have married the Spring!—I am husband to the month of May!" Hawthorne wrote to Sophia, "How strange it is, tender and fragile little Sophie, that your protection should have become absolutely necessary to such a great, rough, burly, broad-shouldered personage as I! I need your support as much as you need mine" (quoted in Newton Arvin, *Hawthorne* [Boston: Little, 1929] 93). Just how conventional Hawthorne was is suggested in a letter he wrote to Ticknor praising Sophia's travel writing as superior to his, but he says, "Neither she nor I would like to see her name on your list of female authors" (quoted in Randall Stewart, *Nathaniel Hawthorne* [New Haven: Yale UP, 1948] 190). Hawthorne was perhaps not only envious of the success of "the scribblers," but may have used the idea of woman and her sphere to justify accusations against them. Certainly Hawthorne renders Hilda completely acceptable to a genteel audience by maintaining her innocence; Martin Green notes that Hawthorne wanted to be a good Victorian writer: charming, cheerful, humorous, tolerant, warm-hearted, bourgeois, full of honest sentiment and stout common sense (*Re-Appraisals* 68). Still, David Downing points out that Kenyon's proposal excludes sexuality, making Hilda his "guide" ("The Feminine Ideal and the Failure of Art in *The Marble Faun,*" *Recovering Literature* 9 [1981]: 12). Leland Person, Jr., notes that Hawthorne uses European women to explore problems in art; Kenyon's union with Hilda is his final separation from Europe, art, and the experience they offer ("Aesthetic Headaches and European Women in *The Marble Faun* and *The American,*" *Studies in American Fiction* 4 [Spring 1976]: 65-79).

11. Phoebe is not a dark lady, certainly, but she is more substantial than Hawthorne's later fair heroines, Priscilla of *The Blithedale Romance* and Hilda of *The Marble Faun.* As Virginia O. Birdsall remarks, Phoebe, unlike Priscilla and Hilda, controls her world ("Hawthorne's Fair-Haired Maidens," *PMLA* 75 [June 1960]: 250-56). Nina Baym delineates three types of heroines, one of which is the strong, cheerful, independent, high-spirited, but ladylike young woman who foreshadows "the American girl" ("Women in American Literature, 1790-1870," *What Manner of Woman,* ed. Marlene Springer [New York: New York UP, 1977] 211-34). Phoebe no doubt belongs here, where Morton Cronin places her as well ("Hawthorne on Romantic Love and the Status of Women," *PMLA* 69 [March 1954]: 89-98). Richard

Brodhead says of Phoebe that she is the actual, the new plebianism, "in which the graces of the lady are combined with a practical talent for home economics" (*Hawthorne, Melville, and the Novel* 83). As Brodhead's assessment suggests, Phoebe may be more corporeal than the fair heroine, but her outer boundary remains home economics, woman's conventional sphere.

12. *Hawthorne* (Ithaca: Cornell UP, 1966) 64.

13. Coverdale's reliability has been frequently debated. See, for example, William Hedges, "Hawthorne's *Blithedale:* The Function of the Narrator," *Nineteenth-Century Fiction* 14 (1960): 303-16; Frank Davidson, "Toward a Re-evaluation of *The Blithedale Romance,*" *New England Quarterly* 25 (September 1952): 374-83; Joan D. Winslow, "New Light on Hawthorne's Miles Coverdale," *Journal of Narrative Technique* 7 (Fall 1977): 189-99.

14. The importance of Coverdale's aspirations to art are discussed by Nina Baym in "*The Blithedale Romance:* A Radical Reading" (*Journal of English and Germanic Philology* 67 [October 1968]: 545-69) and *The Shape of Hawthorne's Career* 190-91; Rudolph Von Abele's *The Death of the Artist* (Folcroft, Pa.: Folcroft, 1955) 75-80; and Frederick C. Crews, "A New Reading of *The Blithedale Romance*" (*American Literature* 29 [May 1957]: 147-70).

15. Jauss, *Reception* 35.

16. My discussion of the significance of *The Blithedale Romance* was published as "Justice to Zenobia," *New England Quarterly* 55 (March 1982): 61-78.

17. Marius Bewley states that the novel accuses Zenobia of sin in rejecting Priscilla's love (*The Eccentric Design* [New York: Columbia UP, 1963] 155), but surely a refusal to receive adulatory love is not sinful. As if failing to take the first person narrator into account and associating Coverdale with Hawthorne, some critics are very severe with Zenobia. James F. Ragan, for example, sees Zenobia as artificial ("The Irony in Hawthorne's Blithedale," *New England Quarterly* 35 [1962]: 239-46), and Newton Arvin thinks Hawthorne condemns the pride that makes Zenobia compete with men and lay claim "to superiority on intellectual grounds" (*Hawthorne* 199). Yet it is Coverdale the narrator who judges Zenobia. Joel Porte insightfully associates the Priscilla-Zenobia opposition with Coverdale's artistic aspirations: "For Coverdale, the choice lies between sexual truth and sentimental deception—between the terrible opportunity to develop into a poet of tragic depth and the comfortable decision to lapse into 'minor minstrelsy' and

fatuous ease" (*The Romance in America* [Middletown, Conn.: Wesleyan UP, 1959] 133).

18. Nina Baym judges that Zenobia's preference for Hollingsworth "indicates that her idea of godliness is controlled by the cultural stereotype of masculinity" ("Hawthorne's Women: The Tyranny of Social Myths," *Centennial Review* 15 [Summer 1971]: 255). This may be so, but it does not change the fact that Coverdale is certainly no viable alternative, even were Zenobia free of cultural stereotypes.

19. Von Abele *(Death of the Artist* 79) argues that Zenobia does not differ substantially from Priscilla and that, as her feminism comes to us second hand, her suicide is predictable. The text of *Blithedale*, however, gives us no reason to discount totally Zenobia's feminism, for her speeches on the subject, represented in the text as quotes rather than paraphrases by Coverdale, express her feminist ideas even if, as Baym contends, she has been influenced by a patriarchal ideal and stereotypes of masculinity.

20. John Harmon McElroy and Edward L. McDonald contend that Zenobia is murdered by Coverdale who, having been rejected by her, kills her "in a burst of dammed-up sexual frustration" ("The Coverdale Romance," *Studies in the Novel* 14 [Spring 1982]: 9).

21. Hawthorne's most recent biographer, James R. Mellow, reveals many dimensions of Hawthorne that make his career with heroines predictable, such as Hawthorne and Sophia's love for Coventry Patmore's "An Angel in the House" (*Nathaniel Hawthorne in His Times* [Boston: Houghton, 1980] 439).

CHAPTER 3. WILLIAM DEAN HOWELLS

Epigraph: Adrienne Rich, "Snapshots of a Daughter-in-Law," *Poems: Selected and New, 1950-1974* (New York: Norton, 1975) 50.

1. "Invalids and Actresses: Howells's Duplex Imagery for American Women," *American Literature* 47 (1976): 599-600. While Howells recognized deficiencies in woman's sphere, in his study of Ann Douglas's *Feminization of American Culture,* David Schuyler asserts that to think of the nineteenth-century genteel woman as idle is to project the twentieth century back onto the nineteenth ("Inventing a Feminine Past," *New England Quarterly* 51 [September 1978]: 299).

2. Many critics have praised Howells as a feminist seeking new avenues for women. See, for example, Edwin Cady, *The Road to Real-*

ism (Syracuse: Syracuse UP, 1956) 232-34; Robert L. Hough, *The Quiet Rebel: William Dean Howells as Social Commentator* (Lincoln: U of Nebraska P, 1959) 100-102; Robert Falk, *The Victorian Mode in American Fiction, 1865-1885* (East Lansing: Michigan State UP, 1965) 49.

3. *Dr. Breen's Practice* (Boston: Houghton, 1881) 161. Subsequently cited in the text.

4. John W. Crowley observes that Howells could not imagine a world without traditional domestic structures, feared woman would lose her moral superiority outside of the home, and hence wished to revitalize the family ("W. D. Howells: The Ever-Womanly," *American Novelists Revisted* 171-88).

5. George C. Carrington, Jr., says: "Idealism to Howells is false sentiment, the opposite of common sense...realism to Howells meant much more than just copying 'reality' (whatever that might be); it involved attitudes toward reality; it meant having the proper, the pious attitude toward the facts" (*The Immense Complex Drama: The World and Art of the Howells Novel* [Columbus: Ohio State UP, 1966] 13). Certainly Howells takes a proper and pious attitude toward "the womanly," and just as certainly he violates common sense and falls into false sentiment about woman's foibles.

6. The New England conscience of Grace is discussed in Paul Eakin, *The New England Girl* (Athens: U of Georgia P, 1976) 97-104; John Roland Dove, "Howells' Irrational Heroines," *University of Texas Studies in English* 35 (1956): 64-80; Delmar Gross Cooke, *William Dean Howells: A Critical Study* (New York: Russell, 1967) 189; George N. Bennett, *William Dean Howells: The Development of a Novelist* (Norman: U of Oklahoma P, 1959) 110.

7. Oscar Firkins, while agreeing with those who say that Howells attempts to refer Grace's ineptitude to the individual rather than the sex, notes that Grace's first case is a test "unfair even to a male" and that her lack of love for her vocation is "a limitation that would cripple a man....A higher sanity than that of the average male is presumed to exist in the male physician; the woman-doctor is entitled to the benefit of the same presumption; yet the sex's competence is tested by a representative who would seem morbid or half distraught to the average woman" (*William Dean Howells: A Study* [New York: Russell, 1963] 96-97). Alma J. Payne contends that Howells was realistic, did not present success when it was unlikely in a given situation, and understood that even when trained professionally many women "would still

find marriage a much easier solution than the struggle against men" ("William Dean Howells and the Independent Woman," *Midwest Review* 5 [1963]: 51). Allen F. Stein claims that in *Dr. Breen's Practice*, as in other novels of Howells, marriage is a key means to mitigate the threat of confusion that works in the outside world and within oneself ("Marriage in Howells's Novels," *American Literature* 48 [January 1977]: 505).

8. *A Selected Edition of W.D. Howells*, ed. Walter J. Meserve et al., 32 vols. (Bloomington: Indiana UP, 1968-1979) 16: 388. Subsequent references to Howells's novels (with the exception of *Dr. Breen's Practice*) are to this edition and are cited in the text by volume. See Mary E. Edwards, "A Portrait of the Artist as a Young Woman: A Study of Alma Leighton in Howells's *A Hazard of New Fortunes,*" in *A Festschrift for Professor Marguerite Roberts*, ed. F.E. Penninger (Richmond: U of Richmond P, 1976) 219-27. Howells may parody, in Wetmore, the American artist William Wetmore Story. Howells's novel *The Coast of Bohemia* treats at length a female artist figure.

9. E.H. Cady claims that Howells worried about women's susceptibility to quixotism and, "a feminist in the best of all senses, he wished to help women become freer psychologically and intellectually, more honest, more mature, more realistic, healthier" (*Road to Realism* 233).

10. According to Gail Parker, Howells wrote in a preface to a collection of stories entitled *Their Husbands' Wives* (New York: Harper, 1906) that his ideal spouse was an impatient Grizzle "who achieves through a fine, rebellious self-sacrifice all the best results of the old Patient One's subjection. It is the wife who has her will only the better to walk in her husband's way" (quoted in "William Dean Howells: Realism and Feminism," in *Uses of Literature*, ed. Monroe Engel [Cambridge: Harvard UP, 1973] 153).

11. See Kermit Vanderbilt, *The Achievement of William Dean Howells* (Princeton: Princeton UP, 1968) 58.

12. *The New England Girl* 114, 116. Ludwig Lewisohn calls Marcia "a predatory and possessive female of a peculiarly dangerous and noxious kind" (*Expression in America* [New York: Harper, 1932] 250). See Olov W. Fryckstedt, *In Quest of America* (New York: Russell, 1958) 226-48, for a discussion of *A Modern Instance* as a novel about the growing disorganization of the family. Ellen F. Wright argues, however, that Howells was not unhappy with the state of American society and did not think American values were deteriorating. Rather, the problems of the novel are peculiar to Marcia and Bartley ("Given

Bartley, Given Marcia: A Reconsideration of Howells' *A Modern Instance,"* *Texas Studies in Language and Literature* 23 [1981]:214-31).

13. Robert Hough claims that Howells seemed to accept the idea of an innate superiority in women and thought of man as an intellectual being and woman as a moral being (*Quiet Rebel* 101). Gail Parker claims that Howells's characteristic method of dealing with the female superiority he proclaimed was to absorb that female principle into himself ("Realism and Feminism" 152). For an excellent discussion of wit, the idea of woman, and Penelope Lapham, see Alfred Habegger, "Nineteenth-Century American Humor: Easygoing Males, Anxious Ladies, and Penelope Lapham," *PMLA* 91 (October 1976): 884-97.

14. Cady 232.

15. William Wasserstrom writes that Howells parades wonderful heroines before us but that "somewhere along the way she loses caste; her loveliness is reduced by veiled disqualification. Typically, she is an angel who is also profoundly tainted" ("William Dean Howells: The Indelible Stain," *New England Quarterly* 32 [December 1959]: 487). Wasserstrom argues that the stain is sexuality.

16. *William Dean Howells* 159-60. See also, however, John K. Reeves, who points out that the sentimentality of Howells's early fiction is a product of his choice of material (in "The Limited Realism of Howells' *Their Wedding Journey,"* *PMLA* 77 [December 1962]: 620). The irrationality of Isabel March is noted by almost all critics. See Elaine Hedges, "Howells on a Hawthornesque Theme," (*Texas Studies in Language and Literature* 3 [September 1961]: 140), on Isabel in *The Shadow of a Dream;* Kenneth Seib, "Uneasiness at Niagara: Howells' *Their Wedding Journey"* (*Studies in American Fiction* 4 [Spring 1976]: 15-25); and Edward Wagenknecht, *William Dean Howells: The Friendly Eye* (New York: Oxford UP, 1969) 156-64.

17. Alfred Habegger says of *Their Wedding Journey* that Howells did not count happily married wives as weak but, on the contrary, ridiculed stereotypes of oppressed wives (*Gender, Fantasy, and Realism in American Literature* [New York: Columbia UP, 1982] 82).

18. In "Types of American Women," *Literary and Social Silhouettes* (New York: Harper, 1894) 3-4, H.H. Boyesen explains that women's goal is marriage and therefore women wish to please men; women's education trains them in "seeming" rather than "being" in order to enhance their charm and pleasingness; and men like this. Boyesen himself identifies woman's gift of pleasing as one of her "most profoundly womanly" traits. In *The Wit of Women* (New York: Funk, 1886) 205-06, Kate Sanborn explains that women do not develop wit

because it is not politic: "No man likes to have his story capped by a better or fresher from a lady's lips." In effect, women must hide their intellects to be pleasing to men, as Boyesen says they wish to be.

19. For titles of utopian novels by women from 1888 to 1900, see *American Literary Realism* 4 (Summer 1971): 227-54. See also Kenneth Roemer, "Sex Roles, Utopia, and Change," *American Studies* 13 (Fall 1972): 33-47. Jean Pfaelzer devotes a chapter to Howells as pastoral utopian in *The Utopian Novel in America, 1886-1896: The Politics of Form* (Pittsburgh: U of Pittsburgh P, 1984) 52-77.

CHAPTER 4. HENRY JAMES

Epigraph: Henry James, *Henry James Letters,* ed. Leon Edel, 4 vols. (Cambridge: Harvard UP, 1974-1984) 4:770.

1. *The Novels and Tales of Henry James,* 26 vols. (New York: Scribner's, 1907-1917) 8:293. All references to James's novels are to this edition, unless otherwise indicated, and are cited in the text by volume.

2. My essay "Isabel Archer and Victorian Manners" (*Studies in the Novel* 9 [Winter 1976]: 441-57) gives a detailed analysis of the novel's instructively parallel proposal scenes. Roy R. Male points out that the figure of the reader haunts the preface of *Portrait* and that the question of Isabel's "value" pertains not only to her intrinsic worth and dignity but to her economic value as well *(Money Talks: Language and Lucre in American Fiction* [Norman: U of Oklahoma P, 1981] 31-49).

3. As Elizabeth Sabiston puts it in her excellent essay, "The Prison of Womanhood" (*Comparative Literature* 25 [Fall 1973]: 336), Isabel's conflict is not only with the world but between the two selves in her own character.

4. *The Ordeal of Consciousness in Henry James* (Cambridge: Cambridge UP, 1967) 357. In a letter to his brother William following the death of Minny Temple, on whom Isabel is said to be modeled, James writes: "She has gone where there is neither marrying nor giving in marriage! no illusions and no disillusions—no sleepless nights and no ebbing strength" (*Henry James Letters* 1:226).

5. See Annette Niemtzow, "Marriage and the New Woman in *The Portrait of a Lady,*" *American Literature* 47 (November 1975): 377-95; F.O. Matthiessen, *The Major Phase* (New York: Oxford UP, 1944) 182.

6. The most recent statement of this contention is in an essay by

Dennis L. O'Connor, "Intimacy and Spectatorship in *The Portrait of a Lady*," *Henry James Review* 2 (1980):25-35. Alwyn Berland, on the other hand, claims that Isabel rejects Caspar because he is unlike her high ideal of civilization (*Culture and Conduct in the Novels of Henry James* [Cambridge: Cambridge UP, 1981] 130).

7. Krook 15-16.

8. Peter J. Conn writes that Rowland alters "facts" to suit his own "vision" and standards, and acts on others through "ideological imposition." Conn asserts that Rowland makes Roderick an ideological extension of himself (in *"Roderick Hudson:* The Role of the Observer," *Nineteenth Century Fiction* 26 [1970]: 65-82). I suggest that Rowland does the same to Mary Garland and to Christina Light. Philip M. Weinstein notes that because Rowland loves Mary, he constantly overinterprets her gestures (*Henry James and the Requirements of the Imagination* [Cambridge: Harvard UP, 1971] 17). Paul Eakin writes that Rowland's assertion that Mary is "a person of great capacity" is undemonstrated by Mary's deeds (*New England Girl* 137). Comparing the first and the New York editions of the novel, Sacvan Bercovitch demonstrates that James meant to draw attention to the inadequacies and delusions that circumscribe Rowland's intelligence ("The Revision of Rowland Mallet," *Nineteenth Century Fiction* 24 [1969]: 210-21).

9. Elsa Nettels points out that Christina Light is a greater puzzle to Rowland than is Roderick (in "Action and Point of View in *Roderick Hudson*," *English Studies* 53 [1971]: 238-47). Alwyn Berland asserts that Christina is James's "most brilliant study of the dark lady" and notes that Christina does not love Roderick but, rather, loves Rowland (*Culture and Conduct* 68, 72).

10. *Henry James: The Lessons of the Master* (Chicago: U of Chicago P, 1975).

11. Christina Light reappears in *The Princess Casamassima*, where she still does not manage to escape the culture's gender limitations. She adopts the life style of the proletariat, but the male leaders of the anarchist movement refuse to take her seriously and persist in the idea that women are intended to be ornamental creatures.

12. Exactly who is saint and who is sinner in *The Golden Bowl* is much debated. Critics have come to Charlotte's defense as they have to Maggie's. Jean Kimball, in "Henry James's Last Portrait of a Lady: Charlotte Stant in *The Golden Bowl*" (*American Literature* 28 [January 1957]: 449-68), argues that Charlotte is the heroine of the novel. Elizabeth Owen, however, in " 'The Given Appearance' of Charlotte

Verver" (*Essays in Criticism* 13 [October 1963]: 364-74), contends that Charlotte is cool and calculating and that Maggie is justified in taking up arms against her. Joseph J. Firebaugh, in "The Ververs" (*Essays in Criticism* 4 [October 1954]: 400-410), contends that the Ververs are distinctly not admirable and that we should sympathize with Charlotte. Maggie, too, has provoked controversy, as in Walter Wright's "Maggie Verver: Neither Saint nor Witch" (*Nineteenth Century Fiction* 12 [June 1957]: 59-71). C.B. Cox finds that Maggie battles for her rights against a wicked Charlotte (in *"The Golden Bowl," Essays in Criticism* 5 [April 1955]: 190-93). Sallie Sears, on the other hand, finds Maggie a "vehicle of destruction and retribution that, in spite of appearances, have nothing to do with the just claims of outraged innocence" (*The Negative Imagination* [Ithaca: Cornell UP, 1968] 171).

13. William Wasserstrom's provocative discussion of Maggie and Adam's relationship (in *Heiress of All the Ages* [Minneapolis: U of Minnesota P, 1959] 87-98) sees Maggie's growth as the product of her increasing awareness of her father's use of her to fulfill his sublime needs, and her consequent exorcising of Adam from her mind. In *Love and the Quest for Identity in the Fiction of Henry James* (Princeton: Princeton UP, 1980) 165 68, Philip Sicker sets out the idea that Maggie has extraordinary psychic sympathies and refuses to devote herself exclusively to one person. She is frustrated by the culture's insistence on single-minded devotion to marriage and would make marriage a sacred but not the sole relation between human beings. J.A. Ward sees the root of Maggie's trouble as her misunderstanding of the meaning of marriage. Ward maintains that she confuses its form and content (*The Search for Form* [Chapel Hill: U of North Carolina P, 1967] 210-11). On marriage and *The Golden Bowl*, see Laurence Holland, *The Expense of Vision* (Princeton: Princeton UP, 1964) 331-407.

14. Leon Edel points out that, whereas in many a novel a heroine in Maggie's place would have made grand scenes, James keeps her faithful to her delicate upbringing and her state of ignorance (*Henry James: The Master* [Philadelphia: Lippincott, 1972] 214). Maggie, however, is no longer ignorant when her greatest opportunities to create scenes arise.

15. Philip Weinstein makes the cogent observation that Maggie exults in an intimacy that has more to do with the exclusion of Charlotte than with closeness to the Prince (*Henry James and the Requirements of the Imagination* 184).

16. *The Notebooks of Henry James*, ed. F.O. Matthiessen and Kenneth B. Murdock (New York: Oxford UP, 1947) 47. Nina Auerbach

observes that "to James, women were simply, and ambiguously, America itself, a land whose men had disappeared either into soldiers' graves or into something mysterious called 'business' " (*Communities of Women: An Idea in Fiction* [Cambridge: Harvard UP, 1978] 123). Sara Davis claims that "women in political affairs during the nineteenth century represented the ultimate conflict between radically opposing values—personal and sexual vs. social and political—and focused ideas of crucial artistic interest to James" ("Feminist Sources in *The Bostonians," American Literature* 50 [January 1979]: 586-87).

17. Lillian Faderman observes that Basil and Olive are alike in their criticism of society, the one wanting it all masculine and the other all feminine ("Female Same-Sex Relationships in Novels by Longfellow, Holmes, and James," *New England Quarterly* 51 [September 1978]: 327).

18. *The Bostonians* (New York: Random, 1956) vi. All quotations are from this edition and are cited in the text.

19. Charles Child Walcutt maintains, uninsightfully, that Ransom's views on feminization are impressive, that Ransom must be judged by what he says, and that "when he speaks he is always lucid, eloquent, witty, judicious" ("Discourse on Feminism," in *Man's Changing Masks: Modes and Methods of Characterization in Fiction* [Minneapolis: U of Minnesota P, 1966] 191-92). Ransom is certainly characterized as being more blind than lucid and more prejudiced than judicious.

20. Gabriel Pearson's remarks on the effort of the Prince in *The Golden Bowl* to overwhelm Maggie with sexual charm apply to the situations of Verena and Isabel as well. Pearson calls the deployment of sexual charm "a form of bullying" ("The Novel to End All Novels: *The Golden Bowl," in The Air of Reality: New Essays on Henry James*, ed. John Goode [London: Methuen, 1972] 322).

21. Abigail Hamblen identifies Verena as James's and any man's ideal of perfect femininity (in "Henry James and the Freedom Fighters of the Seventies," *Georgia Review* 20 [Spring 1966]: 42).

22. This is another echo of Hawthorne's *Blithedale Romance*. Zenobia, however, cast as a writer, recognized and manipulated her tired metaphors. No such claim can be made for Verena.

23. Lyall H. Powers claims, however, that Gabriel Nash is the muse of the novel ("James's *The Tragic Muse*—Ave Atque Vale," *PMLA* 73 [1958]: 270-74).

24. Edward Wagenknecht, in *Eve and Henry James* (Norman: U of

Oklahoma P, 1978) 89, says that he finds James's statement difficult to believe. Daniel J. Schneider, in *The Crystal Cage* (Lawrence: Regents P of Kansas, 1978) 50, notes that Miriam would not dream of giving up her career. D.J. Gordon and John Stokes, in "The Reference of *The Tragic Muse*," *(The Air of Reality* 121), point out that the novel on which James based *The Tragic Muse* (Mrs. Humphrey Ward's *Miss Bretherton*) leads its heroine to abandon art for marriage. Perhaps James confused the two novels when he wrote his retrospective preface, for in his preface he does record "a certain vagueness of remembrance" about its origin and growth. In his *Notebooks*, James records Mrs. Ward's idea for a story and notes that the heroine becomes a celebrity and "soars away and is lost" to her patron (63). No mention of marriage is made. Oscar Cargill, in *The Novels of Henry James* (New York: Macmillan, 1961) 187, and Pelham Edgar, in *Henry James: Man and Author* (New York: Russell, 1964) 284, misread Miriam Rooth's actual character as James did.

25. Quoted in Leon Edel, *Henry James: The Middle Years* (New York: Lippincott, 1962) 90.

26. Henry James, "Miss Woolson," *Partial Portraits* (London: Macmillan, 1905) 188-89. James's review of Woolson first appeared in *Harper's Weekly* in February 1887.

27. Quoted in Edel, *The Middle Years* 90.

28. Quoted in Edel, *The Middle Years* 92.

29. *The American Scene* (Bloomington: Indiana UP, 1968) 345.

CHAPTER 5. EDITH WHARTON

Epigraph: Emily Dickinson, Poem 258, *The Complete Poems of Emily Dickinson*, ed. Thomas H. Johnson (Boston: Little, 1980) 118.

1. New Haven: Yale UP, 1979, 69-74.

2. *A Backward Glance* (New York: Scribner's, 1933) 119.

3. New York: Scribner's, 1908, 41-47.

4. *The House of Mirth* (New York: Scribner's, 1905) 17. Subsequently cited in the text.

5. Lawrence Selden is a major example of Wharton's use, like James's, of a priori ideas of woman as measures of the mind and its stasis or development. Selden fancies that he is unconventional, but his vision is clouded by conventional readings of Lily's manner, her "indiscretions," that keep him from proposing marriage to her. James Gargano

notes, in *"The House of Mirth:* Social Futility and Faith" (*American Literature* 44 [1972]: 143), that Selden cannot reject the ambiguous appearances that induce cynicism. The problem of men's perception of women recurs frequently in Wharton's fiction: in Amherst's view of Justine Brent in *The Fruit of the Tree,* in Merrick's view of Pauline Trant in the short story "The Long Run," in Newland Archer's vision of both May Welland and Ellen Olenska in *The Age of Innocence.* Consequently, heroines are frequently misperceived and therefore underestimated. Cynthia Woolf discusses misconceptions of May Welland in *A Feast of Words: The Triumph of Edith Wharton* (New York: Oxford UP, 1977), 323. (Woolf's analysis of *Age* and of all of Wharton's work is invaluable.) Margaret B. McDowell, in *Edith Wharton* (Boston: Hall, 1976) 98-99, points out that Archer misjudges May. Gary H. Lindberg, in *Edith Wharton and the Novel of Manners* (Charlottesville: UP of Virginia, 1975) 135, makes a similar observation. McDowell's essay, "Viewing the Custom of Her Country: Edith Wharton's Feminism" (*Contemporary Literature* 15 [1974]:521-38), is an excellent overview of attitudes toward women in Wharton's fiction throughout her career. Carol Wershoven, in *The Female Intruder in the Novels of Edith Wharton* (Rutherford, N.J.: Fairleigh Dickinson UP, 1982), also takes up heroines as intruders who bear values and provoke moments of insight in heroes. Lindberg, in *Edith Wharton and the Novel of Manners,* claims that Wharton's characters learn "to perceive reality through the bars of a cage," and that the "major subject of Wharton's fiction is, in fact, precisely how social convention limits the life of the spirit" (36-37). Donald Phelps points out, in "Edith Wharton and the Invisible" (*Prose* 7 [1973]:231), that forces in the society of *The House of Mirth* "do not so much oppress as blindly restrict and control" young women's actions. Judith Fetterley, in "The Temptation to Be a Beautiful Object: Double Standard and Double Bind in *The House of Mirth"* (*Studies in American Fiction* 5 [Autumn 1977]: 199-211), discusses different standards applied to men and women.

    6. *Feminization of American Culture* 44.

    7. *The Gods Arrive* (New York: Appleton, 1932) 367.

    8. Vance's first wife, Laura Lou, is adoring, submissive, and incapable of intellectually stimulating Vance because she is totally unable to comprehend his aspirations and his world. Vance alternately likes and dislikes her submissiveness, dependency, and ignorance. Laura Lou is the female norm from which Vance escapes to Halo for stimulation and understanding, and the norm he finally uses against Halo when it suits him.

9. *Hudson River Bracketed* (New York: Appleton, 1929) 109. Subsequently cited in the text. For Wharton's attitudes toward art and artists and Vance Weston, see Blake Nevius, *Edith Wharton: A Study of Her Fiction* (Berkeley: U of California P, 1961) 225; James W. Tuttleton, *The Novel of Manners in America* (New York: Norton, 1972) 133-40; and Wershoven, *Female Intruder* 139-40.

10. See R.W.B. Lewis, *Edith Wharton: A Biography* (New York: Harper, 1975), especially 50-54, on the intellectual and sexual quality of Wharton's marriage to Teddy Wharton.

11. *The Touchstone* (New York: Scribner's, 1900) 17-19.

12. *Edith Wharton* 206. Nevius reads Pauline's character purely as Wharton's attack on the frivolousness of American women (204-05). Nevius is correct, but beneath the frivolity is the question of what an energetic woman is to do with herself.

13. *Twilight Sleep* (New York: Appleton, 1927) 66-67. Subsequently cited in the text.

14. Adeline Tintner points out that Pauline is a good mother, that her daughter Nona adores her, and that this mother and daughter have a rich relationship ("Mothers, Daughters, and Incest in the Late Novels of Edith Wharton," in *The Lost Tradition: Mothers and Daughters in Literature*, ed. Cathy N. Davidson and E.M. Broner [New York: Ungar, 1980] 154). Carol Wershoven classifies Nona as an intruder figure (*Female Intruder* 134).

15. *A Backward Glance* 207.

16. *The Reef* (New York: Appleton, 1912) 86-87. Subsequently cited in the text. James Gargano argues convincingly, in "Edith Wharton's *The Reef*: The Genteel Woman's Quest for Knowledge" (*Novel* 10 [Fall 1976]: 44), that a woman of Anna's background who had absorbed the mores of her father's society would have immediately terminated her engagement to Darrow. Instead, Anna examines her background and her psyche, proving that she is certainly less puritanical than her forebears. Carol Wershoven argues, however, that Anna, like Darrow, is subject to simplistic classifications of women that cause all the misery. In Wershoven's scheme, Sophy Viner is "the reef," the intruder (*Female Intruder* 98, 107).

17. In "Fairy-Tale Love and *The Reef*" (*American Literature* 47 [January 1976]: 615-28), Elizabeth Ammons dissects Anna's rescue by Prince Charming Darrow.

18. *Edith Wharton* 135, 138.

19. New York: Scribner's, 1913, 149. Subsequently cited in the text.

20. In the cogent and comprehensive *Edith Wharton's Argument*

with America (Athens: U of Georgia P, 1980) 109, and in "The Business of Marriage in E. Wharton's *The Custom of the Country" (Criticism* 16 [1974]: 334), Elizabeth Ammons calls *The Custom of the Country* "one of America's great business novels," in the tradition of *The Rise of Silas Lapham* and others. John Lidoff sees Lily Bart as another example of a Wharton heroine who is sexually immature. Lidoff describes Lily as a sleeping beauty slumbering in a "dormant presexual state from which she never awakens" ("Another Sleeping Beauty: Narcissism in *The House of Mirth," American Quarterly* 32 [Winter 1980]: 522).

21. " 'The Blank Page' and the Issues of Female Creativity," in *Writing and Sexual Difference,* ed. Elizabeth Abel (Chicago: U of Chicago P, 1982) 73-93.

22. New York: Appleton, 1919, 101.

AFTERWORD

Epigraph: Adrienne Rich, "When We Dead Awaken: Writing as Re-Vision," *On Lies, Secrets, and Silence* (New York: Norton, 1979) 35.

1. *The Daughter's Seduction: Feminism and Psychoanalysis* (Ithaca: Cornell UP, 1982).

2. *Toward a Recognition of Androgyny* (New York: Harper, 1973) ix-x. In her very useful and instructive *Sexual/Textual Politics* (London: Methuen, 1985), Toril Moi warns against "taking over the very metaphysical categories set up by patriarchy in order to keep women in their places, despite attempts to attach new feminist values to these old categories" (13). In *Sexism and God-Talk: Toward a Feminist Theology* (Boston: Beacon, 1983), Rosemary Radford Ruether argues persuasively against the notion of androgyny on the grounds that the term "continues to perpetuate the idea that certain psychic attributes are to be labeled masculine and others are to be labeled feminine... there is no valid biological basis for labeling certain psychic capacities, such as reason, 'masculine' and others, such as intuition, 'feminine' " (111). Whether one uses the term "androgyny" or some other term to make the point, it is useful to recall that abilities are not apportioned according to gender.

INDEX